WORK AND THE WORKPLACE

FOUNDATIONS OF SOCIAL WORK KNOWLEDGE
Frederic G. Reamer, Series Editor

Social work has a unique history, purpose, perspective, and method. The primary purpose of this series is to articulate these distinct qualities and to define and explore the ideas, concepts, and skills that together constitute social work's intellectual foundations and boundaries and its emerging issues and concerns.

To accomplish this goal, the series will publish a cohesive collection of books that address both the core knowledge of the profession and its newly emerging topics. The core is defined by the evolving consensus, as primarily reflected in the Council of Social Work Education's Curriculum Policy Statement, concerning what courses accredited social work education programs must include in their curricula. The series will be characterized by an emphasis on the widely embraced ecological perspective; attention to issues concerning direct and indirect practice; and emphasis on cultural diversity and multiculturalism, social justice, oppression, populations at risk, and social work values and ethics. The series will have a dual focus on practice traditions and emerging issues and concepts.

David G. Gil — *Confronting Injustice and Oppression: Concepts and Strategies for Social Workers*

George Alan Appleby and Jeane W. Anastas — *Not Just a Passing Phase: Social Work with Gay, Lesbian, and Bisexual People*

Frederic G. Reamer — *Social Work Research and Evaluation Skills*

Pallassana R. Balgopal — *Social Work Practice with Immigrants and Refugees*

Dennis Saleeby — *Human Behavior and Social Environments: A Biopsychosocial Approach*

Frederic G. Reamer — *Tangled Relationships: Managing Boundary Issues in the Human Services*

Roger A. Lohmann and Nancy L. Lohmann — *Social Administration*

David M. Austin — *Human Services Management: Organizational Leadership in Social Work Practice*

Joan Shireman — *Critical Issues in Child Welfare*

Stuart A. Kirk — *Mental Disorders in the Social Environment*

WORK AND THE WORKPLACE

A Resource for Innovative Policy and Practice

Sheila H. Akabas and Paul A. Kurzman

Columbia University Press   New York

Columbia University Press
Publishers Since 1893
New York   Chichester, West Sussex
Copyright © 2005 Columbia University Press
All rights reserved

Library of Congress Cataloging-in-Publication Data

Akabas, Sheila H., 1931–
    Work and the workplace : a resource for innovative
policy and practice / Sheila H. Akabas and Paul A. Kurzman.
        p. cm. — (Foundations of social work knowledge)
    Includes bibliographical references and index.
    ISBN 0–231–11166–5 (cloth : alk. paper)
    1. Industrial welfare. 2. Social service. I. Kurzman, Paul A.
II. Title. III. Series.
HD7261.A28   2004
363.11′53—dc22   2004059375

Columbia University Press books are printed on permanent
and durable acid-free paper.

Printed in the United States of America
c 10 9 8 7 6 5 4 3 2 1

*To our best friends, and greatest support systems,
Aaron L. Akabas and Margaret F. Kurzman,
with gratitude for many wonderful years*

CONTENTS

FOREWORD

Work and the Workplace

Benjamin Franklin said that there are only three permanent things in life: death, taxes, and change. While I would never seek to modify the teachings of so great a thinker, I feel we must add one other critical element: work. The very fabric of our life revolves around work. Our entire identity encompasses the type of work we are doing—or not doing, for that matter. The type of food we eat, the neighborhood we live in, the clothes we wear, and how we socialize—all somehow are related to our work.

Clearly work has a defining influence. Many people spend anywhere from eight to sixteen hours a day working. This means that one- to two-thirds of their days, and therefore their lives, is spent in activities which define their existence. In Egypt it is said that bread is life. I would posit that work is life. We must be cognizant of what this means to us. We need to understand its influence upon our life. We need to apply the necessary skills, competencies, knowledge, and values in such a way that we are positively influencing this process we call work. Certainly, the social work profession has these competencies. I am glad that Sheila Akabas and Paul Kurzman have written a book which provides a framework for understanding this very important area.

For decades, social workers have all but ignored the second word which defines their very reason for being: work. Certainly the noble roots of the profession put more focus on the disenfranchised and those having mental health issues. This work should never cease. However, as we strive to ensure that every person who is willing and able to work has the ability and opportunity to do so, we should clearly understand more about what work is and how to make it a viable effort for the individual, as well as the organization. We put a lot of focus in our society on getting people employed, but we don't put enough focus on insuring that people can meet their individual and family needs while accomplishing the requirements of the organization.

In my experience, productive workers are those who can meet their individual needs and help the organization meet its goals also. Unfortunately, most organizations do not put enough emphasis on how to help individuals meet their needs. There is not enough of an understanding in some cases, or desire in other cases, to do this. What is required is a professional framework to guide and promote this thinking. Certainly social workers can meet this challenge.

I have been working in various aspects of international human resources for the past twenty-two years. I have worked in senior human resource positions for several companies in Central Europe, the Middle East, Latin America, Western Europe, and the United States. I also have worked for nonprofit organizations in senior positions. There is one common denominator that ties together all of these organizations. People are the most important resource when it comes to achieving the ends of the organization. The company can have money, land, machinery, and products, but it will not be successful unless the right people are helping the organization achieve its objectives.

Organizations typically will rely on line managers to motivate their people. Organizations spend thousands of training dollars to ensure that managers are equipped with the wherewithal to motivate their workers. However, the manager can not do this alone. This is where the human resources department comes into play. Human resource professionals perform functions that take into account that employees have problems and issues that can not be handled by the manager alone. They administer benefits that take into account the needs of the employees and their families. Human resource staff counsel employees and advise them on how they can function harmoniously with their supervisors, coworkers, and supervisees. Human resource people develop work-life programs that take into account the fact that more working mothers need flexibility to deal with family priorities. Policies need to be established that are sensitive and caring, based on employee needs. There is more demographic variety in the workplace, so efforts to attract, retain, and develop diverse populations, while balancing the needs of all employees, is a critical dynamic. Training needs to be implemented continually in order to enable managers to execute their tasks and manage their people with caring, effectiveness, and respect.

I have spent a lot of time ensuring that these functions are well implemented in my work. In fact, my current position as vice president of

Global Workplace Initiatives at Colgate Palmolive focuses on enabling my company to do all of these things well on a global basis. My previous work at Procter and Gamble, Digital Equipment Corporation, and the Triborough Bridge and Tunnel Authority was also informed by occupational social work theory and principles. Although I possess a master's degree in business administration, I would say that my master's in social work has done even more to equip me to be highly effective in these areas. My effectiveness with organizational development is enhanced by an understanding of systems theory and "people dynamics." This is why social workers can bring rich insight to the various human resource functions. The most effective human resource people are those who are sensitive to the needs of the individual and the organization. Unfortunately, many people feel that all too many human resource professionals only care about optimizing productivity and profits. No organization really benefits from such suboptimal thinking and behavior. Research is replete with examples that demonstrate that companies that care for and value their people are the most productive. Social workers have a distinctive ability to care, coupled with a skill set that enables them to help individuals become personally effective. This is an indispensable capability as far as the workplace and organizations are concerned. This is the value added that can ensure that organizations are more effective in meeting both their productivity goals and the needs of their employees. A few concrete examples will illustrate the point.

In chapter 4, the authors take a broad look at the role of health systems as opposed to the traditional view of health. When I was working in southern Africa, there was a need to address the health crisis caused by the AIDS epidemic. When you went to the office one week and returned the next, invariably you would see new workers in certain departments because of so many deaths occurring among the rank and file. Besides the terrible impact on family members, this put a strain on our recruiting efforts. It also meant that it was difficult to maintain continuity with work assignments. We developed a comprehensive health education and awareness program, in addition to giving extensive counseling. The corporation had to take on this role because the governments were either unable or unwilling to take up the mantle. Incorporating the family, community institutions, and relevant nongovernmental organizations into this program was critical to the success of the effort, action that is similar to advice given the reader of *Work and the Workplace: A Resource for Innovative Policy and Practice.*

This same awareness of the broader role that must be played with health systems was evident in Eastern Europe. When I worked in Romania, Hungary, the Czech Republic, and Poland in the early days after the fall of the Berlin Wall, I was involved in starting up subsidiary operations for my company, along with finance, marketing, and manufacturing executives. In addition to establishing the traditional work processes, I saw a need to review the existing health provisions provided by government to workers. While the health systems were good at treatment, they did not provide comprehensive preventative measures. Setting up annual physical examinations to review health broadly, including dental care and vision, became an important part of ensuring the overall well-being of employees. We also offered a healthcare day when the whole family could participate in health education and diagnostic care, if they desired it. This kind of extension of the social service role is recommended throughout *Work and the Workplace*.

This brings us to another area: quality of work life. The authors note that there are more women entering the world of work and suggest the "distinctive presenting problems" that occur when people come to work with "nonwork related concerns" that may impede their productivity. Working mothers are a distinct group that have specialized issues because of their dual status. I have found it advisable to develop policies and programs to improve their quality of work life. An example is a policy to extend the amount of leave that a person can take to deal with personal or family issues beyond that required by the Family and Medical Leave Act. This additional leave, which can be used to supplement leave for childbirth or other personal issues, also applies to fathers who may wish to stay home to expand their parenting role. The company was willing to adopt this policy recommendation when offered evidence of its cost/benefit effectiveness, another verification of the value of the authors' recommendations.

Emergency care is an issue that applies to all workers. This need occurs not only for parents of young children, but also with regard to elder care. Given that many of us now are facing issues of dealing with elderly parents, a need to establish an elder-care information and referral service that would provide employees with information on where to refer a parent who needed temporary or long-term care became apparent. Also needed was the provision of a healthcare worker to offer temporary care for a relative in-house until either the parent was well or could be transferred to a residential facility. The decision was made to offer these services free of cost. Dealing with these quality of work life issues is an extremely important part of helping employees with the "total systems aspects of their lives." In chapter 5, the authors go into some depth regarding the role that occupational social work plays in this process using an appropriately ecological systems approach.

This systems approach is particularly useful when looking at the area of overall organizational effectiveness. Chapter 8 illustrates this well. My previous work at Procter and Gamble and Digital Equipment was informed by a model of appreciating and including key stakeholders in a process of self-determination regarding their workplace systems in manufacturing plant start-ups. Using systems theory and a sociotechnical approach to work, we involved key stakeholders in the design of their work systems and in other design decisions regarding work tasks, reward systems, communication processes, and the ergonomics of manufacturing, among other considerations. Committees of workers and managers representing a cross-section of the organization met before machinery, equipment, and concrete were installed. Worker participation efforts of this type are critical to ensuring that the needs of the organization and the needs of the individual both are optimally satisfied. Naturally, these participation efforts should be maintained after the work system is developed to ensure ongoing effectiveness. In fact, the committees that were established were a source of ongoing problem solving and input. Facilitating such action is within the reach of a social worker in a work setting.

Another good example of using a biopsychosocial assessment and systems approach to work involves the use of employee assistance programs. Without doubt, the EAP has proven to be a remarkably useful organizational mechanism. While at Colgate Palmolive, and previously at the Triborough Bridge and Tunnel Authority and at Digital Equipment Corporation, I was in a position to install EAPs that could partner with me to deal effectively with many concerns of employees. Most recently I took the use of the EAP to another level. During 9/11, I ensured that the EAP was part of our crisis intervention and emergency preparedness. Posttraumatic symptoms needed attention so workers could focus appropriately on their current reality. We put in place a free twenty-four-hour hotline that employees or family members could access. We ran groups for employees to provide comfort and support. We established Web sites that individuals and their families could access for information, education, and resources. Confidential counseling was made available for family members when requested. Since 9/11, the workplace has not been the same. Blackouts, plane crashes, terrorist events, and the Iraq war tend to resurrect similar feelings and fear. Our EAP systems have proven very effective in dealing with these ongoing crises. The authors point out in chapter 6 how crucial the EAP is to the workplace.

That is why this book is so important. *Work and the Workplace* establishes a framework and methodology for applying social work expertise in world of work settings. Over the years that I have known Shelley and

Paul they have provided opportunities for social workers to increase their professional capabilities, while enhancing the effectiveness of their organizations. I found this book to be a very practical guide for continuing this important work. It is a comprehensive text which covers professionals in almost every setting, whether profit, nonprofit, management, union, or university. Lest they are accused of not offering practical suggestions: Pay attention to the case studies that pose real-life problems and provide viable solutions. This book is groundbreaking in all of these aspects. As a reader, you are in for a treat.

Philip A. Berry
Vice President and Corporate Officer, Global Workplace Initiatives
Colgate Palmolive

Work is the best and worst thing we do. Work is a great source of satisfaction and growth and a central cause of distress in people's lives. While the traditionally good things that happen in the workplace are shrinking, participation in the economy is still the best means to escape poverty. Our conviction concerning the significance of work and the workplace is so strong that we, the authors, have devoted our professional lives as social work educators, researchers, and scholars to the pursuit of delineating and clarifying the role of the world of work in the social welfare arena and understanding what work means to different populations and in different settings. In this pursuit we have been fortunate to work as intellectual partners for more than three decades. Often we have been inspired and educated by our colleagues and by our students who have used the knowledge and skill we have tried to impart to develop creative responses to the scene in which they find themselves.

This book represents our attempt to share with the social work community our sense of how occupational social work came to be what it is and what we think are the opportunities for the future. In a sense, this volume is the last of a trilogy. The first book we worked on together was titled *Work, Workers, and Work Organizations: A View from Social Work*, an edited volume in which expert scholars in each dimension of the social work curriculum undertook to look at their areas of specialization through the lens of the world of work and work as a human activity. In its various chapters it supported teaching in research, social policy, human behavior, social administration, community organizing, clinical practice, and of course, specialization in social work in the workplace as a field of practice. Our second volume, *Work and Well-Being: The Occupational Social Work Advantage*, another volume that we organized and edited, and to which we served as major contributors, represented a collection of practice, policy, and research experience in which scholars and practitioners reviewed the experience of using the varied methods of social work practice—clinical, advanced generalist, program development and planning, community organizing, policy, and research—to evolve policies and programs that deal with major problems faced by the profession both in the world of work and in the community as it involves the world of work. In this third book we have taken on the authorship ourselves and have traced the origins, present practice, and future opportunities in social work in the workplace as we have experienced it and as others view it.

Our publications, of course, are not the only writing on this field of practice, although discussion of work and work issues historically has been absent from the social work literature. Work was not a central focus for Mary Richmond in *Social Diagnosis* (1917) or Gordon Hamilton in *The Theory and Practice of Social Casework* (1940), arguably the two most influential social work textbooks in the formative years of the profession. Moreover, with but two exceptions (Reynolds 1975; Weiner, Akabas, & Sommer 1973), no books had been published on occupational social work prior to 1980. The fifteenth edition of the *Encyclopedia of Social Work* (1965) made no general reference to labor or management programs. Skeels's (1965) entry in that edition titled "Social Welfare Programs of Labor and Industry" did not mention occupational social work or any of the programs and services under labor and industrial auspices that are common today. In that same year, Wilensky and Lebeaux (1965: 163) could correctly note that "[i]ndustrial [occupational] social work in the European tradition of social workers offering family and other services from outposts in the plant . . . hailed for the past twenty years as a 'new frontier in social work,' simply has not materialized in America."

Social work textbooks, emerging in the 1950s upon Council on Social Work Education (CSWE) accreditation of master's degree (MSW) programs and expanding after 1974 with the accrediting of baccalaureate (BSW) programs, did not even list occupational social work as a field of practice. The 1980s was a decade of change. Starting with the publication of three landmark books in 1982 (Akabas & Kurzman 1982; Feinstein & Brown 1982; Masi 1982), the literature expanded, with four additional books on occupational social work being published during the decade (Googins & Godfrey 1987; Gould & Smith 1988; McGowan 1984; Thomlison 1983). Additionally, virtually every one of the prominent social work textbooks (widely used in the 165 accredited MSW and 450 accredited BSW programs that now exist) began to feature significant content on "occupational social work," "employee assistance programs," or "social work in the workplace."

This book, in many ways, is the culmination of those efforts. It is presented in nine chapters, which in turn are divided into sections. While serving as a text for the teaching of occupational social work, this book also is intended to be useful in teaching across the curriculum in baccalaureate and master's degree programs. As suggested by its title, *Work and the Workplace,* it should be helpful in the second context because of its focus on the universality of work and on the significance of the workplace in the lives of *all* clients whom we serve in *every* setting for social work practice. It also will support occupational social work concentrations (specializations) in the advanced curriculum that prepare graduates for roles in benefits management, human resource planning, occupational alcoholism and substance abuse services, preretirement preparation, corporate social responsibility, disability management, work-family program development, affirmative action, and employee assistance.

The initial chapter introduces the reader to the themes of the book and the rationale for its publication. With a historic perspective, it looks at the evolution of the field of practice (one of the few new fields to develop in the profession in the last fifty years), as well as at social work's increased interest in recent years in work, workers, and work organizations. Providing boundaries and definitions for central concepts and terms, the chapter attempts to lay out the conceptual framework that will be used throughout and the importance of work, community, and family in this regard.

In chapter 2 we observe the differential meaning of work in people's lives and how this understanding may shed light on contemporary work issues. In describing the economic, social, and psychological conditions extant in the world of work in the United States, we look at how different they may be for particular cohorts of Americans, both in reality and in perception. The "domino impact" of unemployment, for example, on individuals, families, organizations, and communities is cited, along with the inadequacy of the insurances, benefits, and support systems that are intended to respond to personal and systemic crises.

Chapter 3 places these current policy and practice issues in historical context, with an emphasis on the rapidity of change in the closing quarter of the twentieth century and now in the new millennium. Is work an opportunity or an obligation, and from a political perspective, is it a promise made or a promise broken? Using available government and nongovernment data, information is presented that sheds light on the quandaries that workers and work organizations face today; this chapter also reviews the ever-changing role and responsibility of the federal government since the advent of the New Deal in the 1930s.

Building on this policy foundation, the chapter that follows illuminates the corresponding practice issues, in both occupational and traditional social work settings. In comparing practice between the two, the narrative in chapter 4 underscores the importance of a "work viewpoint" for a full appreciation of the significance of practice issues, such as service location, confidentiality, and competing values. Examples from practice at work sites illustrate the similarities and differences in assessment when one chooses to look through a "work lens" at presenting problems that clients (individual and organizational) bring to the social work practitioner. Inherent tensions are discussed, especially in the light of new practice issues, such as the trends toward privatization and managed care.

Chapter 5 discusses the distinct presenting problems that are characteristic of world of work settings. With an equal focus on causes and potential solutions, the chapter looks at the barriers to entry into the work world for many and the risks as well as rewards inherent in participation. The built-in potential for conflict between work and family obligations, the disadvantaged position of some classes of workers and work entrants, the unsupportive (even risk-producing) nature of many jobs and settings, and work implications for people with chronic or acute illnesses each receive attention.

Chapter 6 identifies the models of service delivery extant in the world of work and those targeted at workers and their families from without. Building on an understanding of the occupational social welfare system (chap. 1), the resources uniquely available within this system are cited to illuminate what labor- and management-sponsored social work programs can achieve. Focusing on organizational and individual change, community-based as well as private practice, we outline the interconnection between resources and service delivery systems, and the gaps that persist between them. Illustrated by workplace case examples, successful interventions are presented not only to show service delivery systems in action but also to provide a model that is available for replication.

Using disability as a metaphor, chapter 7 provides case histories that illustrate the great potential inherent in a collaboration of management, labor, social work, and government. Viewing disability simultaneously as an entitlement, manpower, and income-maintenance issue in the social policy realm, the variable becomes a useful template for analysis. Linking policy with program development and advocacy and case finding to direct service opportunities, the chapter underscores how a problem-solving focus and generalist practice perspective can have an impact on the rights and needs of people with disabilities in the world of work.

Since social workers also work (and are the only professionals with "work" in their title), chapter 8 looks at social workers as workers and social agencies as employers. Dealing with most of the same issues as other work sites and workforce participants, employer and employee are conditioned by their mutual commitment to the clients they serve. Issues of productivity, accountability, mobility, and unionization are presented, all framed in part as a reflection of subdominant societal values. Given the reality of relatively low status and a meager array of tangible rewards, the dilemmas of social work employees and employers may be symbiotically intertwined. With the culture of the social agency as a significant intervening variable, some of these problems are resolved in the crucible of a common social ideology and commitment, but often these issues can and do lead to worker burnout or agency goal displacement. Funding sources, professional regulation, and a common code of ethics, however, provide an important mediating function.

Chapter 9 takes a look at the future. Given the achievements and discoveries to date, we try to assess current trends and future potential. Career counseling, manpower programming, and managed-care responsibility, for example, may evolve into important arenas for practice, along with some new alliances with a reinvigorated union movement. Creative methods of social research and new sources for social bookkeeping also may emerge that will strengthen the quality of our evaluation and thereby our capacity for program innovation and accountability. Lessons from the world of work that influence the social work profession in general are noted along with the reciprocal impact of economic and social change in the broader society on the workplace and on work site programs.

As we often tell our students when they are selecting a specialized field of practice, if they are eager to work with children, the elderly, kids in school, individuals facing urban crises, families with health problems, there is a field of practice to meet the specific needs of each of these populations and problems. But if they want it all, and to operate from a strengths perspective, promoting social justice for all, then the world of work is for them because each of those groups and concepts can be served by expertise in the area of work. Children prepare for work; adults struggle with work; the aged reminisce about work; where and how families live and grow is determined by work; and our social policy is directed at getting people to work. Therefore we need social workers to help all those people and policies deal realistically and humanely with work or its absence. Entering work, remaining at work, and leaving work are some of the main passages of life for most of us and being able to find meaningful, rewarding work is the greatest challenge facing individuals and society today. It's the economy, stupid! was the motto of the first Clinton campaign—and it will serve equally for the first presidential campaign of the twenty-first century because, as Camus said, "without work all life goes rotten."

Studying and working in the world of work as a field of practice is about population, sponsoring auspices, legislation, particular presenting problems, and field-related solution sets. This means it is about workers and their dependents (which includes just about everyone); about labor and management and government and their interlocking approaches to work issues; about the Social Security Act and the Immigration Reform and Control Act; about the Ticket to Work, Work Incentives Improvement Act, and the Age Discrimination in Employment Act; about confronting and solving problems of affirmative action and sexual harassment; about finding jobs and helping sustain employment for those disadvantaged by lack of training, immigrant status, or labor market discrimination because of mental health conditions, ethnic group membership, or a history of incarceration or domestic violence. It is also about family/work life balance, child care, elder care, unemployment, and underemployment—about taking on the world and making it a better place for people through the most universal of all activities, WORK. It is about all the reasons anyone becomes a social worker.

As a field of practice, social work in the workplace requires the best of clinical skills to make speedy and accurate assessments and to help people function in all arenas of their lives. It demands good program-planning skills to identify and implement responsive programs; research skills to document needs and use the information as a basis for policy formulation, facilitation, negotiation, and advocacy; ability to take the information and direct attention to the significance of the issues in people's lives—in short, every skill that is required to function effectively as a social worker. But most important, the field, relatively unchartered, calls on the professional to organize creative capacities and go outside the box to find new ways of working in the twenty-first century. If one sees oneself as an activist social worker interested in evidence-based practice, an empowerment model, and strengths perspective, then this is an enticing field of practice. Finally we should speak to jobs—since that is really what many readers are preparing for. The field offers a variety of employment opportunities in traditional social work settings where doing good clinical or generalist work from a workplace vantage is valued but also in specific spots in EAPs (employee assistance programs) and MAPs (member assistance programs) and in human resource departments and planning agencies.

The accomplishments of occupational social workers provide vivid examples of what the profession can do when located at the vortex. Like settlement house or residential treatment workers living in the community they serve, such practitioners become a part of the work organization rather than being external to it. Equally, we argue, the great majority of social work practitioners in traditional public and voluntary settings cannot fully understand their clients unless they appreciate the implications of the presence (or absence) of work as a variable in their clients' lives—and in the lives of family members. Whether viewed as a primary text for specialization in the advanced curriculum or as a supplementary reference for courses in the foundation year, *Work and the Workplace* should fill a current gap in the literature. Adhering to the CSWE Commission on Educational Policy's emphases and expectations, this book looks at direct and indirect practice, values and ethics, and issues of oppression and of social justice. We hope the reader will conclude that this book is able to make a contribution to the Columbia University Press series Foundations of Social Work Knowledge and to the larger organized profession represented by its policy-setting national organizations, its schools, and ultimately, by its practitioners in the field.

Sheila H. Akabas
Paul A. Kurzman

ACKNOWLEDGMENTS

This book, *Work and the Workplace*, is our third together, following publication of *Work, Workers, and Work Organizations* (1982) and *Work and Well-Being* (1993). This new text brings together our more than thirty years of practice, research, and teaching in this arena, and we hope we will provide a useful textbook for occupational social work and meet a pressing need for work-centered content in the social work curriculum.

Sheila Akabas wishes to acknowledge, with deepest appreciation, her invaluable friend and colleague Dr. Lauren B. Gates, the research director of the Center for Social Policy and Practice in the Workplace, who for more than fifteen years has been her partner in building knowledge and understanding of this complex field of social work and the workplace. Many of the findings and insights in this book are a result of this working relationship with Lauren and with the other staff members of the Center, which she has been fortunate to direct for over three decades. To them all, a hearty thanks.

Sheila Akabas salutes the leadership that Dean Jeanette Takamura has provided to the entire Columbia University School of Social Work community and is grateful for the encouragement and support the Dean offers to the faculty in its scholarly activities. Sheila Akabas also wishes to recognize Dr. Cheryl Franks, who has developed innovative and challenging field placements for students in the world of work and has been unfailing in her constructive development of an advisory committee of practitioners for this field of practice. Her work has been a significant contribution to the field's development at Columbia University and nationally.

Finally, Sheila Akabas expresses her gratitude to her immediate family for their ongoing love, interest, and support: her husband, Aaron Louis Akabas, to whom this book is dedicated, Myles and Sharon Akabas, Sam, Leor and Reuben, Seth and Meg Akabas, Shai, Tal, Shoshana and Lev and

Miriam Akabas, and David Kaminsky, Eli, and Ariel. Without them, nothing would be as satisfying.

Paul Kurzman wishes to express his gratitude to his colleague Professor Florence Wexler Vigilante, who has been a partner at the Hunter College School of Social Work over the past thirty years in promoting a work-centric focus for the school curriculum and its World of Work Field of Practice specialization. Dr. Vigilante's unswerving commitment to the field and inspired leadership of Hunter College's Employee Assistance Program, noted in chapter 4, have been a source of insight and inspiration to us all.

Paul Kurzman also wishes to express enduring gratitude to his family for their support of his professional interests and commitments. His wife, to whom this book is dedicated, and his children, grandchildren, and immediate family have consistently provided both sustenance and love—essential complements to the satisfactions of meaningful work. He offers his special thanks and hugs to each of them: Margaret, Katherine, Saïd, David, Shannon, Jacob, and Jenna.

We are grateful as well to our partners and associates at the Columbia University Press. John L. Michel, senior executive editor, Michael Haskell, manuscript editor, and Anne Gibbons, copy editor have all been uncommonly supportive to us during the long incubation and gestation period of this text, and we appreciate their helpfulness, encouragement, and patience. Dr. Frederic G. Reamer, editor of the Social Work Knowledge Series (to which this book is a contribution) has been generous with his sustenance and counsel, and Philip A. Berry has provided us with a most thoughtful and observant foreword to this volume.

We also are grateful to have been able to play a part over the years in making occupational social work a nationally recognized field of practice at graduate schools of social work and in practice settings throughout the country. We appreciate as well the extent to which a discussion of work, workers, and work organizations increasingly has come to permeate most social work curricula, and to assume a prominence in social work practice in more and more settings. We have felt fortunate to have had a modest role in bringing about this outcome for the profession. In our view, the potential of work-sensitive practice is virtually without limit. Moreover, its congruence with promoting the twin goals of our profession—the creative provision of social services and the promotion of progressive social change—we believe will be evident to the reader throughout this book. Indeed, our students and graduates have modeled such holistic practice. We therefore acknowledge our debt to them and pay tribute to them in appreciation for their contributions to the field.

WORK AND THE WORKPLACE

CHAPTER 1

History and Rationale

Work, or its absence, is inevitably a central issue in the lives of the clients social workers serve. When we meet a stranger it is no accident that, after an exchange of names, the first question we ask is "And tell me, what do you do?" with the rest of the question understood to be "for a living." Frequently, it is what we most want to know about the other person before we decide whether we wish to pursue a relationship. If we continue, the next question may be "and so where do you work?" in order to understand the stranger's work in the context of a work organization. It is in the spirit of the centrality of work, workers, and work organizations in the American experience that this book is written.

Work in Legislation

The national agenda of both major political parties has put the issue of "work" on the front burner. Perhaps even at the expense of family life, virtually all adults in America are expected to be a member of a working family. Except for retirees, there will be fewer and fewer exceptions. Additionally, work organizations—employers and unions—play a central role in national and local decision-making and resource allocation. In a peacetime economy, work organizations may influence the family, the community, and the political arena more than any other entity. Moreover, in the past thirty-five years, federal legislation focused on work, workers, and work organizations has altered the American landscape, having an impact on family life and the community as much as on the workplace itself. While the significance of work as a variable in public policy debates is longstanding, the codification of federal laws affecting work institutions and work populations is relatively recent in U.S. history.

Definitions and Boundaries

World of Work

In most countries, and very powerfully in the United States, the world of work is the engine for the production of goods and services that serve the population, create a balance of trade, and sustain the economy. The world of work employs people for wages and benefits under public or private auspices. For most Americans, it is where they will spend up to half the waking hours of their adult life, and yet this world historically has received only modest attention from the social work profession.

A broadly based focus on the "world of work" as a unit of attention for social workers is useful because it insists that we view this arena holistically. Professional practice in world of work settings includes not only workers and their families but also others who wish to prepare for, enter, return to, and retire from the work world. The need for youth employment training, personnel and guidance services, employment programs for people with disabilities, union upgrading programs, dislocated worker services, vocational rehabilitation projects, and welfare-to-work opportunities are core concerns of social workers and natural settings for professional practice.

Conceptually, the world of work is a functional community in which most adults voluntarily participate for a major portion of their lives (Akabas 1983; Ozawa 1982). It is so central that we prepare for it (through education) when young, frequently reminisce about it (in retirement) when old, and see it as the locus of many of our friendships and our social and communal ties. Moreover, within the world of work lies a benefit system for which participants and their families may be eligible.

Richard Titmuss (1968) conceptualized the presence of a third social welfare system over and above the social (voluntary) and fiscal (public) welfare systems that were more commonly understood. He referred to the occupational welfare system of benefits and services as one in which individuals may participate as a result of their employment status. Social work scholars (Weiner et al. 1971: 6) further defined the occupational social welfare system in the United States as composed of "benefits and services, above and beyond wages, directed at social and health needs, provision for which is not legislatively mandated. Entitlement to these benefits and services results from affiliation with a job in a particular company, or membership in a particular union, or a dependent relationship to an entitlee."

In an era when the voluntary sector is overwhelmed by unmet needs and public welfare expenditures are under broad attack, the existence of the occupational social welfare system makes work more attractive. Because of potential eligibility for the benefits and services of a third social welfare system that is funded by employers, voluntary participation may be induced. As Akabas has noted (1995a), if one considers total fringe benefits as the "social welfare provision" of the workplace, approximately one-quarter of all payroll expenses are allocated for that purpose. Moreover, this private social welfare system, often invisible and unacknowledged, grew from only 8 percent of America's gross domestic product (GDP) in 1972 to nearly 14 percent of the GDP in 1992. In absolute figures Kerns (1995: 66) notes that in 1992 "private health care expenditures outstripped government health expenditures, $462.9 billion to $357.5 billion." Hence, the incentives to work may derive in part from the tangible and attractive benefits that become an entitlement for workforce participants.

Occupational Social Work

In the United States occupational social work generally is defined as benefits and services, under labor or management auspices, that utilize professional social workers to serve members or employees, as well as the legitimate social welfare needs of the labor union or employing organization. It also includes the use of social workers, by a voluntary or proprietary social agency, to provide social welfare consultation or services to a trade union or employing organization under a contractual agreement. The employing organizations include corporations, trade unions themselves, government agencies, and nonprofit organizations such as hospitals, churches, and universities (Kurzman 1987).

On an international level, the UN's Department of Economic and Social Affairs (1971: 3) defines occupational social welfare as "the range of programs, operations and activities carried out at any level or by any group which promotes or preserves the welfare of the worker and protects him and his family from the social costs of the work process and work setting." There are three major differences between the international definition provided by the United Nations and the definition commonly accepted in the United States. First, the UN offers a somewhat broader conception of what constitutes occupational social welfare activities. Second, professional social workers are not emphasized in UN guidelines as the principal provider of services. Finally, the international definition places no focus on the auspices of programs and services, which is a central focus of the American definition (Kurzman 1987).

Additional perspectives can be gained from the only two texts written by social work colleagues that have "occupational social work" in the title. Googins and Godfrey (1987: 5), for example, characterize occupational social work as "a field of practice in which social workers attend to the human and social needs of the work community by designing and executing appropriate interventions to insure healthier individuals and environments." In a somewhat similar vein, Straussner (1990: 2) states that it is "a specialized field of social work practice which addresses the human and social needs of the work community through a variety of interventions which aim to foster optimal adaptation between individuals and their environments." In a blended definition set in an ecological framework, the authors (Akabas & Kurzman 1982b: 197) have described occupational social work as a field of practice "where the focus is on the individual in the status of worker, the environment as defined by employing organizations and trade unions, work as the goal of functional performance among client populations, and social policy as a recognition of the interconnection between social welfare and the world of work."

Work in Social Work

While the social work profession has responded to work issues since its inception more than a hundred years ago, the profession usually has intervened from the perspective of the client (the worker) but rarely from the vantage of the employer or union (the work organization). However, the advent of occupational social work as a field of practice has given professional social workers an opportunity to be connected to the same work organization as the clients whom they are serving—clients defined as both workers and work organizations. Starting in embryonic form in the 1920s (Popple 1981) and experiencing some noted success in response to the needs of the armed services and industry during World War II (Reynolds 1975; Bevilacqua & Darnauer 1977), occupational social work began to achieve an entry level of institutionalization during the 1960s. In that decade, two important events occurred. Management at Polaroid in Boston decided to make their innovative employee assistance program a permanent unit of the corporation and to lure additional social workers as human resource consultants to the decision-makers of the firm in areas such as affirmative action, social responsibility, and benefit management ("Counseling and Consultation," 1978). At the same time, Weiner, Akabas, and Sommer (1973) in New York were establishing a successful labor-management–based mental health and rehabilitation program at the health center of the Amalgamated Clothing Workers of America.

Issues and Dilemmas

As occupational social work practice has evolved, issues and dilemmas have become more explicit. Difficult and even paradoxical resolutions have emerged, inevitably shaped by practice experience.

In occupational social work practice the fundamental questions from an ethical perspective are "whose agent are we?" and "what impact does the nature of the host setting have on defining social work's function—in relation to the client and the host organization—when their interests are not the same?" Our answer to such questions has a great deal to do with how we handle the issue of confidentiality when working under proprietary auspices. Our response to these questions requires us to be sophisticated in our mastery of organizational (as well as individual) behavior and to understand that in all settings, confidentiality is always relative, never absolute.

Because a breach of privacy could mean the loss of a worker's job or a stigma that could affect a worker's job advancement, the issue of confidentiality takes on special importance in work settings (Kurzman 1987, 1988b). Because the corporate world is not oriented to human services, the social worker must be prepared to question (even challenge) managers' understandings of confidentiality and, ultimately, their willingness to respect workers' rights. Although experience tells us that instances of actual abuse are rare—some might say they are no more frequent than in more traditional settings (Kurzman & Akabas 1981; Kurzman 1988a)—occupational practitioners must acknowledge and respect workers' apprehensions and be scrupulous in upholding the standards of the social work profession and its code of ethics (NASW 1999).

A second concern is broader in scope and conceptually more complex. Does the emergence and expansion of occupational social work signal a continuing trend, which began with the growth of social workers in private practice, that could lead to an abandonment of public and nonprofit social agencies for the perceived advantages of the private sector? Does a movement toward occupational social work (under labor-management auspices) suggest that the profession has become less committed to serving the poor and people of color, who often are not members of the workforce?

These are powerful and pertinent questions. A national trend toward "privatization" of the economy in general and of the human services in particular already has had a measurable impact on major sectors in which social workers practice, such as psychiatric services, child welfare, geriatrics, substance abuse services, and corrections. Families not connected to the workplace and workforce increasingly are taking on attributes of an underclass that is unserved and unseen. Any abandonment of our historic commitment to organizing on behalf of progressive social change might correctly be viewed as an unacceptable desertion of core functions unique to our profession (Akabas 1983; Walden 1978; Bakalinsky 1980; Kurzman 1983; Akabas & Gates 2000).

In response to the poignancy and centrality of these issues, this book is broadly concerned with "work and the workplace," in title and text. We are committed to a focus on the unemployed, underemployed, and never-employed and to people intergenerationally stuck in marginal employment or on public assistance. Transitions from welfare to work, work reentry for people with disabilities, and the opening of work options for classes of disenfranchised people are central concerns of this text.

The final issue is perhaps the most fundamental. Briefly stated, it is whether social workers' participation in the world of work will be exclusively, or even largely, as providers of social service or whether practitioners also will act as catalysts for social change. This is an old and honored issue in the profession and embraces Richmond's (1917) focus on the inherent tension between "retail" and "wholesale," Schwartz's (1969) discussion of "private troubles" versus "public issues," Wilensky and Lebeaux's (1965) concern with the "residual" and "institutional" and the Milford Conference's (1929) distinction between "cause" and "function."

These questions cannot be answered easily or absolutely, but we will not shrink from them. The world of work is full of contradictions and imperfect propositions, but this is true in great measure of all organizational life and work situations—to which social workers in traditional settings (such as public welfare, school social work, medical social work, and foster care) can attest. Once again, the fundamental questions that social workers must ask are "whose agent are we?" and "what is our professional function?" Practitioners must become comfortable with answers that often are complex and paradoxical. Central to resolution of these dilemmas, however, will be a practitioner's clarity about role and function. In the world of work, no less than in more traditional settings, social workers must hold fast to their dual commitment to being providers of social services and agents of social change. This is a historical mandate of the profession.

Work Organizations

While surely a great deal of what people do represents work, broadly defined—or may be perceived as closer to work than nonwork or leisure—

work that is specifically in exchange for compensation represents "a job." A great deal of mental and physical effort goes into the daily tasks we execute, but such toil may be different from the activities we perform by which we make a living. It is in the latter context that work becomes employment, generating our interest, in turn, in work organizations.

Some workers are self-employed or, increasingly, have an innovative relationship with the provider of their compensation, but most people work for an employer, and some are represented by a labor union. Even those on salary working from home, "on the road," or as consultants have formal relationships with the institutions that pay them in exchange for their work performance. Therefore, it is essential that we understand the organizations that provide the definition, boundaries, and rewards of income, benefits, and services, in exchange for our labor. With civilian employment in the United States currently almost 140 million, work organizations play a pivotal role on behalf of the economy, and more than any other institution, they have an impact on the life of virtually every individual and family.

Despite a vigorous and expanding economy, with little inflation, low interest rates, and low unemployment, union membership has been falling, exacerbating a difference in the balance of power between management and labor. The percentage of workers belonging to unions (35 percent in the 1950s) fell to 12.9 percent in 2003 (U.S. Department of Labor 2004).

Workers

With a decline in unemployment—for example, from 10.8 percent in December 1982 to 5.5 percent in October 2004—more Americans are working than ever before. The work ethic, a product of the Reformation and the Weberian "spirit of capitalism" (Wrong 1971), is strong, and employment increasingly is the societal expectation for all adults, with fewer and fewer exceptions. Welfare rolls are being cut in most states. A mayor of New York City in fact announced in the late 1990s that he was going to end welfare and that the traditional welfare system would be replaced by a "universal work requirement" for any adult hoping to receive financial aid ("Ending Welfare," 1998).

However, the definition of who is a worker is not as clear-cut as it was twenty years ago. A permanent attachment to the labor force in a job with a regular salary and family benefit package is less frequently the prevailing model today (see Chap. 3). Temporary and contingent workers receiving few benefits (or serving as independent contractors, with no benefits at all) are becoming a significant paradigm in a world of work where short-term profit maximization is dominant, long-term investment in a workforce is declining, and fewer workers are protected by collective bargaining agreements (Barker 2003).

Conceptual Framework

A series of conceptualizations provide a context for our view of work, workers, and work organizations, namely, method and model, focus and orientation, and commitment and perspective. By the goodness-of-fit with mainstream social work ideology of the day, social work in the workplace is a practice whose time has come because it makes use of the most evolved conceptual frameworks of the profession.

Method and Model

The roots of professional social work practice are set in the work of the Charity Organization Societies, which evolved into casework practice, and that of the Settlement House Movement, which evolved into group work, research, and community organization. However, in the profession's quest for a generic professional identity and methodology, the concept of generalist practice has been proposed and currently is widely considered to be a venue for reconciliation of this dual focus upon which the profession was founded (Landon 1995). Some scholars (Sheafor & Landon 1987) have argued that social work is "inherently generalist" because of its broad focus on the interface between people and their environments. Nevertheless, with the historic push for scientific specialization to enhance the status of the profession, and an excitement with psychodynamic, psychoanalytic, and measurable social learning techniques, social work has often veered away from a generalist perspective. Similarly, social work's fascination with and active participation in the Great Society social movement programs of the 1960s and the 1970s led (in the language of Porter Lee and the Milford Conference) to an attention to "cause" and a devaluation of "function."

While field-of-practice specific knowledge and skills are needed for successful occupational social work practice, a generalist approach and a strengths perspective are also useful, if not essential. Work organizations need help from a profession that offers advanced generalists who are capable of bringing both evidence-based clinical practice and systems sophistication to bear on their human service needs (Anthony 2003;

Thyer 2002, 2003). Such a generalist perspective fits well with the notion of assessing individuals and organizations in the context of their environment. It also is useful, as Meyer (1987) has observed, because social work needs a unifying perspective that will provide cohesiveness to practice across method. Refined under a National Association of Social Workers' (NASW) grant, the person-in-environment (PIE) system does not lead to a diagnosis, as with the Diagnostic and Statistical Manual of Mental Disorders (APA 1994), but rather to the identification, description, and classification of problems brought to the social work practitioner. The problems are not seen as existing only in the individual or only in the environment but rather in the matrix. Influenced as much by concepts from sociology as psychology, the person-in-environment approach identifies the client's problems in social functioning instead of diagnosing a disease or disorder. With equal emphasis, the PIE system looks at the problems that emanate from the environment and affect the client's social role functioning.

A person-in-situation approach is consistent with, and is further strengthened by, an ecological perspective. In introducing the ecological metaphor to social work thirty years ago, Germain (1973) observed that social work's attention to physical and social environments and culture, and to their reciprocal relationships with people, had been the exception. From a social functioning perspective, however, she argued that the focus ought to be less on questions of client "illness" versus "health" than on enhancing the client's ability to function more effectively (as Freud would remind us) in the critical areas of life, which are family and work. Such an ecological perspective is consistent with what Germain (1973: 327) terms "the life model," which "defines problems not as reflections of pathological states but as consequences of interactions among elements of the ecosystem including other people, things, places, organizations, ideas, information, and values. They are conceptualized as problems in living, not as personality disturbances. . . . Instead of directing a practitioner's attention to the remedial treatment of personal defects, the 'life model' focuses on enhancing people's strengths, modification of the environment and maximizing the level of person:environment fit."

A differential assessment is made of "life stressors," which are generated by critical life issues that clients perceive as exceeding their personal and environmental resources. An emphasis is placed on the ecological concepts of "habitat" and "niche," which serve, respectively, as metaphors for where clients work, affiliate, and dwell, and the status they occupy within those structures and settings (Germain & Gitterman 1995).

Each of the above frameworks—the generalist, person-in-environment, and ecological—is exceedingly useful to social welfare practice, in general, and practice with workers (and in work settings), in particular, because each one builds upon social systems theory. Evolving from the study of biology and ecology, social systems theory looks at the exchanges that take place among individual, collective, and institutional organisms and their environments in an evolutionary context (von Bertalanffy 1968; Morgan 1997: chap. 3). In open social systems, the quest for equifinality creates different challenges from those present in closed biological systems, which generally offer fewer opportunities for intervention in the give-and-take between the organism and its environment. In open systems, such as the family, community, and the world of work, individuals and their environment are in a continuous state of interaction and mutual interdependence. This reality provides both opportunity and challenge for the social work practitioner.

As Parsons (1951) noted, social systems are created and endure because they appear to sustain social functions that are valued. In the spirit of an ecological, open systems paradigm, entropy is replaced by equifinality so long as the system remains open to adaptation and change, and the function that the system performs is one that continues to be valued. Such a structural-functional approach suggests that new structures and systems will be built when new functions need to be performed and sustained, and no structure already in place is deemed equally capable of performance. Conversely, if the function is no longer needed or valued, the social structure that had been created will need to adapt to new social needs or risk extinction. This social systems model, founded upon principles of structural functionalism and systems evolution, helps to explain why some social agencies are created, some close, and others successfully evolve and adapt over time to a changing environment and to altered perception of need.

Hence, we see many Great Society and War on Poverty agencies closing, employee assistance programs being created, and the March of Dimes (Sills 1957) adapting. Indeed, in terms of structural-functional theory, the creation of EAP (employee assistance program) structures in virtually all Fortune 500 corporations during the past twenty-five years can be explained by employers' perceptions that EAPs play a critical function—in health care cost containment, compliance with state and federal statutes, and protection from litigation, if nothing else.

Focus and Orientation

Although there are potential advantages for mastery by the pursuit of practice method specialization (such as clinical services, group work, and community organization), the profession increasingly has observed that social work functions rarely break down in method-specific fashion. The need to embrace both "private troubles" and "public issues" (Schwartz 1969) in all forms of social work practice has led to an appreciation of the practical utility of a multimethod conceptualization for assessment and intervention. Given the typical presenting problems of workers and their families, and the common needs of work organizations, a "mix and blend" orientation to method has proved a happy evolutionary development for social workers interested in the world of work.

Gordon Hamilton (1940) was the first to use the term "psychosocial assessment" in a major textbook, and the conceptualization was given further prominence twenty-four years later by Florence Hollis (1964) in her seminal practice text. With a rapid advancement in the basic sciences and medicine over the past four decades, Hamilton's and Hollis's formulation has been extended and is now known as the "biopsychosocial" focus of the profession. Such adaptation takes note of the increasing appreciation of biological, physiological, organic, and congenital components of development that must be captured in an adequate assessment. As Goldstein (1995: 1948) has noted, the biopsychosocial approach today is committed to professional assessment "within a systems perspective and tries to achieve a balance among biological, psychological, interpersonal, environmental, and cultural factors." As Hollis and Woods (1990) observed, to capture the person-in-situation gestalt, the biopsychosocial approach must use concepts derived from general systems theory and the ecological point of view.

Biopsychosocial assessments, when done in a systems context and with an epidemiological perspective, often lead to effective prevention. Given the public health axiom that the most effective way to address social problems is to prevent them, the obligation of social work practitioners to engage proactively in primary and secondary prevention would seem clear. As Bloom (1995) observes, preventing predictable problems, protecting current competency, and promoting human and organizational potential are at the heart of prevention activities. Because prevention is seen as making economic as well as social sense, some health maintenance organizations (HMOs) today are providing annual cost-free health and wellness examinations and inoculations that traditional third-party health insurance programs refuse to cover. The decision by HMOs to promote and cover routine health prevention tests and examinations is not an eleemosynary gesture; it is a pragmatic response that is cost-effective.

As Akabas and Farrell (1993) note, prevention is an organizing concept for work site services. With greater access to the workplace as occupational social workers than family service workers have to the home, the world of work frequently opens opportunities for practitioners to do primary prevention and early intervention that are uncommon in agency-based settings. In addition, as members of the work organization, one has the insider's advantage to "sensing the system" (Miller 1977) and influencing policy formulation.

Commitment and Perspective

Empowerment is a core function of the social work profession and as much a focus for the clinician as the community organizer. In fact, the current educational policy and accreditation standards (CSWE 2001) and accompanying Council on Social Work Education Commission on Educational Policy guidelines (CSWE 2002) give added emphasis to empowerment, especially of populations at risk. Regardless of method or setting, the practitioner's effort to increase client, group, family, and organizational self-sufficiency is expected to be a primary focus of professional intervention. On the individual level, for example, social workers who engage in empowerment-focused practice seek to develop the capacity of people to understand their environment, make choices, take responsibility for their choices, and influence their life situations through organization and advocacy (Gamble & Weil 1995: 483). For occupational social workers, designing family-friendly job options for working mothers, advocating for work site modifications for applicants with disabilities, promoting the employment of people with developmental disabilities, and ensuring equal mentorship for managers of color are examples of potential empowerment opportunities. In fact, for many people who experience intergenerational disadvantages and discrimination in their family, neighborhood, community, or school, the workplace may be the most likely site for empowerment and equal opportunity.

Work organizations also are an increasingly important locus for our attention because it is projected that, in the first decade of this new century, workers who are women and people of color will constitute 85 percent of the growth of the labor force (Johnston & Packer 1987). Although the prominence of white men in the workforce may not change significantly because there are sufficient new entrants to replace those who leave, it was accurately forecast that in the year 2000 white males would represent only 15 percent of new workers. Almost 66 percent of new workforce entrants are women, and 43 percent are people of color (Bailey 1995).

As Gray and Barrow (1993) observe, the world of work offers social work practitioners an opportunity to mount program-level as well as institutional-level interventions on behalf of minority workforce populations that chronically experience discrimination in our society. Because some attitudes and behaviors are fixed within a culture—Alderfer's (1987) notion of "embeddedness"—social work's location as a peer participant, in the workplace culture, gives it insight, credibility, and potential leverage that would be substantially more difficult to achieve working from a traditional external agency setting. Pluralism and diversity still may be radical concepts in settings bound by tradition. However, a focus on them as strengths (not problems) and as organizationally enriching (not confounding) is a perspective that can be empowering to workers and strengthening to work organizations (Saleebey 2003). As Dunn (1998: 81) has noted, such a practice approach promotes integrative pluralism, a model that "offers the best of all possible worlds . . . because it . . . allows for unity while retaining diversity—diversity with parity."

Akabas and Gates (1993), in fact, argue that diversity is the secret weapon of America's economic strength as compared with the economies of Germany and Japan. As a conceptual framework, social work also stresses that some populations are inherently at-risk and that all individuals experience at-risk moments during their careers. Among the former are older workers, people of color, single parents, people with disabilities, unskilled workers, immigrants, the chronically and continually ill, and people who have been in prison. These are what Gitterman (2001: 1) terms "profoundly vulnerable populations" that may be quietly and persistently "overwhelmed by oppressive lives, and by circumstances and events they are powerless to control." Moreover, all of us may experience poignant and seemingly unmanageable at-risk moments in life if we are suddenly faced with the death of a child, severe physical or mental illness, divorce, economic downsizing, crime victimization, elder-care responsibility, or job jeopardy. While statistics may identify at-risk situations that are more likely to be pervasive for some, the multiple demands of the intricately complex world in which we live presage the likelihood that periods when we are at-risk will continue to be universal. The question for social workers is whether their population-at-risk sensitivity will strengthen them in these instances so that they will be able to serve and empower their clients.

Systems Influencing Policy and Practice

Each of us navigates three worlds that we have been acculturated to conceptualize separately: family, work, and community. Despite Parsonian theory, Kanter (1977: 14) observed that, until recently, policy and practice tended to operate on the basis that work and family and community were separate worlds. "Separation of the occupational and family sectors of society," she noted, "came to be considered . . . essential to the smooth functioning of each institution and thus to the integration of society as a whole." The happenings in one, even if they affected the other, were considered external to it.

This separateness, however, is a myth that must be corrected. If we accept the idea that the job is only a source of income, the family is only a source of affection, and the community is the arena for recreation, we buy into this false notion of "separate worlds." It is simplistic to believe that the behavior of work institutions is only economic, the behavior of families is only supportive, and the behavior of communities is only social. For example, work groups provide interpersonal satisfactions usually associated with the family, and likewise, families produce products and services necessary for their members; thus there is caregiving in the world of work and there are economic issues in the home (Kurzman 1988b). Put another way, we often "live" where we work and we frequently "work" where we live.

The worlds may best be viewed not as congruent, or tangent, but rather as overlapping (see fig. 1.1).

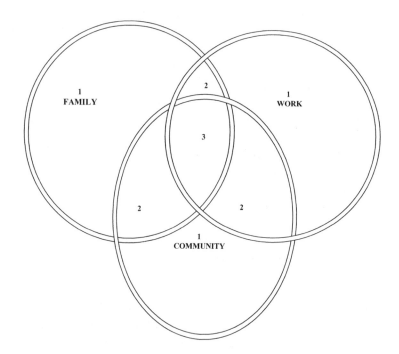

Figure 1.1   The Three Worlds in Which We Live

While to some degree each world is discrete (1), two worlds frequently overlap (2), as do, at times, all three (3). Figure 1.1 allows us to conceptualize the effect of joblessness on the family, adequate family supports on the ability to work, and sufficiency of income and family stability on the possibility for participation in the community.

CASE EXAMPLE

The two-career family often comes up against the problem of finding gratifying work for both members. When one spouse contemplates a move, the issue may become explosive. Recently, a social work intervention assisted a family and the company for which the husband worked.

Mr. K., a sales executive for a large chemical corporation, was offered the opportunity to handle the firm's major sales territory. The position was the steppingstone to top corporate leadership. Yet the vice president, when he informed Mr. K. of the promotion, noted some lack of enthusiasm. In the weeks that followed, sales in K's territory fell appreciably. His assistant often seemed to cover his nonattendance rather than converse about his activities. These changes were easily "explained" in terms of the distraction involved in preparing for the move, but when Mr. K. did not follow his earlier conversation with a timetable for when he would move and take over his new assignments, the vice president became concerned. He approached Mr. K., but the troubled salesman told his boss that he had decided not to accept the transfer and would be happy to start looking for another job; "up or out" was the general corporate policy for managers.

Because Mr. K. was seen as a valued employee (someone on the fast track), this unexpected development caused the vice president to probe further. He elicited little beyond that Mr. K. was declining for "personal reasons." The frustrated officer urged Mr. K. to talk with the occupational social worker in Human Resources.

Mr. K. shared his dilemma with the social worker. His wife, chairperson of the second grade for the school district, had recently received tenure in the local school after working there several years. Although she was delighted by the confidence the corporation had shown in her husband, she was distressed at having to leave her own job, particularly because of the national scarcity of similar jobs due to the declining birth rate in the country. Mr. K. was particularly worried about Mrs. K. losing her job since the family had struggled through a severe adjustment crisis, and he viewed his wife's return to work as contributing to its resolution. He noted an

(continued)

awareness of increasing marital tension and a breakdown of communication at home.

In joint sessions with husband and wife, the social worker drew out their commitment to each other and to retaining each one's career. They realized that if they moved and she could not find rewarding work as an educational administrator, she would have extreme difficulty in adjusting to the dislocation. At the same time, she realized that his refusing this promotion would constitute a sacrifice that might eventually result in great anger and guilt. They had considered an arrangement in which Mr. K. might return to their present home for weekends, leaving the family at its present location, but rejected this option, believing it to be damaging to their marriage and to their teenage children.

The occupational social worker, as a neutral mediator, helped the couple lay out a strategy. They identified the need for more information and agreed that Mrs. K. should visit the proposed town to ascertain its employment opportunities. Her trip confirmed their expectation that only a miracle would produce an appropriate position. They then sought to determine what the corporation expected from Mr. K. Given a certain timetable, they thought that Mrs. K. might be able to take a leave of absence while her husband worked at his new position.

When the social worker conveyed the problem in its multiple dimensions, management shifted its decision. They agreed that Mr. K. was an ideal executive candidate and that the new assignment was an attempt to provide him with management exposure, a goal that could be served in other ways. They found a new, central office promotion for this valued employee. His relief and his appreciation were pervasive. His career became a focal commitment for the entire family.

Social work staff had assisted both the sales executive and the company. Listening well and being able to think "outside the box," the occupational social worker laid the groundwork for an innovative resolution acceptable to both the employer and the employee. Moreover, he established a climate for more flexible solutions to such dual career dilemmas for the future.

In the absence of family-friendly policies, work organizations today frequently put burdens on the family that it cannot independently sustain. The absence of job security, threat of downsizing, requirement of frequent travel, and contraction of fringe benefits can create family instability and dislocation. Similarly, single-parenting, no guarantee of day care for elder parents or young children, a minimum wage set below the federal poverty standard, and the dissolution of the extended family may have a reciprocal impact on availability and willingness to work, and on ability to participate in and contribute to community life. In a six-part series ("Downsizing of America" 1996: 28) the *New York Times* noted that from 1979 to 1996, 43 million jobs were lost in the United States. With the permanent elimination of 185,000 workers at General Motors, 123,000 at AT&T, and 50,000 at Sears, Roebuck "there is the eerie feel of battlefield casualty counts. Like waves of strung-out veterans, psychically frazzled downsized workers are infecting their families, friends and communities with their grief, fear and anger."

In addition to stress-induced illness and a rise in divorce, in city after city, overworked as well as downsized individuals (and families) are withdrawing from the civic activities that hold communities together. Sociologists report that involvement has tumbled at PTAs, Rotary Clubs, Kiwanis, town meetings, and church suppers. Bowling leagues are unraveling, even though more people are bowling. As Lewis (1996: A31) insightfully observes: "A particularly significant phenomenon is the weakening of community life—of the private associations that everyone from deTocqueville on has seen as a crucial factor in American society. People desperate for work do not have the time or the will to volunteer for churches or Boy Scouts or the United Way. Fewer and fewer people feel attached to any community."

Implications

Our goal is to look at the conceptual and functional interdependence among these three worlds: work, family, and community. None of these worlds is static; in fact, over the past thirty years the changes in all three, individually and in relation to each other, have been considered by many observers more rapid than in the previous fifty. The typical family, composed of two parents, with mother and children at home, supported by the working father, has not been the norm now for several decades. A stable workplace that employs full-time workers (frequently for a lifetime, even intergenerationally, father to son) and offers a wide range of family-focused fringe benefits and a one to three likelihood of a strong trade union—these are images of the past. Automation and globalization are work site realities in tandem with feminization and integration. Short-term goals such as profit-taking and productivity-maximization frequently are taking the place of reinvestment and long-term commitment to the development and training of a workforce. With the new five-year federally mandated lifetime limit for public assistance, job centers are replacing welfare centers. Working longer hours for less money and fewer benefits, American workers are also more productive than ever. Outdistancing rivals such as Germany and Japan, the United States appears to have the most efficient and effective economy in the world.

The texture and fabric of the family, community, and world of work also have been altered. Changed not only by the demands of employers but also by new statutes and social movements as well, the family may not be in as good a position as before to respond to the new expectations of the workplace. In addition, there may not be enough well-educated and fully skilled workers available to work organizations at costs they perceive they can afford. With less support from government and fewer volunteers, neighborhood organizations (such as PTAs and ambulance corps) frequently find they too function less effectively. Such are the realities that professional social workers must face as they help to influence public policy and play a pivotal role in providing our society's social services, whether they practice in the world of work or simply with clients who are workers. These realities establish the context and set the stage for the rationale and the "work" of this book.

* * *

In the next chapter we focus more specifically on what "work" means today in America, and the several functions work performs—for the individual and for the country. Why are work organizations so important that they deserve a social worker's attention? Why is "Tell me, what do you do?" so often the opening question we ask someone we are meeting for the first time? Indeed, what is it about this little four-letter word that piques our curiosity?

Study Questions

1. What factors do you feel have promoted occupational social work as a field of practice? What events do you think may have inhibited its growth and institutionalization during the past several decades?
2. Do you agree or disagree with the authors' position that occupational social workers have a dual obligation "to provide social service and act as catalysts for social change?" Explain your answer.
3. How do you feel about trade unions? Do you think the current decline in union membership is a serious issue, or do you feel workers' needs can be met appropriately in other ways?

4. Are the ecological, empowerment, person-in-environment, and populations-at-risk perspectives compatible with your school's educational focus? Do you feel they are fitting frameworks for occupational social work practice?

5. Can you think of other approaches to Mr. & Mrs. K's dilemma that might have been more useful and appropriate than the one that was selected? If so what are they?

6. Do you think Kanter's conceptualization (p. 13) of "work" and "family" as overlapping (rather than discrete) worlds reflects current reality, or would an alternate approach be more useful?

CHAPTER 2

The Meaning and Context of Work

Meaning of Work in America

Human services and mental health professionals focus primarily on individuals and their families; work and work organizations rarely receive equal attention. While there are exceptions—occupational therapists and vocational rehabilitation counselors being possible examples—a review of the literature of the helping professions indicates greater attention to individuals and their adjustment within the family than to the world of work and work functions. This fact is in part a product of culture and context. From the days of the founding fathers, our country and Constitution have valued the individual, glorifying liberty and individualism more than most nations.

Socialization within the helping professions has been influenced as well by psychoanalytic thought and the seminal contributions of Sigmund Freud. Despite his acknowledgment of work and love as the cornerstones of adult functions, his work focused almost entirely on the latter at the expense of the former. Given Freud's preeminence and prevailing impact on mental health education, we should not be surprised that his perspective has been dominant over time. The irony is that we know little about Freud's large family (except the work of his famous daughter Anna), and we know him too almost entirely through his own work, which was an obsession.[1] As Freud himself discovered, work serves many functions.

The early research of Friedman and Havinghurst (1954) demonstrated that work provides financial rewards, opportunities for the expenditure of time and energy, occasion for social interaction, meaningful life experiences,

---

[1] In fact, Freud had *six* children.

and respect and status. In this context, work offers the individual not only income but also an attachment to the larger social system and its realities.

Tangible Functions

As Akabas (1995a: 1780) has observed, in this country our employment defines us more than our ancestors, religious affiliation, or educational attainment. We derive status, self-sufficiency, sense of self-worth, social contacts, and organization of our day from our work. Being in the world of work means that one is swimming with the prevailing current and therefore is likely to be part of the mainstream of America, rather than on the margin. As Ozawa (1985) perceptively remarks, to work is to be a "real" American.

On a manifest level, work is the principal way in which most individuals earn an income to support themselves and a family. In an economic system characterized by a free market, in which goods and services are produced for profit and labor is performed for wages, able-bodied adults are expected "to work for a living" or to be a member of a family unit where such work is performed. To be outside this sphere implies marginality since a capitalist economic system depends upon the explicit exchange between worker and employer to generate its products and services. Lest we become too sociological in perspective, we must first underscore the economic necessity of working and the expectation that every citizen will strive to be self-supporting. Not to work and to earn may result in becoming dependent upon meager and means-tested government payments, and such individuals, to borrow Ralph Ellison's (1952) metaphor, are invisible adults in America.

Work also provides the package of fringe benefits upon which all families depend. Some of these benefits are mandated by law—such as unemployment insurance, workers' compensation, Medicare contribution, and Social Security—and paid in part (Social Security) or in whole (unemployment insurance) by the employer. If one is not in the world of work (or a dependent of one who is), these entitlements are absent and denied; further, if an individual is not formally employed by a work organization, the burden of paying the full cost of some benefits (such as Social Security and unemployment insurance) must be borne solely by the worker.

While there may be other advantages to being an independent contractor, employee status often means that the worker also will be privileged to receive a series of additional fringe benefits. Distinguished from the benefits enumerated above, these additional entitlements are entirely voluntary (or collectively bargained) and result solely from affiliation with a job with a particular employer, membership in a union, or a dependent relationship to a benefits recipient (Weiner et al. 1971). Expanding after the Second World War, and becoming commonplace in many settings by the 1960s, these benefits may include health insurances, paid vacations, pension contributions, and an array of services such as educational reimbursement, day care subsidies, and employee assistance services. These nonmandated employee benefits and services (over and above wages) are generally far more expensive for individual workers to purchase on their own in the marketplace, if they can obtain them at all. These employer-sponsored payments have the considerable added value of representing wage supplements on which workers (unlike income) do *not* have to pay taxes, because they are provided as pretax benefits.

Until recently, some Americans may have taken these voluntary benefits for granted. Social historians, however, will remind us that these benefits have no long-term precedent in the American workplace. For most of our history, even after the industrial revolution and the evolution of formal employer-employee relationships, workers enjoyed no legislatively mandated benefits; these commenced, albeit in embryonic form, with the New Deal and provisions of the initial Social Security Act of 1935. At that juncture in American history, of course, the nonmandated benefits and services, which many workers today take for granted, were few, meager, and ephemeral. Fringe benefits also include being paid a wage or salary for days when one does no work at all. Many employees, for example, enjoy some measure of paid vacation, paid holidays, paid sick leave, and perhaps paid personal days as well. Cumulatively, they often add up to twenty or more days a year, or nearly a month of wages without working.

Intangible Rewards

Sigmund Freud (1930) noted the importance of work to the individual's connection to society. For "work has a greater effect than any other technique of living in the direction of binding the individual more closely to reality; in his work he is at least securely attached to a part of reality, the human community." Indeed, Freud's autobiography is not about himself as a person or about his family, but rather is an account of his work. It should, therefore, be no surprise that Studs Terkel (1972) concluded, after three years of interviewing workers all across America, that people feel passionate about their work, regardless of their occupation. As Solzhenitsyn (1963) observed, even forced laborers in Siberia, like Ivan Denisovich, care about their work. At day's end, Ivan ventures one more look at his work on a construction gang. A moment of satisfaction is felt for he sees that despite having had few tools and no leveling string, his bricks lie even. The wall is straight as a die and he feels genuine pride in his accomplishment.

Jahoda (1988) has spoken of the tangible and intangible functions of work. According to Jahoda, jobs fulfill manifest goals, such as securing an income (and usually fringe benefits) for individuals and their families. Never having (or suddenly losing) these tangible resources may lead to loss of social and psychological stability as well as financial equilibrium. Because a job also fulfills latent functions for individuals and their families, the absence or loss has intangible implications too. In the context of Freud's (1930) earlier observations, Jahoda (1988: 17) explains: "Whether one likes or hates one's job, it structures time for the day, the week, the years; it broadens the social horizon beyond family and friends; it enforces participation in collective purposes; it defines one's social status; it demands reality-oriented activities."

Bringing manifest and latent functions together into a unitary conceptualization, Perlman (1968: 81) concludes that work offers not only a social identity and linkage with other people but also "a socially recognized function; an occupation—in the sense of a use of oneself and time towards some end; some purchase power for necessities or compensatory pleasures; the right to self-governance and choices; and an underpinning of other valued life roles. Further, by its regularities, its stipulated requirements of time, behaviors, and production, work provides essential conditions for the stabilization and ordering of daily living."

To be part of a working group, recognized and appreciated by one's workmates, united with them whether by bonds or gripes or by general camaraderie, fulfills the ever-present human need to be accepted, supported, even to be authenticated by others. Sharing and exchange take place in this arena as well since the world of work is as much a community as the neighborhood in which one lives. For many, who have little time left for neighborhood activities once commitments to work and family have been met, the workplace serves a primary group function. It is here that the newly married share confidences and tips on adapting to marriage; young mothers give and receive suggestions on raising children; parents barter babysitting so they all can enjoy additional leisure without cost; divorced and widowed workers select roommates and traveling companions; and young singles arrange time-shares so they can all afford a summer vacation. In a world where demands are great, free time is circumscribed, and spare resources are scarce, the world of work frequently functions as a community, more even than the neighborhood and its traditional institutions, such as church, political clubhouse, scouts, or civic association. These are important latent benefits of association that the unemployed do not enjoy.

Nonwork Meanings

A number of literature reviews (Feather 1990; Kates, Greiff, & Hagen 1990; Leana & Feldman 1992; Vosler 1994; Warr, Jackson, & Banks 1988) identify consistent findings in research on the mental health and social consequences of unemployment. Many of these studies show a clear pattern of negative effects of unemployment on both mental and physical health: reduction in self-esteem, higher levels of anxiety, and increases in substance abuse, depression, and psychosomatic symptoms. Common feelings include pessimism, apathy, and fatalism about life, especially as unemployment persists over time. Also common are increases in somatic illnesses such as sleeping and eating disorders, as well as in physical problems such as ulcers, tics, colitis, and hypertension. Those who experience financial strain due to unemployment are at especially high risk of suffering from these physical and psychological symptoms. Social isolation and increased loneliness also are common consequences of being unemployed, since people lose not only their jobs but supportive contact with coworkers. The lack of a daily routine often leads to feelings of boredom and purposelessness among the unemployed and in extended cases to feelings of anomie (Gilberto 1997). Many scholars and clinicians who have studied work therefore have focused on nonwork and on unemployment. The best way to understand the meaning of work, they contend, is to observe what happens when it is denied or taken away.

The epidemiologist M. Harvey Brenner (1973) conducted a 125-year review of mental hospital admissions in New York State and concluded that the single most important source of fluctuations over time could be correlated to instabilities in the economy and rates of unemployment. He later expanded his research to document a similar lagged relationship between the rate of unemployment in the country (1950 to 1980) and a rise and fall in the annual number of heart attacks, imprisonments, suicides, and cases of cirrhosis of the liver (Rosenbaum 1984). Researchers at the National Institute of Mental Health also studied anxiety and depression associated with three of life's most important adult roles: worker, spouse, and parent. In their study they uncovered ten "life strains" linked to these roles and concluded that by far the greatest number of "life strains" were associated with work and occupation (Bishop 1979).

The centrality of work and nonwork has been noted by practitioners as well. Betty Carter, a social work clinician and family therapist, is quoted as stating (Bielski 1996: 25): "In this society, work has replaced religion and community as the main source of meaning, and with all the economic contradictions we're seeing, it now breeds enormous anxiety."

Fear sets in, even when economically marginal individuals are working, which in turn may affect work performance, increasing vulnerability in the overwhelming percentage of workplaces (87.1 percent in 2003) that are not protected by a collective bargaining agreement. Since work and family are inextricably interconnected, an impact on marriage, partnerships, and parenting often is inevitable, as Brenner's research confirms. Hence, Perlman (1968: 69) notes that workers, even with modest jobs and marginal job security, rarely measure their work against nonwork. Rather, they measure it against some image of the work they would like to do under conditions they would like to set—against some ideal of work.

When nonwork occurs involuntarily, whether through downsizing, global relocation, or dismissal for cause, the meaning of work comes into focus. In a study of skilled and unskilled workers faced with unanticipated unemployment, Madonia (1983: 484) concluded, "Without day-to-day accomplishments, people accustomed to work and the psychological gratifications it offers feel insecure and inadequate. Dependency increases and autonomy diminishes. Self-esteem is significantly affected and the basis for depression is established." Psychodynamically, involuntary unemployment represents the loss of a significant object to which the ego is attached, and thus there initially is the need to grieve, as with loss through death of a loved one, or in rehabilitation settings, with the loss of a limb. Sherraden (1985: 407) confirms this reality, stating that "clinical observations of recently unemployed persons . . . found grief reactions, anger, guilt, feelings of loss, and a sense of losing a part of the self . . . responses not unlike bereavement."

Interventions

When working with such clients, social workers must establish the right to mourn during treatment, since the family and community seldom will offer the sympathy that is common custom with sudden death or disability. Such intervention and permission may help clients marshal their adaptive resources and avoid "psychic numbing" (Lifton 1980: 173), which could lead to feelings of chronic deprivation, resignation, and disengagement.

Permission to grieve the loss is essential for two reasons. First, one must help individuals to mourn because it is normal and healthy to do so, and it is essential to functioning well again and to marshaling one's resources for entrepreneurship or for education, retraining, and a job search. Second, if the loss is not worked through it is likely to be relived in the future when another loss takes place, at home or at work. The new loss usually will reactivate the earlier loss—creating a psychodynamic fusion of the two, which may promote profound depression. Such pathological forms of grief may create long-term suffering and immobilization. Wilson (1996) sees this phenomenon as a characteristic of the African American underclass. Where jobs are scarce, many people may eventually feel no connection to work in the formal economy. They no longer expect work to be an option in their lives, and they participate in society with little or no labor force attachment. Feeling like dehumanized, insignificant nonpersons, such individuals may lose faith in our political and economic system altogether, blaming (perhaps correctly) larger forces for their personal predicament. Even when they find new jobs, they may not fully recover their self-esteem and a sense of "learned helplessness" may set in (Barker 2003: 245). They may feel permanently estranged from society, and their subsequent loss of attachment to work, family, and community may lead to pathological levels of anger and aggression or to passivity, major depression, or substance abuse.

With respect to the meaning of work and nonwork, Feather (1990) recommends that intervention be viewed in the general framework of interactional analysis. This approach is consistent with an ecological model that focuses on the person as an active agent who construes and interprets information from the environment and may have the capacity to alter environmental conditions. An interactional analysis sets the context for action. According to Feather (1990: 5–6), "Whether an unemployed person becomes depressed; changes his or her lifestyle; persists in looking for a job; modifies his or her beliefs, attitudes or values; withdraws from social contacts; suffers psychological distress and physical symptoms, or reacts in other ways to the condition of unemployment depends on both the person and the situation and the way they interact. This interaction is a two-way process. The situation can affect the person and the person can in turn influence or modify the environment." By viewing the unemployed from a person-in-environment perspective and with the advantage of a life model maxim (Germain & Gitterman 1996), the social worker has additional options for intervention. However, some clients may respond to individual, group, and community-based help more readily and ultimately more effectively than others, and some may simply react to the new work mandates embedded in social policy. Research has identified the advantage of a fast track to reemployment for those who experience such job loss, particularly for those with mental health and substance abuse conditions. Evidence-based best practice now is focused on a more assertive placement and training model, rather than on support for long-running vocational exploration and education, which was traditionally thought to best serve individuals experiencing job loss (Gowdy, Carlson, & Rapp 2003; Bond 1998; Ridgeway & Rapp 1999).

THE MEANING AND CONTEXT OF WORK 27

Kobasa's concept of hardiness offers an additional avenue for understanding the influence of personality traits on job reentry potential (Kobasa & Purccetti 1983). In an effort to appreciate the effects of stressful events on illness, Kobasa developed a theory of personality disposition in which hardiness is defined as "a constellation of personality characteristics that function as a resistance resource in the encounter with stressful life events" (Kobasa, Maddi, & Kahn 1982: 169). Since loss of a job can be expected to create a stressful life situation for most workers, this "hardy" personality disposition may act as a buffer against such stress and also lead to more effective job search behavior and reemployment.

The meaning of work therefore ultimately can be understood both by focusing on its manifest and latent functions in our society and, conversely, by looking at what happens to the individual, family, and community when work options are withdrawn. As our values and our statutes increasingly make employment the norm and expectation for every American family, the social and economic pressures to work may make nonwork an increasingly unsatisfying option. More than in most industrialized countries, our tangible rewards are attached to the workplace, and leisure is suspect for the able-bodied adult. In an economic system such as ours, however, there will always be a significant percentage of Americans who are unemployed or underemployed, and an appreciation of the meaning of work should help us as we serve them. Such understanding also reminds us that we must influence the public policy agenda toward the goal of minimizing the problem and maximizing client options.

Relating Practice to Work Issues

That a setting in which individuals spend the majority of their waking hours would be given only passing consideration by human services professionals who attempt to understand such people's lives is ironic. But this is all too often the case. Vocational issues frequently are viewed by social workers and other psychotherapists as being the province of other professionals, such as career counselors. This may be, in part, a consequence of our feeling poorly trained to explore this dimension of a client's life or our perception that authentic clinical issues lie in the sphere of affect, sexual function, and family. As Chestang (1982) suggests, social work practitioners have tended to pay more attention to love, eros, and intimacy than to work, creativity, and performance. Just as we might acknowledge that career counselors would be handicapped by overlooking the role of family and affection, however, we too may be hampered in our practice if we choose to overlook the importance of workplace issues (Ulrich & Dunne 1986). Ultimately, if we are to reach a synthesis in which neither love nor work dominates our explanations, work and love must merge and be conceptualized as complementary.

Contrary to popular belief, such insights are not recent observations. More than sixty years ago, Menninger (1942: 172) stated flatly that "three-fourths of the patients who come to psychiatrists are suffering from an incapacity of their satisfaction in work or their inability to work. It may be their chief complaint." As a result of her research, Lantos (1943) moreover reminded her colleagues that, in clinical practice, disturbances of working capacity are second in importance only to disturbances of sexuality but that very little attention is being paid to *work* in the practice literature. There is evidence to support her claim. Grinstein (1960) documented that among the thousands of titles listed in a comprehensive index of psychoanalytic writings, fewer than a dozen papers related to work or labor. This is despite the fact that disruption of the ability to work is seen as a significant diagnostic criterion of severe mental disorder. For the social work profession, however, the emergence of original, research-documented conceptualizations over the past thirty years has finally provided a disposition to address this clinical imbalance.

Germain's (1973) innovative ecological point of view has led many social work practitioners to accept a "life model" of practice in which all elements of a client's ecosystem are subject to study and assessment. Moving away from a prior reliance on diagnosing disorders, Germain's orientation is to look broadly at problems in living, not at illnesses or personality disturbances. This approach provides an alternative to the medical model and to dependence on a diagnostic manual developed mainly by physicians and promulgated by psychiatrists. The ecological perspective is the first of many uniquely social work models that focuses on a client's social functioning: at work, in the community, and at home.

In 1981 the National Association of Social Workers (NASW) funded a two-year project to develop a system for classifying the problems of social functioning experienced by social work clients. This study gave birth to the person-in-environment (PIE) system, a ground-breaking event for the profession (Karls & Wandrei 1994, 1995). The centrality of PIE then was codified in NASW's definition of clinical social work (Swenson 1995), which underscores the use of a person-in-situation focus and assessment of clients' social functioning in all aspects of their lives.

In this context Meyer (1987: 414) wrote that "[i]t is important [for social work] to find a unifying perspective that will provide greater cohesiveness to social work practice. Such a perspective would have to reflect the person-in-environment focus that has become central to the purpose of social work practice." Further, in developing an influential "needs-resources" paradigm for assessment, Vigilante and Mailick (1988) applied a social constructionist approach that further supports viewing the family in the context of culture and community.

The creative decade of the 1980s also witnessed the refinement of the genogram in family assessment. Defined, in part, as a diagram used in family therapy to depict relationships over several generations (Barker 2003: 178), the genogram is a social network mapping that expands the unit of attention beyond the immediate nuclear family and addresses the need to look broadly at social functioning over time. Equally helpful has been the development of the ecomap, which shows, through graphic social network mapping, the quality and quantity of nurturing supports present in a client's life. The ecomap also expands the unit of attention from the family to relevant social institutions and environmental influences (Barker 2003: 136; Meyer 1995; Hartman 1978). The next step might be a genogram that specifically maps the intergenerational work history of a family and an ecomap that traces the relationship of all adults over time to their preparation for, entry into, participation in, and retirement from the world of work. Such adaptations of these innovative diagrammatic mappings would be useful additions to clinical social work practice from a work-sensitive perspective.

Practice Issues

Although clinicians historically have tended to see family as a source of support and work as a source of stress, these new practice models look beyond such easy codifications of life spheres and events. While work may be seen by some clients as a necessity and family participation a positive choice, reality once again is rarely so simple. As Vigilante (1982: 298) has observed, "Work itself can be relatively conflict-free and growth enhancing. While individuals may have difficulties in intimate familial or social relationships, it is not unusual for them to find a more neutral environment at work." For example, a truck driver who has a local route, returning home each night, may choose to switch to cross-country driving in order to enjoy more independence from his dispatcher and more freedom from family obligations. Whether a clinician would assess this decision as a sign of strength or weakness is less important than viewing it as an important adaptation to life events in the larger ecosystem in which he functions.

Individuals make such decisions, consciously or unconsciously, in their selection of a vocation. Lawyers with a public persona may choose litigation while those who are more comfortable with data and analysis may select tax law. While there is a common denominator to sales, some may select the structure present while selling behind a counter in a store, while others may prefer a sales territory or route in the community. One person may want to become a physician because she is fond of working with people, selecting family practice as a specialty. Another may have an equal desire to become a doctor but is also aware that a bedside manner is not her greatest asset. Choosing to become a hospital-based pathologist, she states: "I know I don't have a great personality—but given my specialty, I find none of my patients complain!" The secret of success is in the goodness-of-fit.

Research by social psychologists also has provided valuable insights with respect to workers' adjustments to their work environments. They note that such adaptations should be viewed as normal and must be reciprocal. Often it is the inability of work environments to adjust to the legitimate needs of workforce participants that diminishes the goodness-of-fit. For example, despite an increase in the number of women in the workforce and the emergence of an increasingly androgynous workplace, gender stereotype and discrimination persist. If employers are unwilling to adopt family-friendly policies, such as job-sharing, flextime, and support for day care, women surely will be disadvantaged so long as family and societal expectations are that women assume primary responsibility for performing (or arranging) child and elder care. Moreover, employers who tolerate gender bias at the work site will impede the normal process of accommodation requisite to a healthy and well-functioning workplace.

It is considered normal, however, for employers to expect workers to adapt to the tasks, routines, and relationships of the workplace. Efficiency in the performance of the central tasks assigned, the ability to adapt to change, and a commitment to a specified quality and quantity of output are part of the workplace bargain and exchange. In a competitive market environment, and in an era of lean government, productivity is a universal expectation, and flexibility in adapting to change is a workplace norm. Neff (1985), a social psychologist, has documented that it is in this context that maladaptation to work can be observed. Workers who show a chronic inability to meet employer expectations in the area of task performance, compliance with work site routines, or maintenance of normal intraorganizational relationships may have great difficulty in holding a job (see chap. 5). This observation provides a useful paradigm in which occupational social workers, for example, can help supervisors identify a worker who may need help from an employee assistance program. A worker whose task performance unexpectedly declines from the norm only for a brief period, however, simply may be adapting to or recovering from a period of change, at work or at home.

If a decline in productivity, an increase in errors, or both should continue over time, administrative referral to an EAP may be warranted. Using a biopsychosocial assessment, a person-in-environment focus, and multimethod intervention, the occupational social work practitioner may be able to restore the equilibrium—not only for the worker but also between worker and work organization. Like family and community, the workplace has its legitimate routines. Arriving on time, using one's sick leave fairly, signing out at lunch, and wearing appropriate safety equipment are routines endemic to the world of work. An employee who suddenly appears unwilling or unable to comply may be evincing troubles associated with work or with issues at home; the interest of the supervisor is in securing professional expertise in making this assessment and in the employee's return to a respect for the legitimate routines of the work site. Finally, the workplace is a functional community in which individuals have roles and relationships. Supervisors need to be able to elicit the compliance of supervisees; interdependent work teams must collaborate and converse; and peers expect to be able to interact, for business and pleasure. Employees unable to participate in such relationships may impede work performance or challenge a cohesive and communal culture that others built and value. An incapacity in the area of job performance, adherence to work routine, or maintenance of appropriate relationships with others therefore are all signs of disequilibrium that may require a professional social worker to intervene, individually or systemically, in order to restore the prior symbiosis. Equally important, the occupational practitioner must make a differential assessment, since the problem may be located not with the worker but with the work organization.

CASE EXAMPLE

Mr. Ralph Pulaski had been working for a large Midwestern firm since he had graduated from high school twenty-five years ago. Bright and eager from the beginning, he had risen through the ranks from a starting position as laborer to the top mechanic's job—electrical wiring trouble-shooter. He helped train new workers, was depended on to undertake the most complex jobs, and was one of the few men who could lead a team or be sent out alone to any location. He dealt well with customers and with the technical content of his job.

(continued)

But in the last year or two, he had become difficult to work with. He alienated young trainees because of his lack of patience, often behaved rudely to customers, and although still a top technician, seemed unwilling to undertake any jobs supervising a team. Then one day he called in ill and a medical report filed by the attending physician indicated that he would be out for six weeks with a mild coronary. When Mr. P. was called in at the end of four weeks by the medical department for a physical evaluation to verify his continuing disability, the doctors certified him as ready to return to work (in fact they found no evidence of cardiac damage). Mr. P. was irate, insisted his health would be endangered by such return, stating the company wanted to "kill him," and he wasn't going to let them do that. He applied for early retirement based on disability. Although the company had a "twenty-five and out" plan for retirement at half pay, it was reluctant to lose a good worker and to absorb the long-term expense they would incur if Mr. P. retired at forty-three. His supervisor referred him to the benefits specialist in Human Resources.

At the first interview, Mr. P. presented a picture of a tense, upset person. He sat on the edge of his seat, leaned toward the interviewer, and talked loudly in response to questions. He reported that he was "very sick" and always knew he would die young. His own father had died when he had been just Mr. P's age. As they talked about the job, Mr. P. said: "This company doesn't need me. Everything's going digital and getting computerized. If I weren't sick and having to retire, I'd be sent out to pasture any day anyway. And these new kids coming in . . . they've been to the community college . . . know a lot about wiring systems . . . what can I teach them . . . ? Besides, it takes too much out of me."

The benefits specialist, a social worker, viewed Mr. P. as a complex person, frightened of aging, unsure of his own present and continuing worth, obsessed with ideas of death related to his father's early demise, and therefore somatizing his fears. In addition, the practitioner suspected that Mr. P. had a hearing problem that was exacerbating his insecurity and withdrawal.

The social worker was able to reassure Mr. P. that if he chose to, he had a right to retire and she would help him. She mentioned, however, that sometimes a person gives up a good job and regrets it later. She suggested that they meet a few times to talk about the plans Mr. P. had made, just to be sure that everything was organized and clear. The social worker's enthusiasm for such a plan brought out considerable ambivalence in Mr. P. concerning retiring. Mr. P. gave permission for her to talk with his supervisor and attending physician. At the same time, Mr. P. accepted a referral for a hearing test, and an appointment to return to Human Resources again in a few days.

As information from the various "systems" started to collect, the complexity of the problem was confirmed. The general practitioner admitted to being puzzled at what he described as the patient's report of severe chest pains with no clinical evidence of coronary disease. He had, therefore, ordered the six-week rest although he felt there was a psychosomatic overlay. The audiologist reported that Mr. P. had a hearing loss, and Mr. P. then admitted that he found it an increasing strain to communicate with others, and saw coworkers who talked with each other as "talking about him and his declining skills." Together, he and the social worker were able to identify that his death ideation and difficult middle-age "passage" had shaken his belief in himself and retiring was an attempt at flight.

Mr. P. had no plans beyond retiring. As he began to understand his concerns and ambivalent feelings, a new arrangement proved feasible, and looking at alternatives to early retirement seemed desirable to him. Work meant a great deal to him, and he really didn't want to give it up. Once Mr. P. was able to distinguish between his fantasy, his physical complaints, and his real problems, it was possible to offer counseling to deal with some aspects of his situation. He began to feel that he would like to continue working. A hearing aid helped him feel less "out of it," less threatened by work groups. His supervisor was alerted to Mr. P.'s need to feel valued and secure in the importance of his skills and was able and eager to provide such support. He had been deeply concerned about losing the trouble-shooter that he depended on—and viewed in many ways as irreplaceable. The benefits administrator calculated that the potential savings if Mr. P. remained productive and on the payroll rather than retiring would cover the benefits specialist's salary for several years.

Freud (1930) has implied that, as a path to happiness, work is not valued very highly. Such a pessimistic view of work is understandable, given Freud's emphasis on human sexuality and the pleasure principle. As in the above case example, it also reminds us as practitioners that work does not have the same meaning for everyone, and as in all issues of social living, some people may be far more advantaged than others. Also, given the still prevalent discrimination in our society against, for example, gays and lesbians, people with disabilities, immigrants, and racial minorities, a social worker must be prepared to adapt generic practice models to different client needs and expectations and to advocate for social justice.

Responsiveness to Difference

In a nation where all its people (save Native Americans) emigrated from some other country, one should expect a sensitivity to diversity and the richness of cultural pluralism. The "melting pot" spirit of America, however, hides many realities that we are hesitant to recognize. One reality is that the obscuring of difference takes away what many Americans value and is not universally desired. Another truth is that the melting point for the pot may be higher than is the popular wisdom; in fact, some melting (race, gender) rarely takes place. Historically, moreover, some groups of Americans have started off with a dramatically differential status, such as African Americans (approximately 13 percent of the current population). They came to America not voluntarily in search of freedom and opportunity, but involuntarily and enslaved, to be auctioned by others as property. Whether one looks at the forced placement of Native Americans onto reservations, internment of Japanese Americans in camps, or the holding of African Americans in bondage, in America, racial and ethnic difference often has been perversely accentuated rather than munificently melted or blended. These groups have discovered the value of recognizing and promoting their differences to achieve personal and collective authenticity and respect but frequently find themselves having to struggle for this in the workplace.

Differences in America are evident in wealth and income as well. A sharp increase in inequality in the past two decades has made the distribution of wealth in this country even more unequal than what previously prevailed in the class-focused societies of Europe. As noted in a 1995 research publication of the Twentieth Century Fund, the United States is now the most unequal of any industrialized country both in terms of income and wealth (Herbert 1996). Given the dearth of unskilled and semiskilled jobs in the United States today, the fabled working class feels threatened. Fewer young people, regardless of their ideological commitment to work, can count on full-time employment at a job that pays a wage and provides a benefits package that together can support a family. A high school diploma, willingness to learn a trade, and a good work ethic are no longer the guarantee of middle-class or even working-class status.

Gender

There are gender-specific changes as well—most dramatically, the marked increase in this country in the percentage of women who make up the workforce, from 17 percent in 1890 to 30 percent in 1950 to 47 percent in 2000 (Roark et al. 1998: A62; Toossi 2002: 27). For women of color, work for pay has been a historical norm. For example, in 1940, 32 percent of married African American women worked outside the home, while only 14 percent of married white women did so (Abramovitz 1996). The overall change in both age and labor force participation for women in recent decades has been remarkable. For example, approximately 75 percent of all women ages twenty-five to thirty-four participated in the labor force in 2000—up from about 50 percent in 1975 (DiNatale & Boraas 2002: 3). Mothers are the fastest growing group within the labor force, showing that women are choosing work in addition to (not in lieu of) a family. While in this country many women have held jobs before having children and then after their children were grown, the fact that women are maintaining a permanent attachment to the labor force, just as men do, is largely a phenomenon of the past few decades.

Interestingly, research shows that while the need for income is the primary reason for women's participation, personal satisfaction is also a powerful motivation. A 1983 *New York Times* poll of American women found that even if they could afford not to be employed, 58 percent of the women surveyed said they would rather work outside the home than stay home. They generally regarded employment and independence as elements of life that were as satisfying as husband, home, and children. The poll showed that men and women are growing much closer in their attitudes toward work, pointing up a dramatic shift since 1970 when a similar national poll found women still clinging to hearth and home (Dowd 1983). Despite substantial improvement in recent years, however, women in America earn only about seventy-seven cents for every dollar a man earns (Leonhardt 2003). Indeed, the roots of gender inequality are historical and run deep.

Race

Work opportunity and compensation are unequal as well for people of color. African Americans and Latinos have incomes considerably lower than whites, and the disparities have changed remarkably little over time. In recent years, racial inequality actually has increased. African Americans and Latinos now earn less relative to whites than they did in 1979. As a result, in 1992 only 12 percent of African American households and 15 percent of Latino households had annual incomes over fifty thousand dollars, compared with 27 percent of white households, and Latino and African American families had a median net worth of about a tenth that of white families (Folbre 1995: 45). Work opportunities also would appear to be less for people of color than for whites. At the end of 2001, when the national unemployment rate stood at 5.6 percent, the rate for whites was only 4.9 percent; however, it was 7.5 percent for Latinos and 9.9 percent for African Americans (Langdon et al. 2002: 15).

People of color also are likely to work in settings where their foreperson or supervisor is white, even though coworkers share their race, language, folkways, and culture. This reality may foster problems. Latinos, for example, may view the workplace as an extended family where people work hard but also laugh, share, and cover for each other in a fashion that a white supervisor may view as inappropriate, even insubordinate. Latino men, even if their work is humble, will look forward to *respeto* (respect) from others so that they retain their *dignidad* (dignity) and *machismo* (manhood). As Mayo-Quiñones (1998: 51) points out, the idiomatic definition of manhood in Spanish interestingly is *un hombre cabal y responsable en su trabajo* (a trustworthy and responsible man on his job). Such a definition designates him among his family and community as the epitome of male achievement and success. Such are the cultural differences that must be understood and respected, especially since Latinos have now become the largest minority population in America.

The Asian American population is diverse and growing. Composed of Chinese, Japanese, Asian-Indian, Vietnamese, Korean, Filipino, Pacific Islander, and others, the religious, language, and cultural differences are many. However, there are cultural norms that most share in common that are distinct from those in the West. Silence, humility, modesty, privacy, and control of emotion organically flow from Taoist, Confucian, and Buddhist teachings. Union activity (and engaging in strike action) may be very uncomfortable, and the bravado of a coworker or supervisor may seem inappropriate, even alienating. While our nation and culture were founded on a spirit of individualism and independence, Asian American workers may prefer a culture of interdependence, cooperation, and mutuality. Their preference may be for equilibrium, homeostasis, and harmony (See 1998). In a culturally diverse workplace, it is important for managers and coworkers to understand, appreciate, and respect these differences from a strengths perspective.

For African Americans, the issues have deep historical roots. Students of American history will recall that article 1, section 2 of the U.S. Constitution states that African Americans would be counted in the census as only 3/5 of a person, even where they were free. (American Indians—now Native Americans—were not to be counted at all.) Such institutional roots of racism are profound in American history and provide an essential backdrop for understanding the meaning of work (and opportunities for work) in the black community.

THE MEANING AND CONTEXT OF WORK 37

William Julius Wilson, perhaps the most noted African American sociologist today in America, has observed that the technological advances and global economic shifts of the past thirty years have had devastating effects at the bottom of American society in general and on black America in particular. "The disappearance of work in the inner-city ghetto presents a serious challenge to society," he writes; "today, it appears that inner-city residents who are not in the labor force tend to be beyond the reach of monetary or fiscal policy" (Wilson 1996: 146). While not taking as pessimistic a view about the opportunity structures for African Americans as his colleagues, Andrew Hacker (1992) and Derrick Bell (1992), Wilson is a realist when it comes to documenting the black experience. In the opening sentence of his book *When Work Disappears* (1996: xiii), Wilson states simply: "For the first time in the twentieth century most adults in many inner-city ghetto neighborhoods are not working in a typical week." In the 1950s, he notes, black neighborhoods were just as segregated as today, but they had employment rates of nearly 70 percent. Currently, Wilson (1987) emphasizes that children in the black ghetto often grow up never having seen family or neighbors organize their day around a job. Neighborhoods that are poor and jobless, he concludes, are entirely different from neighborhoods that are poor and working.

Technological advances and global economic shifts in recent decades have had devastating effects on what Derrick Bell terms the "faces at the bottom of the well" (1992). In agreement with Wilson, Bell emphasizes that it is the lack of suitable jobs—not the lure of welfare—that has kept minorities in general and African Americans in particular from working. As working role models have gradually disappeared from economically depressed ethnic minority communities, there has been an entirely understandable disruption in the socialization of youth to the world of work. As Wilson (1991) argued, such jobless ghetto communities do not transmit the ideas of scheduling, regularity, and organization of daily routines necessary to be successful in the world of work. This represents a challenge to social work practitioners and to the social work profession.

Mandatory welfare-to-work programs, stimulated in part by the Personal Responsibility and Work Opportunity Act of 1996, may be capable of moving a modest number of ghetto residents (currently on public assistance) into employment who would not have done so on their own (Coulton 1996). Even the most successful programs, however, leave more than half the participants jobless at the end of three years and do little to raise incomes above the poverty line (Friedlander & Burtless 1995). Indeed, positive results of such mandatory programs have been achieved so far only when there has been a high demand for low-skill labor in the local economy (Bane & Ellwood 1994). As Hagen (2003) observes, initial implementation of such compulsory "work first" strategies was facilitated by the strong economy of the late 1990s. A study by the nonpartisan U.S. General Accounting Office (1998) however emphasizes that it is not yet known how such state welfare-to-work programs will perform under weaker economic conditions. As Wilson (1996) suggests in the final chapter of *When Work Disappears,* the only viable long-range solution may be an ambitious agenda of educational and social reforms, centered on a WPA-style federal program that would guarantee work to all who seek it. The Works Progress Administration (WPA) cost America $10 billion—in 1935 dollars—and even at that rate of expenditure, the WPA could not afford to employ all of the employable unemployed from the Federal Emergency Relief Administration (FERA) rolls due to insufficient funds (Kurzman 1974). Asking government, therefore, to serve today as the employer of last resort would clearly be very expensive and probably politically untenable; hence, it would appear alone to be an unrealistic solution to a vexing economic *and* social problem.

Sexual Orientation

For the approximately 20 million people in the United States who are gay, lesbian, or bisexual (Seck et al. 1993), participation in the world of work sometimes is problematic. Despite widespread American support for their right to participate in the workplace, they are, at the least, rendered invisible by policies that fail to include them individually or as part of a familial relationship (with the small exception of some employee benefits plans that may offer coverage to domestic partners). Worse still, gays and lesbians are sometimes harassed, and often they are subject to discrimination (Kivel & Wells 1998). In Winfield and Spielman's terms (1995), bias may be a product of personal, interpersonal, institutional, or cultural homophobia, or a combination thereof.

As Poverny & Finch (1988) observe, overt job discrimination can take many forms. Individuals can be fired from their jobs, forced to resign, relegated to invisible support positions, or not hired in the first place. Only ten states (California, Connecticut, Hawaii, Massachusetts, New Jersey, New York, Rhode Island, Maryland, Vermont, and Wisconsin) have enacted laws to protect gays, lesbians, and bisexuals from discrimination in the workplace (Kivel & Wells 1998: 110). The Civil Rights Act of 1964, the most comprehensive federal legislation offering injunctive relief to victims of discrimination, only prohibits policies and practices that discriminate on the grounds of race, creed, gender, religion, or national origin. The courts have refused all requests to apply the act's Title 7 prohibitions to cases involving sexual orientation. In addition, the U.S. Equal Employment Opportunity Commission, through which most discrimination cases are filed, has declined to accept any such discrimination claims (Poverny & Finch 1985).

Some activists see a glimmer of hope for judicial support of gays in the 1996 U.S. Supreme Court decision of *Romer v. Evans*. In a six to three decision, the Court struck down a Colorado law that would have discriminated against homosexuals, saying that it would represent a violation of the equal protection clause of the Fourteenth Amendment to the U.S. Constitution (Roark et al. 1998: A47). A subsequent 1997 attempt to pass a federal law that would have made it illegal for employers with more than fifteen workers to discriminate against gays, lesbians, and bisexuals in hiring, firing, promotion, and compensation (the Employment Nondiscrimination Act) failed however by a Senate vote of forty-nine to fifty (Kivel & Wells 1998). At present there are relatively few federal or state statutes (and scant common or case law) establishing sexual orientation employment discrimination as a legal wrong (Achtenberg 1985). Moreover, existing local laws are few, confusing, and incomplete.

Impact of Employment and Unemployment

The preeminent economic order in the world today is capitalism—characterized by a free market, open competition, and the predominance of the production of goods and services for profit. With the fall of the Iron Curtain and the dissolution of the Soviet Union, market economies have become the prevailing norm. While capitalism has made America what some economists call "the envy of the free world," it also has produced casualties for which America has made only modest and dissonant provision.

Economic Impact

If one cannot achieve entry into the world of work and maintain one's gainful employment (with a regular wage and fringe benefits) one is at a distinct disadvantage in America. In the absence of universal health care, family allowances, or generous unemployment insurance, nonworking individuals and their families are placed at the very margins of life. In fact, unless a second wage earner is present in today's nuclear family or one can qualify for open-ended social insurance protection (e.g., Social Security, SSI, Medicare), economic vulnerability for some families is likely to be severe, immediate, and predictable. Despite the demands that the world of work typically makes on its participants, it provides economic rewards not available anywhere else in the American social system.

A variety of the most favorable entitlements are tied exclusively to the employment of a family member—including social insurance and private employee benefits. The importance of these occupational benefits and services—"new property" in Charles Reich's terms—cannot be overestimated because they constitute the primary "family protection" system in this country (Reich 1966). These fiscal benefits, in cash and in kind, are so central that if they are lost through unemployment or disability, families often experience a painful period of economic readjustment. Family members have not only lost an income but also primary benefits coverage for the family, which is often not affordable, even if available, to Americans outside the workforce (Kurzman 1988b).

A stable, full-employment economy is probably the best form of primary prevention that America can offer. While economists used to believe that low unemployment could only be achieved at the expense of high rates of inflation (the principle known to economists as the "Phillips curve"), recent experience has proved that this equation is not inevitable and perhaps is no longer even valid. During 1998, for example, America experienced an unemployment rate of 4.5 percent concurrent with an inflation rate of under 2 percent. Macroeconomic policy—controlled as much by decisions of the Federal Reserve Board as by global economic judgments or private corporate determinations—plays a pivotal role in deciding how employment (and unemployment) will be distributed in America. No one who is interested in occupational issues should underestimate the importance of macroeconomic decisions.

As Brenner noted in his study of economic cycles in America (1973: 232), "stresses brought about by large-scale economic change are likely to fall most heavily on those in lower socioeconomic strata." Since the 1970s more than 8 million manual labor jobs have been lost in machine tools, glass, rubber, textiles, and similar industries, largely due to advanced technology and use of cheaper labor in developing countries overseas. The *Wall Street Journal* reports that between 1 and 2 million American jobs a year are being lost to such "corporate re-engineering" (Bielski 1996). One sociologist cites a light bulb factory that now employs eight people on a shift that used to require more than fifteen hundred. He predicts that in just a few years voice mail, fax machines, e-mail, the Internet, and similar innovations will render unnecessary more than 25 percent of those employed today as secretaries, clerks, administrative assistants, and middle managers (Aronowitz 1994).

Psychological and Social Impact

The old rules were clear and unambiguous: if Americans respected the work ethic, the work ethic would respect them. The rules have changed, however, and the consequences are evident to society in general and to social work practitioners in particular. For work and a job have not only an economic meaning in this society but also a pragmatic social and psychological meaning. When work is not available, is denied, or is taken away, practitioners must anticipate a reaction, generally of anger, depression, or both. In psychodynamic terms, the loss of work and all it entails suggests the loss of a significant object to which there is ego attachment. As Jahoda (1988) reminds us, work has many profound levels of meaning (even when not ideal) and performs many dynamic functions (even when stressful). Hence, social workers need to understand that clients who have experienced the loss of work may need professional help to work through this loss so they can function again and pursue appropriate job-seeking behavior.

By looking through such a work-specific lens we can see that work not only is a way to make a living and support one's family but also constitutes a healthy and desired framework for patterns of interaction because it imposes discipline and regularity to social living. As Bourdieu (1965) observed, in the absence of regular employment, however modest, a person lacks not only a place to work and the receipt of income but also a coherent organization of the present. Regular employment provides an anchor for the spatial and temporal aspects of daily life. Work not only binds the ego, in a psychodynamic sense, but also, sociologically, binds an individual to the larger society as well.

Income Maintenance Alternatives

Many of the government benefits available in our society are means-tested and only available to people with little or no income and few tangible resources. One of the principal benefits of workforce participation is eligibility for income maintenance alternatives that are provided as forms of social insurance. These work-related benefits include disability insurance, Social Security, unemployment insurance, and workers' compensation. They are available to workers when they retire, become disabled, face unemployment, or incur a work-related illness or injury.

Retirement

Passed by Congress on August 14, 1935, during a period of the Great Depression that historians call the Second New Deal, the Social Security Act was America's first federal social insurance legislation. Evolving over time through adjustments and amendments, Social Security is best known as an insurance for retired workers. These monthly cash benefits for retirees, eligible family members, and survivors of insured workers are the oldest and most widely accepted feature of Social Security and today cover almost all wage and salary jobs in America. At the end of 1992, for example, an estimated 93 percent of men and 84 percent of women age 20 to 64 were fully insured for old age and survivors benefits (Tracy & Ozawa 1995: 2186). Compulsory contributions by workers and their employers are pooled to fund the program on a modified insurance principle. Benefits are provided as a matter of earned right, without the means test that is present when applying for public assistance or Supplemental Security Income (SSI). While the qualifying age in 2002 for full retirement benefits was 65 (gradually increasing to 67 by the year 2027), the majority (69 percent) of new awards to retired workers go to people who apply early (age 62 to 65) and, in exchange, accept a reduced monthly payment.[2] Social Security's Old Age and Survivors Insurance (OASI) is one of the three principal forms of financial support for retired workers, providing more than one-third (38 percent) of total income for people age 65 and older (U.S. Department of Health 1992). Retired workers, however, also depend on income support from savings and pensions.

Although employer pensions are not legislatively mandated and were uncommon prior to the Second World War, by 1970 more than half (52 percent) of all full-time workers were covered by a private pension plan (Beller & Lawrence 1992). Concern for workers was only one reason for employers' voluntary establishment of pension plans. Originally, such initiatives were viewed by employers as a way to avoid government imposition of pension coverage, as a management tool to retire workers who were no longer efficient, and as a means to dampen the influence of unions (Williamson 1992). During World War II, pension plans gained popularity as a mechanism to circumvent strict wage and price controls, and after the war they became a routine part of the collective bargaining

---

[2] While Social Security kicked in at age 65 when it was enacted in 1935, the average person then didn't even live to age 62. Current life expectancy, however, is 77 and still rising. The need to move up the date for full benefit eligibility therefore became a fiscal and demographic necessity.

process in unionized industries and a management strategy to avoid unionization in nonunion settings. The passage of the Employee Retirement Income Security Act (ERISA) in 1974 gave recognition to the prevalence of private pensions and built insurance safeguards to protect the pension benefits of workers, in recognition of how many employees would be counting on this retirement income and the fact that private plans (unlike Social Security) were not managed with the same care as those under government auspices.

The adequacy of retirement income depends on careful planning early in the work cycle. Ensuring that one has adequate "quarters of coverage" under OASI; creating an early and systematic plan for savings, carefully invested and properly insured; and seeking employment where there is a private pension that can be vested, all are components of a strategy to provide for retirement income for oneself and one's family. Social workers should recognize, however, that half of American workers are not covered by private pension plans, are not able to accumulate significant savings, and may receive well under the average monthly Social Security benefit for retired workers, which was $922 in 2004 (Social Security Factsheet 2004). Private pensions have not grown as much as was hoped, particularly for low-income workers and people of color who increasingly are employed in the service sector or in part-time work—settings and conditions where private pension plans may not prevail. Moreover, the average monthly OASI for female workers was only 77 percent of the benefits of male workers, highlighting the significance of gender. Overall, however, it is important to note that Social Security (along with private pensions) has played a major role in reducing poverty among the aged.

Disability

Entitlements differ for labor force participants, whether the disability is or is not work related. (See chap. 7 for a more comprehensive discussion of disability.) If a workforce participant's disability results from a work-related injury or illness, a social insurance benefit is payable through a state workers' compensation program. Covering individuals who are prevented from working as the result of a job-related disease, disability, or accident, workers' compensation is wholly a state program. Started in some states early in the twentieth century and extended to all states by the 1940s, workers' compensation laws require employers to insure their workers through the purchase of coverage from a private insurer, a state insurance carrier, or through an approved self-insurance plan. Coverage and payments are not insignificant. Disbursing more than $34 billion in medical, hospitalization, and cash benefits to eligible workers in 1989, workers' compensation programs generally pay out each year more than double the dollar benefits of unemployment insurance (Wolf-Jones 1995). Essentially, workers' compensation benefits are intended to replace lost earning capacity and to cover medical and hospital costs associated with work-related illness or injury. It is an expensive program due to the rising cost of hospital and health care and because workers with permanent work-induced disabilities may receive a lump sum or a monthly payment in perpetuity (Asch & Mudrick 1995).

Workers who incur an injury or illness that is not job-related may be covered by disability insurance. Four states (New York, New Jersey, Rhode Island, and California) have short-term disability insurance to cover employees who need to be out of work for less than a year, but the major program of insurance for totally and permanently disabled workers is federal and comes under the disability insurance provision included in the 1956 amendments to the Social Security Act. To receive such insurance benefits "a worker must be unable to engage in any substantial gainful activity because of a severe physical or mental impairment that is expected to last for at least 12 months or to result in death" (Tracy & Ozawa 1995: 2188).

Monthly benefits are payable to the disabled worker and eligible family members (including unemployed spouses and children under sixteen years of age) as a form of long-term income support for workers and their families when disability prevents employment, regardless of the cause. Because it is a social insurance rather than a public assistance entitlement program, assets and earnings of other family members do not affect eligibility for or the amount of the benefit paid.

Income support for low-income people with disabilities who have little or no labor force experience does not take place through Social Security, since insufficient employee and employer payments (by payroll deduction) would deny eligibility to such applicants. Income support for such people with disabilities is available through a means-tested public assistance program entitled Supplemental Security Income (SSI). Although financed essentially by the federal government from general revenues, by 2000 all states (except West Virginia) supplemented the basic federal benefit. While having the appearance of a social insurance program, because it is operated by the U.S. Social Security Administration, SSI actually is an income-tested form of public assistance. In this spirit, there is a dual system of income support for people with disabilities, based on work attachment (Asch & Mudrick 1995).

Unemployment

While Social Security operates as a federal program and workers' compensation as a state program, unemployment compensation is conducted as a joint federal-state endeavor. Established by the original Social Security Act of 1935, it is intended to provide temporary, partial wage replacement to involuntarily unemployed workers. There are broad federal guidelines to which the states must adhere, but the terms of eligibility and the amount and duration of benefits vary widely from state to state. Financing of the program comes from a payroll tax on employers (Wolf-Jones 1995).

To be eligible for unemployment compensation benefits an individual must (1) be unemployed, (2) be covered as a consequence of prior work, for a specified period of time, in an insured employment setting, and (3) meet federal and state qualification requirements. In general, for eligibility purposes, the "unemployed" are defined as people sixteen years and over who had no paid employment at all during the referenced week, took some specific step to obtain a job in the prior four weeks, and are currently available for work. Approximately 98 percent of all wage and salary workers currently are covered (Wolf-Jones 1995).

Jobless individuals who (1) do not meet the above definition of "unemployed," (2) are among the small percentage of workers not covered, (3) have not been employed long enough to qualify as insured, (4) were discharged from employment for misconduct or left without a good cause, or (5) have received benefits for the limit of benefits coverage (generally twenty-six weeks) will not be qualified for unemployment compensation payments. For example, people who have a work history but are not currently employed and have given up looking for work (often referred to as "discouraged workers") are not considered to be "in the labor force" and, therefore, are not classified as "unemployed." Such jobless individuals, who do not meet the federal government's definition of unemployed, are not eligible for benefits despite the fact that they may appear by lay standards to qualify and to be in need. Similarly, workers who remain unemployed after twenty-six weeks may be in great need of unemployment insurance income but find that their benefits period has expired. As Robert Reich (1998) has observed, unemployment insurance was designed to respond to a temporary layoff; hence, six months of benefits generally was thought to be sufficient. With the downsizing and reengineering of the economy today, millions of Americans use up their unemployment insurance but still find themselves unemployed.

In short, there are substantial gaps in the provision of the income maintenance alternatives to work in America, and this reality is not unintentional. Work is the centerpiece of the American promise. Lest we forget, efforts to build a safety net are an experiment that began recently in American history—with the New Deal of the 1930s—and still are questioned by many in this country who consider such arrangements to be alien to our heritage and traditions.

Practice Issues

The centrality of work in our culture implies that organizations should adapt their policies and practices to fit this reality. If our government benefits and entitlements are designed to encourage work, support workers, and facilitate the productivity of work organizations, one might expect that social agencies would promote services in this spirit. Social work services, however, often are designed as much for the convenience of staff as they are for the comfort of clients—most of whom are working, looking (or training) for work, or supporting the needs of their working family members. Social agencies, usually closed at night and on weekends, when workers are available to seek help, have to examine whether their hours are set for the accommodation of staff or for the needs and availability of clients. Too frequently the operation of goal displacement (Merton 1968) places the preferences of staff ahead of clients—when staff's raison d' être and stated goals should be to respond to client need. The responsibility of social workers and social agencies to adapt to the want of working families must take precedence if work is a priority in America.

Bertha Reynolds's (1975) decision to provide social work services to merchant seamen at their union and under its auspices was a recognition of the centrality of work in seamen's lives. If agency days and hours posed a dilemma for workers seeking help, Reynolds surmised that perhaps location could be a problem as well. By gaining the sponsorship for services from the trade union that seamen had chosen and trusted, she ensured that seeking help became acceptable and safe. Because social workers were stationed at the "crossroads of life," services became easy to access.

Such outposts in the world of work ease and normalize the help-seeking process by recognizing both the demands of work on the one hand and the centrality of the workplace on the other. As Meyer (1976: 189) has noted: "Assuming that potential customers of social work service are 'out there' and as yet untouched and unknown, the matter of location of social workers is a crucial one, for availability at the 'crossroads of life' is essential if the practitioner is to meet the citizen." In this spirit, the impetus for occupational social work practice can be understood as a need to "be where the action is"—at the center of life for working Americans.

However, as Vigilante (1982: 300) has observed, whether the services are "offered in a community agency, in the workplace, or in private practice, failure to utilize the potential for growth inherent in the work experience itself may be considered a deficiency in practice." While Vigilante (1982: 299) adds that the social worker "located in the work setting has direct access to the environment and concurrently is a part of it," the obligation to understand the meaning of work (or the wish to work) in a client's life is universal to sound practice, despite the tendency of the clinical professions to focus on the family. Bargal and Katan (1998: 257) concur by noting that "[w]ork plays a central role in the lives of adults in Western societies. However, until recently most of the publications and research produced by social scientists and interventions implemented by helping professionals have focused on issues and problems related to personal and interpersonal relationships within the family."

By not looking beyond the family in the process of assessing our clients, we demonstrate our professional naïveté since we are choosing to bypass the arena in which our clients function generally for more waking hours than they do at home. In addition, work often is a relatively conflict-free area for clients, and thus initially they may be more comfortable in discussing it, fostering a therapeutic alliance in which all issues can be shared and examined. While clients may feel some shame or conflict about their performance as child, spouse, parent, or sibling, they may feel pride about their accomplishments at work. In such instances, assessment and intervention can begin from a strengths perspective.

As social workers come to understand the meaning and content of work in their clients' lives they also need to appreciate how work opportunities, work expectations, and the very texture of work itself have changed in recent decades. Work and work organizations at the beginning of the twenty-first century have undergone rapid transformations that are likely to continue in the new millennium, as we shall see in the next chapter. Understanding this "changing landscape" will be essential for good practice.

Study Questions

1. Do you agree with Friedman and Havinghurst's list of what "work" provides for individuals and with Ozawa's statement that "to work is to be a 'real' American"?

2. What do the authors mean when they state that a practitioner must observe both the manifest *and* latent functions of work in a client's life?

3. Would you agree or disagree with the assessment and intervention by the social worker in Human Resources who served Mr. Pulaski? Was her professional use-of-self consistent with a generalist approach to practice that utilizes an ecological framework and a strengths perspective?

4. Based on your experience, would you support the observations made here with regard to the variables of race, gender, and sexual orientation? Why or why not?

5. What do you see as the inherent *strengths* and *limitations* of providing services under the auspices of labor, management, or both at (or through) the workplace?

CHAPTER 3

The Changing Landscape

The Historic Context

Once perceived only as a principal function in adulthood for working- and middle-class men, today employment is almost equally the expectation of women in America.[1] In an increasingly androgynous society, work is a common denominator—whether from the motivation of preference or necessity. Indeed, as Shostak (1982) has observed, work has in fact been an expectation in Western society since Greek and Roman times. As Sir Keith Thomas (1999: v) has written: "Dreary or not, work is a virtually inescapable part of the human condition. Many of us spend most of our waking hours engaged in it. It absorbs our energies and preoccupies our thoughts. It involves us in close relations with other people and gives us our sense of identity. It provides us with the means of subsistence, and it makes possible all the pleasure and achievements of civilization."

Whether under principles of socialism (where government may be the employer) or of capitalism (and its reliance on private arrangements and the marketplace), work for pay is viewed as the norm during the course of adult life. In Alexis de Tocqueville's words (quoted in Heffner 1956), "Among a democratic people . . . everyone works to earn a living, or has worked, or is born of parents who have worked. The notion of labor is therefore presented to the mind, on every side, as the necessary, natural and honest condition of human existence." Much of the responsibility of parents and teachers is to prepare children for skill and commitment to this core adult function (see chap. 4). Implicit in this context is an understanding that appropriate jobs will be available and that employers will properly compensate employees, in cash and in kind.

---

[1] However, poor women have *always* worked from necessity.

In addition to a wage or salary, employers generally are expected to meet some of the personal and family needs of workforce participants. This "social welfare" relationship can be traced to the Middle Ages. In medieval English guilds, funds were set aside to ensure workers' economic security in case of accident, poverty, old age, or death. Laws soon replaced guild levies, but the guild continued to maintain schools and almshouses and was, along with the church, the principal social welfare organization for such workers and their families until the advent of the Poor Laws of 1601 (Kurzman 1970b, 1987).

By the twentieth century, in addition to the expansion of social welfare provisions as supplements to wages and salaries, another implicit social compact had evolved between employers and workers: as employers prospered they would share a measure of this prosperity with the employees who made the financial success possible. As companies became more profitable, wages and benefits would rise and jobs would grow more secure. A crisis is occurring today, however, because the social contract is perceived as having been broken. As Hedrick Smith (1995) notes, too many American companies see labor merely as an expense of production rather than as capital to be nourished by loyalty and education. Some employers (like General Motors) have a tendency toward short-term views that blight the cooperation with employees (shown by Honda) generally required for long-term success.

For example, when Honda had to trim production in 1993 in response to a decline in demand, the company did not lay off workers; Honda saw this as a time to teach its workers new skills, reasoning that this decision would become an investment in future productivity (Levin 1993). Understanding that its workforce (not its plant or equipment) was its most valuable resource, the corporation gave up the option of layoffs and short-term savings. Instead, Honda made a long-term investment in worker loyalty and in enlarging employee skills and flexibility in expectation of future profits.

America and its corporate culture frequently find themselves torn between the historic promise of work opportunity on the one hand and the commitment to a free market economy on the other. Even the available jobs frequently do not provide customary fringe benefits and often do not pay enough to sustain a family. Hence, work may in fact be available but compensation may not be sufficient to achieve a principal social goal—support of the American family. This is a complaint often voiced by women who have moved from welfare to work (Lens 2002). Most of these women have shifted from being poor and on welfare to being poor and working.

The American economy grew steadily during the 1990s. Productivity (measured as output per hour of work) increased and corporate profits were at record levels. Average wages and salaries (after accounting for inflation) declined, however, and total compensation (which includes fringe benefits) fell as well. Wages did not keep pace with the growth of output; therefore, the proportional share of income going to workers decreased. Where did the profits go? A 1995 report by the Economic Policy Institute noted that more and more profits went to shareholders (in higher dividends and stock price increases) and to corporate executives (in wages, stock options, and bonuses). This trend was confirmed by an even larger national study published in 2004 by the Center for Labor Market Studies at Northeastern University titled "The Unprecedented Rising Tide of Corporate Profits and the Simultaneous Ebbing of Labor Compensation." The authors concluded that the bulk of the gains did not go to workers but instead were used to boost profits, lower prices, reward shareholders, or increase CEO compensation (Sum et al. 2004). As the economist Lester Thurow (1995: 11) observed: "No country without a revolution or a military defeat and subsequent occupation has ever experienced such a sharp shift in the distribution of earnings as America has in the last generation. At no other time have median wages of American men fallen for more than two decades. Never before have a majority of American workers suffered real wage reductions while the per capita domestic product was advancing."

Moreover, as Wilson (1996: 154) points out, the issue in America for the last quarter of the twentieth century was not the absence of work opportunities. The U.S. economy created 35 million jobs between 1973 and 1991. Europe added just 8 million during the same period, despite having about one-third more people. However, most of America's new job growth occurred outside central cities and in the low-paying and benefit-scarce service sector. As a result, the United States has fallen far behind most of its industrialized trading partners in several measures of working and living standards. For example, in hourly compensation for production workers, the U.S. ranks twelfth. In public spending for job creation, training, and placement—ninth place. In unemployment compensation—dead last (Kameras 1997b).

The issue in America for the twenty-first century then is not the promise of work and a job for anyone who wants one. Nor perhaps is it even a question of the nation's historic but wavering commitment to "full employment." In fact, Pres. Franklin D. Roosevelt proposed an economic bill of rights back in 1944 seeking to establish full employment as a national goal, and he voiced a willingness to engage in Keynesian fiscal policies to support it. The subsequent Full Employment Act of 1946 stated that this would be a primary goal of the federal government, and despite wide fluctuations in the official unemployment rate since then (to a high of 10.8 percent in December 1982), unemployment generally has hovered between 5 and 6 percent in recent times. The breach of promise has been the relative distribution of employment opportunity and employment rewards.

African Americans, Latinos, and other people of color customarily have rates of unemployment double that of whites; minority teenagers experience rates triple those of white adults. Women earn only 77 percent of what men earn when performing the same or comparable jobs (Women at Work 2003: 49). Despite passage of federal legislation (such as the 1967 Age Discrimination in Employment Act and the 1990 Americans with Disabilities Act), workers age forty and over or with physical or emotional disabilities are routinely victims of workforce discrimination. As opportunity is unequally present to such classes of workers, so too are the rewards uneven. With the current minimum wage set at $5.15 an hour, full-time employees (working forty hours a week) could (and often do) receive a gross annual wage of $10,712—which is well below the U.S. Department of Health and Human Services' 2002 poverty threshold of $18,392 for a family of four (Clemetson 2003: 10).[2] When a prominent politician, addressing a group of blue-collar workers during the 2000 presidential election campaign, noted that "there are plenty of jobs out there to help you support your family," it is reputed that one worker in the audience replied, "Yes, and I have three of them!" President Roosevelt's pledge to the American people that there would be good jobs so that men and women could support their families is a promise that many Americans perceive as having been broken. The opportunity and reward structures have changed over time, creating dependency even for those wanting to work and for many who are employed full-time at a legal wage.

CASE EXAMPLE

A medium-size insurance company in a major metropolitan area of the Northeast was proud of its progressive personnel policies. Other companies respected it as a leader in innovative insurance plans for meeting changing demographic conditions.

---

[2] In 2002, 34.6 million Americans were living below this poverty line.

With an increasing number of women entering the workforce, and with affirmative action guidelines and litigation settlements in mind, the firm decided that the time had come to employ more women in its principal professional departments, beginning with the actuarial function. (Although many women worked in the sales and administrative areas, few had entered the actuarial arena.)

The company hired qualified women and placed them in line and in some first-level coordinating positions. They performed well overall in a wide variety of challenging situations. Human Resources and departmental supervisors reported that the newly hired women were pleased with their career opportunities, and the firm was justifiably proud of its continuing reputation as a leader in personnel management.

Nine months later, however, reports came to senior management that an unanticipated number of women were visiting the employee counseling program for help with managing their dual commitments to work and family. Attracted by the salary, good working conditions, and career advancement opportunities, many women had taken these positions without knowing how they would manage their responsibilities at home. Initially, many asked favors from friends and extended family or made temporary arrangements with neighbors. Perhaps they had not fully believed they would succeed in their new jobs, or perhaps they presumed that long-term solutions would somehow evolve as the need arose. Whatever mistakes they had made, these women now felt vulnerable—aware that the family life they treasured was endangered by their careers and that, conversely, their absenteeism and lateness to "take care of emergencies" imperiled their future at the firm.

The social work staff of the employee counseling program responded. They recognized that the mutual investment the new actuaries and the company had in each other justified efforts on both sides to work out the conflicts. The counselors met at a weekly staff conference and agreed that many of the new actuaries needed individual counseling time because each woman found herself in a situation slightly different from those of her peers. The staff, however, also recognized that many of these employees shared much in common. The social workers concluded that they also had to take organizational responsibility for identifying the community resources for this critical new corporate population of working mothers.

After confirming that the women's task performance was excellent (when not pulled away from work by family emergencies), the social work staff realized that the success of the firm's workforce initiative depended

(continued)

on locating and building appropriate systems of support. The staff identified resources that were needed in the critical arenas that the women who had come for help had mentioned—child care for their preschool children, after-school programs for school-age youngsters, and housekeeping and home-making services for themselves and for their aging parents and in-laws.

Aware of the clout of the company in the community (as a major tax-payer and principal employer) the staff approached community facilities. When agencies realized who was calling, they were responsive (to both the problems identified and the affiliation of the social worker). Once they rec-ognized the importance of backup services to the success of the company's program, they made special arrangements. After the social workers had secured these tangible services, they arranged informal lunchtime meetings for the women so they could discuss their feelings, share their adaptations to a dual career (or single-parent) lifestyle, and build a mutual aid network at work to support one another.

Management was delighted at the high quality of the new actuarial workforce, pleased at retaining its reputation for enlightened personnel policies, and proud of solving the problems cost effectively through the ini-tiative of its own employee counseling program.

Work as Opportunity

A huge amount of the world's work historically has been done by slaves and captives. "This was the case in classical Greece and Rome," notes one social historian, "and continued to be so in the age of European expan-sion, when millions of people were forcibly transported from Africa to work as slaves in the Americas" (Thomas 1999: xiii). The voyage from Africa to America, known as the Middle Passage, began as early as 1619, and by the 1680s laws designating most African Americans as slaves (the Black Codes) were firmly in place (Leashore 1995). In addition, a large number of early European settlers were poor or working-class blacks and whites serving under contracts of indenture. For example, in 1625 virtu-ally 40 percent of Virginia's population was indentured servants (Axinn & Stern 2001: 26). While the choice to come to America was their own, they did not enjoy many civil liberties, including the right to chose their employer or their working conditions.

Most other immigrants to America, however, came as free people, able to choose the work they wanted to do, the employer they would work for, and often the terms of employment. However limited or harsh the condi-tions might prove, the status and work opportunities for most "new

Americans" were significantly different from those of slavery or indenture. An opportunity to enjoy economic freedom often was as important an incentive for immigration to America as was the prospect of experiencing freedom of speech, politics, or religion. America was (and still is) perceived as the "land of opportunity," and frequently the opportunity most valued continues to be employment.

In the early agricultural era, most new Americans lived on farms. Children had real economic value at a very early age, especially during planting and harvesting seasons. For both parents and children the family was the economic unit and the social welfare net. Parents knew that children were their only pension system, and families stayed together because it was difficult to survive independently. Today, however, most work opportunities exist outside the family; in the language of today's economy, children generally have shifted from being "profit centers" to being "cost centers."

At the start of a new millennium, America is experiencing a period of profound economic transition, analogous to the shift from an agricultural to an industrial economy at the end of the nineteenth century. Two major transitional phenomena are taking place in the world of work that affect the opportunity structure. Unskilled (and even semiskilled) labor is becoming surplus, and skilled labor has become cheap and plentiful abroad. Technology and cybernetics have reduced our prior dependence on manual labor, and a global economy—where anything can be made anywhere and sold everywhere—means that less costly labor in the third world is having a big impact on first world wages. In addition, 10 million immigrants entered the United States from 1985 to 1995, competing for America's jobs and lowering wages (Thurow 1995).

While these newest immigrants are doing what generations of predecessors have done—seeking work opportunity in America—the consequences are different today because the United States frequently cannot absorb these new workers as rapidly as it did in previous decades. The current combination of an increased supply of labor in this country, greater efficiency and productivity reducing demand, and the availability of cheap labor abroad have created a situation where America may not continue as a "land of work opportunity" for future generations. The implied American covenant of intergenerational occupational mobility has been broken, and today we may presage a generation where, for the first time, children will *not* do as well as their parents. In a nation where the words "work" and "opportunity" have usually been linked, the above conundrum has profound implications. As Wilson (1996: 153) observed: "In the highly integrated global marketplace of today, economies can grow, stock markets can rise, corporate profits can soar, and yet many workers may remain unemployed or underemployed. Why? Because capital and technology are now so mobile that they do not always create good jobs in their own backyard. Corporate cutbacks, made in an effort to streamline operations for the global economy, have added to the jobless woes of many workers. In short, economic growth today does not necessarily produce good jobs."

Although there are signs in the first decade of the new century that the equation of supply and demand may alter these trends, work in America in most of the 1980s and 1990s was characterized by job insecurity, stagnant wages, and declining benefits. (Poignantly, as the national minimum wage rose to $5.15 an hour in 1997, its real inflation-adjusted value remained below what it was in the 1960s.) As Thurow (1995) notes, each year more than a half million good jobs are being eliminated by the nation's most prestigious companies. Most new jobs are being generated in the service sector, with lower wages, less union protection, and fewer fringe benefits. While still modest in number, a greater percentage of workers have been forced to become independent contractors (e.g., self-employed), having to purchase their fringe benefits, when feasible, on the open market and paying the mandatory full cost of their Social Security coverage. While the country and its corporations have prospered during the past two decades, the economy has grown steadily less egalitarian. As Robert Reich (2004: 103) has emphatically stated, by 2004 "America had become the most economically stratified society in the advanced democratic world." Passell (1998: D2) notes that virtually all the bounty of growth has gone to the educated and already-affluent. The real income of the bottom tenth of American families fell by 13 percent between 1973 and 1995 as the inequality of income and opportunity became more pronounced. The chairman of the Board of Governors of the Federal Reserve System, Alan Greenspan, has commented that layoffs and cutbacks were the major factor in this slowdown in labor compensation. Sensing job insecurity, employees have sought to preserve their jobs by accepting smaller increases in wages and fewer fringe benefits. There have been few countervailing forces in play.

Furthermore, regulations and tax changes have allowed corporations and the wealthy to keep more of their income and earnings. In the 1950s federal taxes averaged about 45 percent of corporate profits but by the mid-1990s averaged only about 24 percent (Folbre 1995: 5.12). However, it can also be argued that, while some individuals and groups have been favored and others have not done well, capitalism continues to be widely perceived as a superior concept of macroeconomics and was kind to this nation as a whole in the twentieth century. America has emerged as the world's major economic superpower and the country's overall standard of living has risen dramatically. For most of the last century, the United States has been the economic envy of the world, despite a quiet yet pervasive malaise. There are only a few pure noncapitalist economies remaining in the world, and none could be said to be flourishing.

There is a lively debate, nonetheless, in American intellectual magazines (such as the *Nation* and *New Republic*) as well as in respected journals of the profession (such as *Social Work* and *Social Service Review*) as to whether capitalism has promoted opportunity or exploitation. The truth is that the two concepts are not mutually exclusive and the American experience throughout the twentieth century featured both phenomena. Today, profound changes are affecting the country as a consequence of its economic doctrine, producing a dominant middle-class culture with conservative aspirations; a decline in mid-twentieth-century welfare state ideology and the political structure to support it; and the emergence of what Edwards, Cooke, and Reid (1996) call a "new consensus" that promotes smaller government, the end of "unnecessary regulation," greater use of free-market mechanisms, and belief in the inherent superiority of private (nongovernment) initiatives. In this model, the government defines social objectives but it no longer promises to protect citizens as often from the excesses of capitalism.

Following this paradigm, public and nonprofit provision of jobs and services is perceived as less efficient, less effective, and less responsive to change than market-driven programs of the private sector. It should, therefore, prove no surprise that by the 1980s about 30 percent of programs and services in child welfare, correctional services, home health care, and residential treatment were being provided directly by (or through purchase-of-service agreements with) for-profit institutions. The involvement of proprietary organizations in employment training, nursing home, day care, substance abuse, and health and mental health services has been expanding as well (Abramson & Salamon 1986; Frumkin & Andre-Clark 1999; Stoesz 1986; Clark 2003).

Privatization and the dominance of free-market economic thinking, of course, have implications not only for traditional social welfare institutions but also for workers. These principles work in tandem with one another and are mutually reinforcing. Government intervention (whether to provide, regulate, or reward) is to become the exception; the profit motive is seen as superior to other forms of incentive; and the "invisible hand" of the market generally is trusted more than the hand of elected and appointed officials. However, as the noted Princeton economist Paul Krugman (1999: 6.25) observes, "A market economy—even the Goldilocks economy of America in the 90's—requires that a certain number of people who want to work be unable to find jobs so that their example will discipline the wage demands of those who are already employed." In Karl Marx's (1967) terms, labor supply must always be greater than demand if wages are to be held in check. Creating a "reserve army of the unemployed" competing for the same jobs brings a greater opportunity for owners to cut labor costs and to have larger profits available to shareholders. It is also useful to keep unemployment benefits low, eligibility tight, and weeks of coverage limited. It should be no surprise that unemployed workers in America generally can only collect about 50 percent of their lost wages for twenty-six weeks, much less by both measures, for example, than in France, Sweden, or Spain (Nasar 1999).

Given the reduced role of government as the protector of work and equal opportunity, labor unions frequently are looked to as a countervailing force on the side of workers and their families. In this sense, unions are perceived not only as social institutions that can bargain for wages and benefits but also as organizations that can fight for a more equitable balance of power in the world of work. Establishing a legally binding collective bargaining agreement, securing safe working conditions, ensuring fair and impartial grievance procedures, and lobbying for progressive (prolabor) legislation are part of the trade union agenda. The union contract is an equalizer of central import in America today for that portion of the labor force (12.9 percent in 2003) that is unionized. In addition, unions quietly serve as a restraining force in industries that are not organized (and in settings that remain nonunion) since employers generally want to offer comparable wages, benefits, and working conditions as a disincentive to unionization.

From a pocketbook perspective, one observer notes, workers are absolutely better off joining a union (AFL-CIO 2003: 14). Economists across the political spectrum agree: turning a nonunion job into a union job very likely will have a greater effect on lifetime earnings than all the advice employees will ever read about for investing their 401(k) plans, buying a home, or otherwise making more of what they earn. Johnston (1997: 3.9) notes: "Overall, union workers are paid about 20 percent more than nonunion workers and their fringe benefits are typically worth two to four times as much, economists with a wide array of views have found. The financial advantage is even greater for workers with little formal education and training and for women, blacks and Hispanic workers." This statement draws no argument even from Leo Troy of Rutgers University, who is known for his hostility toward organized labor. "From a standpoint of wages and fringe benefits," Professor Troy states, "the answer is yes, you are better off in a union" (Johnston 1997: 3.9). And as leaders of the national AFL-CIO have emphasized, workers also want and need unions to promote job security and to have a greater voice in the American workplace.

Work as a Promise Broken

Work is a paramount value in American society. One is told that if one is willing to work hard the rewards will be available—a "slice of the American pie"—regardless of where you were born or who your parents were. The unspoken promise—breached only temporarily during periods of recession—is that if an adult is available to work, an employer will offer a job with compensation (wages and benefits) that is adequate to support a family. All of this is possible because America has the strongest economy, which offers the highest wages, greatest job opportunities, best technology, and the loftiest standard of living.

Since the late 1970s, however, the U.S. model of export-led growth, tax breaks for the affluent, and weakened unions has caused mass layoffs of workers and managers alike, reducing the number of jobs available that will compensate a worker sufficiently to support a family. Some 43 million employees, for example, were the victims of "corporate downsizing" between 1979 and 1995, and for those who found new jobs, only one in three could match their previous pay and benefits. Moreover, one out of eight Americans who lost their jobs in the first part of 1998 lost them to corporate mergers (Kameras 1997a). While such job loss through corporate downsizing, mergers and acquisitions, and "permanent layoffs" had been present during intervals of recession, now it is tending to occur in large numbers even during periods of economic recovery and high corporate profit, such as the decade of the 1990s and into this new millennium.

In modern America, loss of what economists term "a permanent attachment to the labor force" has become commonplace for lifelong workers. The phenomenon has many causes and is known by different names. Business leaders speak of the necessity for merging, acquiring, relocating, contracting, downsizing, privatizing, outsourcing, and offshoring in order to stay competitive in the global marketplace. In order to pay off the loans incurred in a leverage buyout of another firm, a new corporate entity usually has to markedly reduce its operating costs to have cash to cover the new debt it has assumed. Staff at all levels may be summarily dismissed and replaced by less expensive personnel or workers without employee status. Loyalty, experience, and seniority become irrelevant in the transition because cost becomes the key factor upon which decisions are made for employee termination. (At their subsequent job, workers may reciprocate, of course, with less commitment to their new employer.) Nevertheless, the consequences for whole classes of workers are devastating—economically, socially, and psychologically—such that some observers feel that a new classification of disorder, "downsizing terror disorder," should be added to the next edition of the *Diagnostic and Statistical Manual of Mental Disorders* (DSM) (Bielski 1996; Lawson 1987).

Many of these "involuntarily severed" workers have skills the firm values. The employer often does not want to lose their work participation—just their expensive employee status. As a result, many involuntarily retrenched employees (termed "preferred workers" in Akabas's 1970 study) are encouraged to return to work—not as employees but as freelance or contract workers. As freelancers they work as independent contractors with none of the legally mandated, employer-financed benefits (e.g., Social Security, Medicare, unemployment insurance, workers' compensation) or customary occupational social welfare benefits (e.g., health insurance, vacation pay, sick leave, pension contribution) that they previously enjoyed. As contract workers they are day laborers on the payroll of one of the many temporary-help agencies that rent workers to the corporation, even as it sheds its employees. As the Princeton economist Alan Krueger has observed (quoted in Uchitelle 1996: 1): "Many companies don't want to lose experienced people and they don't want to keep them on expensive career tracks. So they have come up with contract-worker status for ex-employees. And that is an important step that companies are taking toward rewriting the implicit contract that bound them to their workers."

As they grow in number, these former employees, returning on provisional or contract status, become a subculture in the workplace. They are people with an employee's mindset spliced centaur-like to an outsider's role as a rented worker. Often they are doing precisely the same job as when they were salaried employees, but at a fraction of their previous pay, with few benefits (if any), and no job security, contractual or implied. In Fabricant and Burghardt's (1992) terms, this growing practice represents a "proletarianization" of the workforce, where worker control, career expectation, and reward all are reduced as a systemic change occurs in the balance of power at the workplace.

While the overwhelming majority of Americans have always supported capitalism and its reliance on free-market principles (even during the Great Depression, when 25 percent of Americans were unemployed), there has been an implicit understanding that even when companies must downsize in order to stay in business they would honor their responsibility to help all their stakeholders adapt, not just their creditors and shareholders. As (Reich 1998: 300–301) asserts: "Americans always assumed that when companies did better, the people that work for them should do better, too. They'd have higher wages, better benefits, more job security. This was the implicit moral code that guided the economy for more than three decades after World War Two. It was reinforced by the unions, but it was enforced in the first instance by public expectations. It would have been considered unseemly for a company that was doing better to fail to share the good times with its employees. But that compact has come undone."

Typically, when Chemical Bank and Chase Manhattan Bank in New York merged in 1995 they decided they would immediately fire twelve thousand employees. The news (of 16 percent fewer workers) sent the value of the two bank stocks up 11 percent (Norris 1995: 4.3). Shareholders were thrilled; the directors offered large bonuses to senior management; and investors were lining up to purchase the new stock. Bank employees, once described as their greatest asset, became merely a cost of doing business. Therefore, when the new corporate entity was looking to cut expenses, the first "cost" that was discarded was people. This in not an exceptional instance. In a merging and downsizing corporate environment, short-term financial gain often takes precedence over long-term investment in human capital.

As a result, a new phenomenon emerged in the final decades of the twentieth century. As permanent, full-time jobs declined (even disappeared) we witnessed the emergence of "alternative work arrangements." This euphemism describes what now is known as America's new "nonstandard job sector," a seemingly inoffensive term that covers work outside of the traditional contractual norms to which Americans became accustomed and that many, if not most, preferred. Participants in this work arena are known as part-timers, temporaries, freelancers, on-call workers, day-laborers, consultants, casuals, contract workers, provisionals, supplementals, or independent contractors. The U.S. Bureau of Labor Statistics estimated that in 1997, 30 percent of the nation's workers were employed in some form of nonstandard work—the largest group in part-time jobs. The fastest growing sector of the nonstandard workforce, however, is that of temporary workers, who numbered only 800,000 in 1986 but grew to 2.4 million in 1997. Such temporary workers in the manufacturing workforce rose from approximately 1 percent in 1990 to 4 percent in 1997, with high-technology industries reaching nearly 6 percent. Not surprisingly, only 2 percent of temporary workers are covered by union contracts (cited in AFL-CIO 1998: 10, 1999: 9).

The new American workforce can best be conceptualized as having three tiers or concentric circles (see fig. 3.1).

At the center (tier I) is a core workforce composed of managers and valued workers with "permanent" full-time jobs. They are favored with a customary package of occupational social welfare (fringe) benefits, a degree of job security, and opportunities for lateral and upward mobility.

Rapidly expanding during the last two decades of the twentieth century was a cadre of tier II regular, part-time, and supplemental workers. In 1997, despite a booming economy, 17.8 percent of all American employees (21 million workers) reported that their primary job was part-time. Some were at work 40 hours a week but still were being treated by employers as part-time (Kahne 1994). A 1998 AFL-CIO report (based on federal figures) showed that such part-timers earned four dollars less an hour than full-time workers doing similar or identical tasks. In addition, while 67 percent of the full-time workers received health benefits, less than 20 percent of part-timers were covered. Moreover, 57 percent of full-timers were covered by employer pensions but only 20 percent of female and 11 percent of male part-time workers enjoyed this privilege (UAW 1998a: 2).

Replacing full-time workers with part-timers was the central issue in the landmark United Parcel Service (UPS) strike of 1997. Before 1982 full-time and part-time workers at UPS were paid the same hourly wage. When the International Brotherhood of Teamsters first agreed to a lower pay scale for part-timers at UPS there was to be only a four-dollar an hour wage differential. By 1997, however, the full-timers were earning nearly twenty dollars an hour and part-timers only nine dollars (the same hourly wage as in 1982). Moreover, most of the new UPS jobs during the economic boom from 1993 to 1997 were part-time. That category of workers at UPS thus grew from 54 percent in 1993 (and 42 percent in 1986) to 60 percent by 1997 (Uchitelle 1997). In addition to the marked wage differential, most part-timers received little or no health insurance, sick pay, or vacation days, and worked the least desirable "graveyard" shift.

The UPS workforce composition change roughly mirrors what has happened to workers elsewhere. At many companies, a relatively small upper tier of full-time core workers enjoys the best combination of pay, benefits, hours, mobility, and job security that a company can offer. Below them is a second tier of less-valued and less-rewarded part-time employees who, in addition to being less expensive, can be discharged more easily—giving corporate managers the flexibility that they say is essential to compete in an increasingly global economy. The fact that Bureau of Labor Statistics data show that the number of part-time workers in the United States rose to 19.5 percent in 1994 (from 14 percent in 1968) is telling. These part-timers are

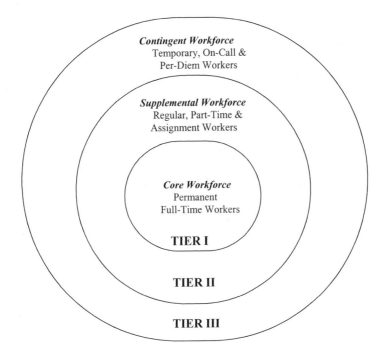

Figure 3.1 A Conceptualization of the New American Workforce

further supplemented on a professional and managerial level by a cadre of "assignment workers"—people hired to accomplish a specific assignment to be completed over a specified period of time. While they sometimes receive more benefits than part-timers, these assignment workers have no job security (beyond their assignment), no upward or lateral mobility, and no eligibility for stock options, bonuses, or union membership.

Considered by unions (and some prospective workers) to be the most insidious "alternative work arrangement" of all is the growing third rank of contingency workers. Such tier III temporary, on-call, per diem workers usually do not have employee status at all. Instead, they work for corporations as independent contractors. They are working not only with no job security, mobility, pension, or health coverage, but also without the protection of the major and hard-won labor legislation of the twentieth century: unemployment insurance, minimum wage assurance, occupational safety and health coverage, protection against age and disability discrimination, fair labor standards, and similar state and federal laws that workers often take for granted. Labor unions, and other opponents of the drift toward "casualization," claim that companies are using the trend to convert workers usually considered to be employees, like truck drivers and middle-level managers, into an independent contractor category, which traditionally referred only to people in business for themselves. Microsoft, for example, is reported to have developed a new rule requiring all their temps—often referred to as "permatemps"—to take a thirty-one-day break in their work at least once a year to ensure that they cannot be viewed as regular workers (Greenhouse 1999b). The federal government has rarely challenged these practices.

Such a strategy not only gives companies more flexibility to shrink their workforces, it also saves them thousands of dollars per worker because employers do not have to make Social Security, Medicare, unemployment insurance, or workers' compensation contributions on behalf of their contingent workers defined as independent contractors. This kind of strictly contractual (rather than employer-employee) relationship creates many cost advantages for corporations, pushing competitors as well toward "casualization," in domino fashion. This trend is especially worrisome for organized labor, which is struggling to increase its ebbing numbers, because contingent workers (such as independent contractors) are not allowed to form or join unions under federal labor law. Indeed, American labor law and benefit structures are completely out of sync for this tier III segment of the workforce. If the rules of the game are changing and workers increasingly are going to become independent contractors, America may need to form a new safety net that serves this portion of the labor force as well.

The increasing use of temporary, per diem, and contract workers has given birth to a new industry—the temporary staffing business—led by Kelly Services, the Olsten Corporation, and Manpower Incorporated. These firms—each multibillion-dollar-a-year businesses traded on the stock exchange—would appear to be permanent fixtures in the workplace today, ironically providing "impermanent" labor for the world of work. Responding to corporate trends, such temp agencies are an intermediary that supply the bulk of transient workers to large corporations. Indeed, as temporary jobs expanded by 211 percent between 1970 and 1990 (compared with 54 percent for all employment), these temp agencies became very profitable new entities in the workplace (Folbre 1995: 2.4). Bureau of Labor Statistics figures show that from 1982 to 1997 the number of workers employed by temporary agencies increased more than 530 percent, from 417,000 jobs to more than 2.5 million (Heintz & Folbre 2000: 105). Furthermore, workers with independent contractor (rather than employee) status expanded to 8.5 million by 1997, but 59 percent of such workers said they would rather have full-time jobs (AFL-CIO 1999: 10).

Companies find that the use of office temps is not only less expensive but also less encumbering. The advent of just-in-time inventory systems, for example, demands a just-in-time workforce. Employers therefore increasingly rely on this highly flexible labor pool, which can quickly be adjusted to stay in sync with the rise and fall of business demand. One major 1998 study found that, as a result, 74 percent of new jobs in America do not pay a "living wage," that is, one that can support a family, even minimally (UAW 1999: 2). The expansion of tier III has helped to foster a growing cadre of working poor in this country, which Rocha (1997: 332) cites as "the fastest growing population in poverty in the United States." Rocha further notes that African American and Hispanic workers are about three times more likely to fall into poverty than non-Hispanic whites, and about 53 percent of the working poor are women. Nonetheless, there are times when part-time, temporary, and freelance work are fair and voluntary. Indeed, there are advantages to contingent work arrangements for many current workforce participants, including women, students, entrepreneurs, and a growing percentage of American workers over age fifty-five. A set schedule at a fixed place of work, thirty-five or more hours every week, for example, does not suit all prospective workforce participants, given their commitment to education, child (or elder) care, career autonomy, or leisure time (Barker 2003).

As one observer remarked, "Temp work can be great when it's voluntary, fair and equitable. But for many, it's none of the above" (Bravo 1999: 4.14). A vivid example is provided by a vignette in former U.S. labor secretary Robert Reich's memoir (1998: 170). Reich is stopped on the street by a middle-aged man:

"Excuse me, aren't you the Secretary of Labor?"

"Yes, but. . . . ," Reich replies.

"Look," the man says, "I wanted to tell you that I don't care what they say. I think you're doing a pretty good job."

"Thanks, but . . . "

"Problem is," the man persists, "the economy sucks. They made me a *contract worker.* You know what that means? I'm doing exactly what I did before, but now I get no health insurance, no pension, no unemployment, no nothing."

"I'm sorry but I just can't . . . ," Reich responds.

"It's happening all over. That's all I want to tell you. You're Secretary of Labor. You need to know these things."

Manpower Incorporated, the leading office temp agency, is now, in fact, the largest private employer in America.

Work Options

Women increasingly are full participants in the world of work, with the same career goals as men. Nevertheless, women who work are often mothers as well, caring for young children (as well as aging parents and in-laws) in a world that is not as gender neutral or androgynous as the male-directed media might claim. Flexible hours and the option of working part-time at home often are welcome options, supported by today's technology and the nature of twenty-first century jobs. For many career women, the potential conflict between family and work may be mitigated by the accommodation and alternatives that are available today to both employer and employee. Hudson's (1999) study of people in alternative work arrangements found that married women frequently preferred part-time, temporary, and other alternative arrangements, including the autonomy and flexibility that come with being an "independent contractor" rather than an employee.

A quarter century ago, Kanter (1977: 77) asked, "What do individuals bring home of their jobs, and what do they bring to work of their families?" Today, that question might add "when home and workplace are one and the same" (Levinson 2003: 11). The home office once seemed a perk exclusive to professionals like doctors, accountants, and visual artists. Today, with e-mail, high-speed data networks, broadband cable connection, instant messaging, digitization, overnight mail services, and faxes, business often can be conducted from home—the ultimate extension of flextime. While still a relatively small percentage overall, home-based employment is expanding because it frequently serves the needs of business and skilled workers (particularly women with dependent care commitments) in a symbiotic way. "Telecommuting"—using cable and telecommunications technology to work without commuting daily to an office—is becoming increasingly common given the nature of emerging twenty-first century jobs (Judy & D'Amico 1997). As Giuliano (1998: 1077) has observed, new technology means that "the shipping of information can be substituted for the shipping of workers."

Similarly, students and many young workers find they need part-time and seasonal employment when they are not in classes or preparing for exams. They too need to "multitask," and the ensuing mutual lack of long-range commitment (employee to employer, and employer to employee) may provide a practical and conceptual framework that best suits the needs of both parties. Upon graduation, many of these new workers, confident in their skills and career prospects, eschew employment in traditional, bureaucratic settings to escape what they perceive as the downside of becoming what Whyte (1972) once termed "the Organization Man." Instead, many well-educated young men and women today opt to work for what Rubery and Grimshaw (2001: 170) call "network organizations," which are smaller entities, with less job security and fewer promises of career advancement. Or they willingly choose contingent work arrangements "in which an individual does not have an explicit or implicit contract for long-term employment," (Polivka 1996: 4). Such highly skilled young workers may then move among network organizations, building careers without boundaries, often referred to as "portfolio careers." What they lose in security they gain in flexibility and autonomy. In this fashion, more and more new workers are charting their own journeys through the labor force rather than depending on the traditional pathways provided by government bureaucracies, unions, and multinational corporations.

Contingent work opportunities also often are embraced by men and women over the age of fifty-five—who increased (in 2002) to 12 percent of the American workforce. Many of them want (or need) to continue working part-time throughout their sixties and into their seventies to stay active and to supplement their savings, pension, and Social Security. Living longer and often maintaining good health, older workers frequently find that a transition to temporary, seasonal, or freelance work is their preferred option (Mutchler et al. 1997). With the average age of the American workforce estimated to continue to increase until about 2020 (when the baby boomers are expected to fully retire), the flexibility and the accommodations provided by such alternative arrangements may suit the needs of a growing sector of participants in the world of work seeking to balance labor with leisure.

The expanding use of "disposable workers," however, seen by corporate leaders as a necessary business practice, has led to a degree of economic, social, and psychological instability for a whole portion of the American population that our country has not experienced on such a pervasive, decade-long basis since the Great Depression. In traditional economic terms, we now see not only the division in the country between the primary and the secondary labor markets but also the emergence of a third or tertiary labor market (Greenhouse 1997: 18). While secondary labor market participants usually work for wages at or near the federal minimum ($5.15 an hour in 2004), with few fringe benefits and little job mobility, the tertiary sector is comprised of "disposable workers" who involuntarily endure concomitant casual, provisional, and transitory work arrangements. In contrast, the primary labor market is characterized by relatively permanent, full-time jobs paying wages or salaries sufficient to support a family at a moderate (working- or middle-class) level. These positions come not only with the legally mandated fringe benefits and a significant number of voluntary occupational social welfare benefits and services (Weiner, Akabas, & Sommer 1973: 102) but also with employee status and the protection of many state and federal labor laws.

Postulation of a tertiary labor market disproportionately composed of women, teenagers, immigrants, and people of color is a new phenomenon in the world of work that defies more traditional categorization (Root 1993b; Sherraden 1985). The economist Richard Freeman (1996) suggests that the emergence of this tertiary workforce underclass implies that America may be moving toward an "apartheid economy." Hidden by a relatively favorable unemployment rate (in 2004) hovering between 5 and 6 percent, workers in what is euphemistically called this new "nonstandard job sector" are not enjoying the rewards received even by traditional secondary labor market participants (Burghardt & Fabricant 1987: chap. 7). One of these rewards is health insurance. The United States, despite its bounty, stands alone among industrial nations in not providing free basic health care for all. By contrast, Otto von Bismarck established a national health insurance system in Germany in 1883; Great Britain initiated a National Health Service in 1946; and Canada launched a universal and comprehensive health care program in 1985 (Barker 1999).

While people in the United States who are permanently disabled more than two years or have reached age sixty-five are covered under Medicare (Title 18) and people who have few assets and little income may qualify for Medicaid (Title 19), most Americans today expect to receive coverage for themselves and their families through employer-sponsored health plans. As a result of changes in the world of work and recent legislation, however, more and more Americans have no health care coverage at all. The percentage of Americans covered by employment-related health insurance, for example, declined from 63.6 percent in 2000 to 61.3 percent in 2002 (with the figure at only 45 percent for workers in private industry), and the number of people without health insurance rose from 41.2 million in 2001 to 43.6 million in 2002. As a result, the proportion of Americans lacking coverage increased in one year from 14.6 to 15.2 percent (Pear 2003: A-1; Health Care Benefits 2003: 2).

The principal reasons for most of these changes are work specific. First, Medicaid rolls are down, as stringent new laws (such as the Personal Responsibility and Work Opportunity Reconciliation Act of 1996) have pushed people from welfare to work. While most states permit families to remain on Medicaid for a year after leaving welfare, many families then lose income eligibility once a family member becomes employed, even in a low wage job. At the same time, they often find that the employer either does not offer a health benefit or will charge them far more for employer-based coverage than they can afford to pay (Mishel & Bernstein 1994). While new legislation allows for a Medicaid buy-in for some low-wage workers, this purported remedy fails to be as comprehensive as necessary.

A second reason for a swelling in the numbers of uninsured is the rising cost of health care, making it the most costly optional fringe benefit for employers today. A study by the Kaiser Family Foundation showed that in 1985, nearly two-thirds of all businesses with one hundred or more employees paid the full cost of a worker's health care. A decade later, only a third did so. The study also found that employers who now ask workers to pay part of the cost through payroll deduction raised the workers' shares to 22 percent in 1996, from only 13 percent in 1988 (Pear 1998). Furthermore, as workers move from employee status to being contingent workers, employers often no longer feel any obligation to provide health insurance, and these workers frequently cannot afford to purchase coverage in the marketplace from their after-tax income. These changes, analysts conclude, have spawned the largest segment of the uninsured—the working poor.

Among this large cohort of the uninsured, people of color have been affected disproportionately. Data show that in 1998, 34 percent of the nation's 31 million Hispanics had no health insurance, compared with 22 percent of African Americans but just 12 percent of whites. The study points out that for most uninsured Hispanics the disparity in coverage results simply from a decline in jobs that offer benefits. In addition, only half of all Hispanics in America are covered through employment, compared with two-thirds of African Americans and three-quarters of whites (Kilborn 1999: A1, A16). Hispanics are also more likely to be noncitizens, and under the Personal Responsibility and Work Opportunity Reconciliation Act of 1996 even legal immigrants now must wait five years before achieving Medicaid eligibility. It is no surprise therefore that rates of infant mortality in the United States are approximately double for people of color in contrast with whites, and with respect to infant mortality among the 27 most developed countries, the United States ranks thirteenth for whites and twenty-sixth for African Americans (Giovannoni 1995: 437).

In sum, despite the fact that we spend a much larger portion of our gross domestic product on health care than any other advanced industrialized nation, many Americans are uncovered; infant mortality is high; and minorities of color are disproportionately affected (Heintz & Folbre 2000: 133). As Jansson and Smith (1996: 446) note, perhaps a fundamental change is needed, such as the transfer of primary financing of health care from employers to government. After all, such a pattern of financing has been in effect since 1965 (as Medicare and Medicaid) for the elderly, impoverished, and disabled. Such an innovation also would no longer place American companies at a competitive disadvantage with corporations in other industrialized nations where there is government-funded health insurance.

Transferring the core responsibility for health insurance for all—especially for working Americans—historically has had only modest support and much organized opposition. When Harry Hopkins led the fight within the Roosevelt administration in 1934 for inclusion of national health insurance in the original Social Security Act of 1935, intense pressure from the American Medical Association (AMA) led President Roosevelt to decide not to push further in fear that such a provision, which he supported, could endanger passage of the Social Security Act as a whole (Hopkins 1934; Witte 1962). The fear of AMA resistance did not change in ensuing years. After the U.S. Federal Security Administration published a book entitled *Common Human Needs* by social work leader Charlotte Towle in 1945, the government stopped its publication (in 1951) and burned the remaining copies because of complaints by the AMA that Towle was advocating government-funded health care. More recently, the effective opposition in 1994 to President Clinton's proposal for government assurance of universal health care reminds us that popular support for such a proposition, and hence its political viability, has not changed substantially over the passage of time.

In his 1937 inaugural address, in the midst of the Great Depression, President Roosevelt said, "I see one-third of the Nation ill-clad and ill-nourished." With apologies to FDR, he today might say: "I see one-third of the workforce ill-paid, ill supported, and ill-protected." In a period of economic crisis, such as the 1930s, one can explain such realities. It is more difficult to rationalize such facts today in an era of relative economic prosperity. In his 1998 memoir Robert Reich states: "For more than fifteen years, people in the bottom half of earnings distribution have lost ground. The middle class has been squeezed. The very poor have become even poorer. The wage gap is widening at alarming speed. . . . The whole economy has been transformed from high-*volume* production (based on repetitive tasks) to high *value* production (based on thought and knowledge). And only those with the right skills are flourishing" (12; emphasis in original).

Equally important, Reich observes that this economic transformation is occurring in tandem with technological innovation (computerization and cybernetics) that permits work to be done anywhere and thus for investors to be able to move capital quickly to wherever it earns the most.

To serve this end, even highly profitable companies are modifying and slashing payrolls in order to boost their stock prices rather than sharing profits with workers and investing in them as a corporate asset.

For the first three decades after the Second World War, prosperity was widely shared. Most people in the top fifth of incomes in America saw their real incomes double—and so did most people in the bottom fifth. Adjusted for inflation, however, in 1998 half of all workers earned less than they did in 1988. In short, the 1990s witnessed greater polarization of income than any other decade since World War II. Nowhere is this more evident than in the comparison of compensation for chief executive officers with that of wage and salaried workers. One labor study has shown that CEO compensation has risen from 28 times the average worker's salary in 1978 to 149 times in 1998 (UAW 1999: 2). Another independent Washington-based survey documented that in 1998 "big-league C.E.O.s pocketed, on the average, four hundred and nineteen times the earnings of a typical production worker" (Cassidy 1999: 32). By comparison, in 1992 in Japan, CEOs earned only 32 times as much as workers (Folbre 1995: 1.6). As a result of such phenomena, working and middle-class income loss occurred during the 1990s, while the wealthiest 1 percent of the American population amassed the greatest proportion of the nation's wealth in the twentieth century ("Underground Economy" 1998; Madrick 1995; Mishel et al. 2003). The richest 1 percent of Americans now own half of all stocks, bonds, and other assets in this country (Johnston 1999), and the average American corporate chief executive now makes more in one day than the typical American worker makes in a year (Leonhardt 2000: IV.5).

Role of the Labor Movement

For the past seventy years, labor unions have been an important countervailing force in enforcing Reich's "social compact." Representing workers in their collective negotiations with management, unions have added to the wealth of workers when measured both by wages and the value of employer-financed fringe benefit programs. As the economist Rebecca Blank (1994: 17) has pointed out, "unionized workers typically receive not only higher wages, but also more non-wage benefits." However, 87.1 percent of the working population today in the United States is not represented by a labor union. The annual shrinking in the size of union membership is undisputed, despite the fact that the trade union movement has been actively working since 1995 toward increasing its rolls.

In the 1930s three major pieces of federal legislation gave rise to a new role for organized labor in America. First, passage of the Norris-LaGuardia Act of 1932 provided support for unions that engaged in peaceful strikes and restrained federal courts from issuing injunctions against such activity. Enactment of the historic National Labor Relations Act (the Wagner Act) in 1935 guaranteed workers the right to organize and bargain collectively. The act gave the newly formed National Labor Relations Board (NLRB) authority to supervise union elections and determine the appropriate bargaining unit, to hear complaints of unfair labor practices, and to petition the federal courts for enforcement of NLRB orders, and it effectively outlawed company-sponsored unions. Finally, passage of the Fair Labor Standards Act of 1938 codified laws that dealt with the minimum wage, child labor, and work hours. The forty-four-hour work week was reduced to forty; sixteen was set as the age below which a child could not work in industries whose products entered interstate commerce; and a minimum wage was established at twenty-five cents an hour (Axinn & Stern 2001). Buoyed by enactment of such supportive legislation and by the strong economy following World War II and the Korean conflict, unions grew to represent 35.5 percent of all workers in 1954.

The labor movement was strengthened further in 1955 when the two major union federations—the American Federation of Labor (AFL) and the Congress of Industrial Organizations (CIO)—merged into one national confederation of unions. Paralleling a pattern that had been set by corporations, mergers among AFL-CIO member unions began to take place in the 1980s and 1990s, because smaller unions were becoming less viable as the industries they represented either disappeared or diminished. The ILGWU and ACTWU joined forces to become a single union (called UNITE) to represent clothing workers; the communications workers swallowed up the newspaper guild; and the steelworkers took over the rubberworkers, and then agreed to merge with the United Automobile Workers (UAW), forming a new union of more than 1.5 million members. In addition, the major unions that had been outside of the federation—the mine workers, longshoremen and warehousemen, automobile workers, locomotive engineers, and the Teamsters (the largest union in the country)—all chose for pragmatic reasons to become AFL-CIO members. Furthermore, in 1996, under special arrangements that would preserve its autonomy, the 125,000-member New York–based National Health and Human Service Employees Union (known as Local 1199) rejoined the AFL-CIO union confederation. Finally, a new president of the AFL-CIO was elected in 1995. He ran on a campaign to increase the size of the labor movement by organizing new settings and recapturing sites that had disaffiliated (Hardesty 1995; Greenhouse 1996b).

While union membership registered small gains in the late 1990s, these increases did not kept pace with growth in employment. For example, the AFL-CIO reports that unions recruited nearly 400,000 new members in 1997, but nonetheless, according to the Bureau of Labor Statistics, union membership was down by more than 200,000 (Greenhouse 1998b). The percentage of Americans holding union membership in the 1990s continued to fall each year. Despite this decline, unions in the public sector have grown and remain strong, consistently representing more than 40 percent of federal, state, and local government employees (Tambor 1995). Labor's biggest organizing victory in recent decades, for example, was the Service Employees International Union's gaining the right to represent 74,000 Los Angeles County home care workers who previously had no health insurance and earned the California minimum wage of only $5.75 an hour. With the growing tendency of government agencies to contract out to the private sector and to rely on temporary workers who are not eligible for civil service status or union membership, further unionization of this job sector now is in doubt.

Only a small fraction of the nation's 2 million computer and software developers, programmers, and engineers today belong to trade unions (Greenhouse 1999b: C1). If the American labor movement is to reverse the decades-long slide in percentage of workers belonging to unions it must rapidly make membership headway in high technology, the economy's fastest-growing sector. At the same time, labor leaders will need to continue to reach out to the growing number of workers in personal services positions—in retail, hotel, university, restaurant, insurance, and hospital jobs—that cannot be moved overseas. As Robert Reich observes (2004), personal service workers currently hold more than 30 percent of the jobs in America, and what he terms "symbolic analytic workers" hold at least 20 percent. Together, they constitute more than one-half of the workforce in the United States today.

This will not be easy to accomplish. Despite passage over the years of progressive legislation, American labor law has always given management the upper hand in labor relations. The common law concept of "employment at will" means that most private employers can hire and fire freely, unless a specific statute is in place to prohibit such an action as discriminatory or illegal. Deliberate strategies toward casualization and growth through expanding the contingent workforce have given employers further means to minimize worker eligibility for union membership. A management threat to contract-out work (often to suppliers located in southern states, where wages tend to be lower and unionization less common) can be supplemented by floating a proposal to outsource labor-intensive functions to developing countries on the Pacific Rim, where there are few labor laws, no unions, and substandard wages. Ultimately, some manufacturers can announce a need to downsize or relocate, making union recruitment substantially more difficult. Workers in high technology industries, furthermore, often believe they will be stigmatized if they join a union.

Labor unions also were significantly more cautious in the 1990s about using their most powerful weapon, the strike. In this regard, Pres. Ronald Reagan's actions in 1981 against the air traffic controller's union is considered a watershed event. When 12,700 controllers rejected the federal government's final contract offer and went out on strike, President Reagan secured a back-to-work court order. Two days later, when the traffic controllers (with their union's support) refused to return to work, they were dismissed and replaced by "permanent replacement workers." Many labor observers say that this action gave private employers the green light to take similar actions when confronted by strikes. "It wasn't something that management did until the 1980s," noted David Lipsky, dean of the Cornell University School of Industrial and Labor Relations; however, "[i]t had a chilling effect on unions and their propensity to strike" (Greenhouse 1996a: 12).

During the 1980s such well-known companies as Greyhound, Phelps Dodge, Eastern Airlines, and the Detroit Free Press successfully combated strikes by following this now established model of hiring permanent replacements—while the original union workers lost their jobs. Unions also began to shun walkouts because they saw several big ones fail, like the eighteen-month UAW walkout against Caterpillar. While unions recently have had success with strikes in a few instances, notably the machinists in 1995 against Boeing and the package handlers in 1997 against UPS, these achievements have been the exception not the rule. Faced with employers' greater use of automation and consequent ability to operate successfully during a strike and labor's continuing fear of management's deployment of permanent replacement workers, the number of strikes in 1996 nationwide fell to the lowest level in fifty years. In 1997, continuing the trend, there were just twenty-nine strikes involving a thousand workers or more, about half the amount of ten years before and one-eighth the level twenty years prior to that (Greenhouse 1996a).

While the strategy of striking has indeed abated, unions have convinced some workers in previously unorganized service settings to join, which is essential for the success of the labor movement as traditional manufacturing jobs continue to decline. While workers seek increased job security, safer workplaces, and better fringe benefits through unionization, the customary quest for better wages is always present as well. Such a focus continues to be necessary, for despite modest wage gains, the average worker's inflation-adjusted wages in 1997 remained 3 percentage points below 1989 levels (Greenhouse 1998b), and by 2003, average workers' take-home pay, as a share of the economy, was at its lowest level since the government started keeping track in 1929.

In contrast, Bureau of Labor Statistics data for 1996 show that the average weekly earnings of *union workers* was 33 percent higher than those of nonunion workers; furthermore, government statistics indicate that the median earnings for full-time workers in America in 1997 were $640 per week for union members, but only $478 for nonunion employees. Union members were also more likely to be covered by health insurance, disability policies, and defined-benefit pension plans, and they enjoyed significantly greater job security, measured by the number of years on their current job (AFL-CIO 1997; UAW 1998b). A 1999 research study (Ellin 2002) found that young union members are more likely than young nonunion employees to have full-time permanent jobs (74 percent versus 49 percent), earn more than $20,000 a year (70 percent versus 38 percent), be covered by a pension plan with an employer contribution (63 percent versus 39 percent), and have an employer-provided health plan (76 percent versus 40 percent). In terms of fringe benefits, the union advantage has been greatest in the private sector. In 1995, for example, nonunion members received benefits worth $4.35 an hour—only 54 percent of the amount ($7.99 an hour) awarded their unionized colleagues (Gold 1996: 5). The "union difference" has been especially important to African American workers who are represented by unions at a significantly higher percentage than whites or Hispanics (Heintz & Folbre 2000: 46).

Unions play additional roles that are helpful to their members and also to the smooth functioning of government in a democracy. The AFL-CIO and member unions contribute to candidate campaigns as a balance to the large contributions made by corporations, and labor participation includes contributions of not only money but also of manpower. Unions encourage their members to run for office, work for progressive candidates, and register to vote. In 1996 union households accounted for a larger segment of the overall vote nationwide than in the 1992 and 1994 elections. The number of union members who voted increased by 2.3 million over the 1992 election, even as the overall voter turnout dropped by more than 8 million (Allen 1996: 8).

In the increasingly dehumanized, downsized, and provisional work-place today, replete with contingent workers and "alternative work arrangements," workers find they desperately need the collective voice and the sense of stability and community that unions provide. "The organizations that have traditionally provided advocacy, understanding, fellowship, and links to entitlements (such as schools, churches, political clubs and community centers)," Molloy and Kurzman observe (1993: 55), "appear to be markedly less effective in doing so today." In Bielski's (1996: 26–27) view: "Work, the place and the people we find there, are now the closest we come to genuine community, to a network of friends and associates who gossip with us, laugh at our jokes, encourage us, lis-ten to our troubles; our work mates have become a kind of family that often seems closer to us than those people whom we [happen] to have married or given birth [to]. Certainly we spend more time with our coworkers than with our families." It is for these reasons, economic and noneconomic, that we value trade unions and regret their decline.

Some of the bases for the reduction in union members are embedded in macro- and microeconomic forces. Other reasons may have more to do with the public's declining respect for the union movement and its lead-ers, as evidence of widespread discrimination is proven (especially in craft unions) and instances of internal corruption are disclosed (such as with the Teamsters). It is therefore important that unions in America ensure the integrity of their elections and their operations so that they once again can secure the recognition and respect they deserve in the workplace. In an era when many employer promises appear to have been broken, the need for labor unions in the world of work has never been greater.

Work as a Federal Responsibility

Under federalism, there are checks and balances between the rights and responsibilities of the three branches of government, and there is the con-cept of limited government, especially on the federal level. The principle of state sovereignty has been firmly established, and a preference that pub-lic issues—when they cannot be resolved by responses from the private and voluntary sector—be resolved at a local level. Our appreciation for federal response to need must be understood in this constitutional con-text. Americans were not surprised when Pres. Franklin Pierce vetoed leg-islation in 1854 to provide national programs to assist the mentally ill, stating a popular view at the time that this was entirely the responsibility of the states and localities. This philosophy and public policy remained in effect until the Great Depression of the 1930s. There were only very modest and limited exceptions. The federal government, for example, established the Freedmen's Bureau at the end of the Civil War explicitly to assist newly released slaves to pursue education and employment, and at the end of World War I, the first Vocational Rehabilitation Act was passed to provide occupational training (and prostheses) specifically for disabled veterans. However, when the first federal Child Labor Act became law in 1916, forbidding interstate commerce of goods manufactured by child labor, legislators were not too surprised when it was overturned by the U.S. Supreme Court as being unconstitutional.

Historically, areas where the Constitution explicitly authorizes federal responsibility and expenditure, such as military defense, have been supported and favored. (Every year about one-fourth of federal spending goes to the armed forces, with the United States spending much more in 1992 on its military, for example, than France, Great Britain, Germany, and Japan combined [Folbre 1995: 5.9].) In understanding the federal government's resistance to viewing work as an arena of federal responsibility at the start of the twentieth century, one must look beyond federalism and the ideology of limited government to the always controversial issue of taxation. The primary sources of revenue at that time were customs duties and excise taxes on liquor. Not until passage of the Sixteenth Amendment to the Constitution in 1913 did the U.S. Congress achieve the power "to lay and collect taxes on incomes." The initial income tax, which followed the constitutional amendment, only affected the richest 5 percent of Americans, and it was not revised to impact most wage earners until the beginning of World War II. Consequently, the federal government simply lacked the resources to fund programs to redress poverty and unemployment, not only at the start of the 1900s but also during most of the 1930s. Even when faced in 1942 by the massive expenditures needed to fight simultaneously on two continents to win the Second World War, Americans funded more than 60 percent of the costs not by raising income taxes (i.e., current revenue) but by increasing borrowing (i.e., future debt) sixfold. Federal monies for funding human service programs also were scarce at the end of the war. Saddled now with a large national debt, President Truman had to fund veterans benefits, make interest payments on the war debt, and provide aid to devastated nations in Europe and Asia with taxes that were being slashed by the Congress over his vetoes (Jansson 2001).

In 1933 when Franklin D. Roosevelt assumed the presidency and found unemployment peaking at 25 percent, the federal government took the initiative to respond to Americans' desperate need for income and employment. Two months after his inauguration, President Roosevelt

approved the Federal Emergency Relief Act (FERA). Half of the $500 mil-
lion congressional appropriation was made available to the states, on a
matching basis of one to three; the other half was to form a federal dis-
cretionary fund from which sums could be granted to those states whose
relief needs exceeded their ability to meet the matching provisions. As
Axinn and Stern (2001: 186) have noted, "In authorizing direct grants to
states for relief, the legislation set a major precedent for a new fiscal relationship between the federal government and the states and for a new
interpretation of the responsibility of the federal government for social
welfare" that shattered the principles laid out in President Pierce's 1854
veto—which had prevailed for seventy-nine years.

During the first two years (1933–34) the FERA primarily gave direct
relief. Families needed money to buy food, pay the rent, and clothe themselves and their children. In the short run, it was also less expensive to give
people cash relief than it was to create jobs. In the second phase
(1934–35), however, the agency converted from a cash-relief project to an
emergency work program. Understanding the centrality of work in people's lives, President Roosevelt (Rosenman 1950: 19) told Congress in
January 1935: "The lessons of history, confirmed by the evidence immediately before me, show conclusively that continued dependence upon
relief induces a spiritual and moral disintegration fundamentally destruc-
tive to the national fiber. To dole out relief in this way is to administer a
narcotic, a subtle destroyer of the human spirit. It is inimical to the dic-
tates of sound policy. It is in violation of the traditions of America. Work
must be found for the able-bodied but destitute workers."

To this, FERA administrator (and social worker) Harry Hopkins
(1935a: E5) added his own belief that people in America have a conviction that there is something intrinsically good in earning a living. "It is, in
fact, such a deep-seated conviction" he noted, "that without work men
actually go to pieces." But why spend billions of dollars on employment,
Hopkins was asked; would it not be cheaper to keep on with a cash dole
(Hopkins 1935b: 7)? "Of course it would be cheaper in terms of money!
Cheaper, in all probability, by a full 50 percent; but, when you count up
in terms of pride, courage, self-respect, ambition and energy, a direct-relief
program is a thousand times more costly than a work program, for it ends
inevitably towards the creation of a permanent pauper class, hopeless and
helpless, an increasing and crushing weight on the backs of the gainfully
employed."

This belief in the importance of work continued during the 1930s when
the FERA was supplemented by the Civil Works Administration (CWA)
in the winter of 1933–34 and replaced by the Works Progress Adminis-

tration (WPA) in the spring of 1935. The WPA abandoned the grant-in-aid system in favor of a direct federal program (in funding and operations) and continued until 1939, when industry began to absorb the unemployed as war and lend-lease production activities accelerated. Spending more than $10 billion (86 percent on wages), the WPA gave employment to nearly 8 million Americans, one out of five of all the nation's workers (Kurzman 1974).

During the 1940s and 1950s, America experienced low unemployment. As war production became the paramount economic (as well as military) focus of the nation, men either joined the armed forces, held critical positions in their communities (police officer, farmer, banker, civil servant), or worked in the private sector producing the goods and services needed to support our troops abroad. They were supplemented, frequently working full-time for the first time, by women who assumed many critical jobs that men had held before the war. After the Allied victory in 1945, men returned to the States and assumed their old jobs, and women (immortalized in films such as *Rosie the Riveter*) returned home to start families. While unemployment began to rise at the end of the decade (to 7.9 percent in 1949), the advent of the Korean conflict in 1950 lowered employment to 2.9 percent by 1953 and kept rates low until late in the decade.

In the late 1950s and early 1960s unemployment once again was clearly a national problem. Moreover, America's new leaders, Presidents Kennedy and Johnson, both had put forth a public commitment to reaching out and serving the traditionally disadvantaged including the rural and inner-city poor and people of color. At President Kennedy's instigation, the first major federal employment legislation since the New Deal was enacted in 1962 as the Manpower Development and Training Act (MDTA). This new federal program was intended to provide training or retraining for workers displaced by economic or technological change. Conceptually, the emphasis on preparation for labor market participation and enhancing occupational potential were extensions of the intent of the Servicemen's Readjustment Act—the famous GI Bill. The MDTA, however, specifically focused on classroom and on-the-job training for dislocated workers and became the forerunner of the employment initiatives that emerged as part of President Johnson's subsequent Great Society programs.

Foremost among the employment-centered ventures of the Economic Opportunity Act of 1964 were the Job Corps and the Neighborhood Youth Corps, offering training, stipends, and subsidies for work-related expenses to severely disadvantaged youth and young adults. These programs functioned under the ideology that, for most American families, work is the antipoverty program of choice. In the 1967 amendments to the Social Security Act, a Work Incentive Program (WIN) was created to further this ideology for recipients of AFDC. For the first time, nonexempt welfare mothers were required to enter a job-training or work-placement program, with the promise of help with child care, employment, and support services. (WIN II, enacted in 1971, added punitive sanctions for non-participation.) "By all accounts," Abramovitz (1995: 190) observes, "the WIN program was a dismal failure. It placed too few women in jobs, was too costly and was plagued by administrative flaws, inadequate child care services, numerous labor market barriers, and a host of other problems." While the WIN amendments resulted in little discernable increase in labor force participation among welfare recipients, they were symbolically important as the initial salvo in America's search for a "work-based" public assistance system (Reid 1995).

In 1969 President Nixon's urban affairs adviser, Daniel Patrick Moynihan, persuaded the president to sponsor a Family Assistance Plan (FAP) to nationalize welfare policies and payments. The FAP would replace state-administered and subsidized AFDC programs with a federally run and financed minimum benefit payment for all indigent families with children. The new plan would include work incentives, even stronger and potentially more punitive than in the preceding WIN program. Opposed by many conservative Republicans, who feared a major expansion of welfare provision at the federal level, and by liberal Democrats, who believed the benefits were too low and the work requirements too stringent, the legislation passed in the House of Representatives but failed in the Senate (Dickinson 1995). Four years later, however, President Nixon was successful in getting Congress to pass employment legislation.

Stung by the "federalization of public welfare" concept explicit in the Nixon-Moynihan FAP proposal, the Senate was pleased with President Nixon's new proposed legislation. It would consolidate and transfer the operations of earlier training programs from the federal to state and local levels. The 1973 Comprehensive Employment and Training Act (CETA) would use the mechanism of special block grants (revenue sharing) so that prime sponsors (state and local governments) could contract with employers to provide training and subsidized jobs. Reminiscent of the New Deal employment programs of the 1930s, CETA jobs were not means-tested because applicants only had to prove their unemployment. CETA was widely viewed, however, as deeply flawed legislation. Rather than providing extensive training to millions of workers who were becoming displaced from manufacturing jobs in steel, automobile, and other industries (as American corporations moved plants abroad and as

Japan and Europe increased their exports to the United States), CETA mostly provided temporary jobs to unemployed people (Jansson 2001).

When President Carter assumed office he sought to revise the nation's welfare system by proposing legislation titled "A Better Jobs and Income Security Program." In its essential thrust, President Carter's 1977 plan was remarkably similar to President Nixon's 1969 proposal for a Family Assistance Plan, and it too met with defeat in Congress. President Carter's proposed legislation, however, provided for universal coverage whereas the Nixon proposal was for families only, and the new 1977 program would have included a provision for job creation. Failing to get congressional support for the legislation, President Carter proposed the Youth Employment Demonstration Projects Act of 1977, which was enacted into law. It funded pilot employment programs for disadvantaged youth and incorporated an ambitious commitment to experimental program design and comprehensive research.

The Job Training Partnership Act (JTPA) of 1982 reflected the approach of a new president, Ronald Reagan, and the leaders of the Republican party. Replacing the public service–oriented focus of CETA, the JTPA provided education and training for dislocated workers and promoted the transition from welfare to work. The emphasis was away from work experience and toward vocational exploration, skills training, job search assistance, and vocationally centered remedial education. Equally important was a requirement that closer relationships be built between state government and private industry. Private Industry Councils (PICs) had to be established in each service delivery area to oversee implementation of JTPA operations and to contract with community-based organizations. Emphasizing the president's preference for private sector job placement, rules dictated that at least 51 percent of PIC membership in each community had to come from the private, for-profit sector.

As part of President Reagan's overall Family Support Act of 1988, a new program, Job Opportunities and Basic Skills Training (JOBS) was established, directed at mothers on welfare. With the introduction of the Work Incentive Program in 1967, work requirements for women on AFDC had been imposed for the first time. With rapid changes in the desires and demands of employers during the intervening decades, there was now a need for a more sophisticated program of education and skills training if these low-income women were to be qualified for job openings, which were no longer likely to be low-skilled positions in manufacturing but rather high-skilled opportunities in the growing communications and technology industries. As Edwards and colleagues (1996: 472) cogently observed: "The U.S. economy, which was built on large-scale standardization and manufacturing, moved dramatically to service and communications, a shift in emphasis from skill and labor to speed, knowledge, abstraction, analysis and planning. Whereas the new economy is increasingly based on the manipulation of words and numbers, the U.S. population as a whole is not well suited by education or social experience for this new world."

The aim of the JOBS program was to increase the emphasis on education and training as components of a welfare employment program and to guarantee the availability of child care to all mothers entering the workforce. The states were required to invest their own funds, but the federal matching rate was 90 percent of each state's previous WIN allocation. Subsequent studies favorably noted JOBS' new emphasis on a "human capital investment strategy and on a refined implementation of focused training and remedial education" (Hagen 1995: 1549).

During the last forty years, a wide variety of federal legislation has been enacted, with a significant focus on work, workers, and work institutions. Fifty of these laws are noted in table 3.1.

Some of the new laws were focused on employment opportunity; several, on promoting workplace health and safety; a few, on protecting employee benefits; some, on opening up employment equity and employee options; and still others were targeted at eliminating workplace discrimination. Indeed, as one reviews the seminal federal legislation over these forty years under nine presidents—five Republicans and four Democrats—it is noteworthy how often work-centered issues have been the focal point for new federal statutes.[3]

As Seymour Lipset (perhaps the most thoughtful contemporary authority on American exceptionalism) has observed, public policies are deeply rooted in American perceptions and values (Lipset 1985). While feeling overtaxed, for example, Americans actually pay substantially less personal taxes than Europeans. Similarly, American corporations pay less federal taxes—down from approximately 45 percent of corporate profits in the 1950s to only about 28 percent in the 1990s (Folbre 1995: 5.12). Put a different way, corporate taxes shrank from 23 percent of all federal tax receipts in 1960 to merely 11 percent in 1998 (Heintz & Folbre 2000: 94–96). The U.S. government therefore simply undertakes much less in

---

[3] Additionally, some significant changes in federal employment policy were enacted through executive orders, especially in the area of affirmative action, such as the 1965 executive order no. 11246 codified by the Affirmative Action Rule 41CFR (part 60) in 1970, which requires all employers conducting business with the federal government to develop and implement an affirmative action plan.

TABLE 3.1 Major Work-Centered Federal Legislation, 1962–2003

1962	Manpower Development and Training Act (MDTA)
1963	Equal Pay Act
1964	Civil Rights Act of 1964: Titles 6 and 7, "Workplace Discrimination"
1965	Senior Community Service Employment Program of the Older Americans Act
1967	Age Discrimination in Employment Act (ADEA)
1967	Work Incentive Program (WIN): Title 6 of the Social Security Act Amendments
1969	Federal Coal Mine Health and Safety Act
1970	Occupational Safety and Health Act (OSHA)
1970	Comprehensive Alcohol Abuse and Alcohol Prevention, Treatment, and Rehabilitation (Hughes) Act
1971	Emergency Employment Act
1972	Equal Employment Opportunity Act
1973	Rehabilitation Act of 1973
1973	Comprehensive Employment and Training Act (CETA)
1974	Employee Retirement Income Security Act (ERISA)
1977	Youth Employment Demonstration Projects Act
1977	Public Works Employment Act
1978	Full Employment and Balanced Growth Act
1978	Federal Employees Part-Time Career Act
1978	Pregnancy Discrimination Act
1978	Civil Service Reform Act: Title 7, "Right to Collective Bargaining"
1980	Employment Eligibility Provisions of the Refugee Act
1982	Job Training Partnership Act (JTPA)
1984	Retirement Equity Act
1986	Earned Income Tax Credit of the Tax Reform Act
1986	Federal Employee Health Benefits Improvement Act
1987	Employment Opportunities for Disabled Americans Act
1988	Drug Free Workplace Act
1988	Job Opportunities and Basic Skills Training Program of the Family Support Act (JOBS)
1988	Federal Employees Leave Sharing Act
1988	Worker Adjustment and Retraining Notification Act
1988	Employee Polygraph Protection Act
1988	Economic Dislocation and Worker Adjustment Assistance Act
1990	Older Workers Benefit Protection Act
1990	Americans with Disabilities Act (ADA)
1991	Civil Rights Act of 1991: Title 1, "Employment Discrimination"
1991	Government Employee Rights Act
1992	Job Training Reform Amendments Act
1993	Family and Medical Leave Act (FMLA)

(continued)

TABLE 3.1 (continued)

1994	School-to-Work Opportunities Act
1994	Uniformed Services Employment and Re-employment Rights Act
1994	Federal Employee Family Friendly Leave Act
1996	Small Business Job Protection Act
1996	Mental Health Employment Parity Act
1996	Personal Responsibility and Work Opportunity Reconciliation Act
1996	Health Insurance Portability and Accountability Act
1998	Veterans' Employment Opportunities Act
1998	Workforce Investment Act
1999	Ticket to Work and Work Incentives Improvement Act
2002	Job Creation and Worker Assistance Act
2003	Jobs and Growth Tax Relief Reconciliation Act

terms of worker retraining, maternity leave, day care for working mothers, health insurance, and programs to aid the unemployed (Bok 1996). Reactive rather than proactive, employer-oriented as opposed to worker-centered, and individually directed rather than family-focused, our government has adopted a generally laissez-faire attitude, hands-off approach toward the needs of workers and their families (Kurzman 1988b).

Current workforce benefits and services frequently are not only too few and too modest but also often out of date with current need. Unemployment insurance was designed, for example, for workers who were temporarily laid off, until the economy picked up and the company would rehire them. That process might take up to six months, so that is how long the benefit was designed to last. A great number of the unemployed since the 1980s, however, have become structurally unemployed, as employers merge, downsize, restructure, and relocate abroad. Rather than merely collecting unemployment benefits for six months, a more responsive alternative might be to create a "reemployment system" whereby those who lost jobs that probably would never reappear could immediately start education and skills training for new jobs in expanding economic sectors (which Thurow [1999] terms the "knowledge-based economy") such as communications, professional services, and technology (Reich 1998). While some support is available under the 1988 Worker Adjustment and Retraining Notification Act, the resulting programs have been underfunded, and the opportunities have not proved sufficient to meet contemporary need.

One of the most controversial recent changes in public employment policy came through provisions of a statute entitled the Personal Responsibility and Work Opportunity Reconciliation Act of 1996. An important piece of compromise legislation (following President Clinton's veto of a relatively similar bill earlier that year), this law is perhaps the most pivotal welfare- and employment-focused legislation for America at the beginning of the new millennium. Among its central provisions are

- replacing AFDC, a federal guarantee of cash assistance to all eligible low-income mothers and children, with a block grant to states for Temporary Assistance for Needy Families (TANF)
- setting a five-year lifetime limit on assistance and requiring the head of the household to find work within two years
- requiring future legal immigrants to wait five years before gaining eligibility to receive most federal benefits
- prohibiting a single parent with children older than age five from claiming lack of child care as a reason for not working
- continuing Medicaid coverage for families one year after the head of household finds a job
- requiring able-bodied recipients with no dependents to work at least part-time after they have received food stamps for three months
- increasing financial assistance for child care by $3 billion over the succeeding six years

Not surprisingly, reactions to the new law have differed widely. Liberals predicted it would push millions of people (including children) into poverty, while conservatives felt it would give independence and a future of hope to generations previously trapped by dependence and poverty. Undisputed, however, is the explicit preference here of work over welfare and that public assistance (like unemployment insurance) should be viewed as a temporary measure. Unfortunately, TANF's provisions not only set time limits on assistance but also narrow the definition of work activities the government will fund, ruling out many skills-building and training options, including higher education, allowed by the landmark 1988 JOBS program (Abramovitz 1997).

When the twentieth century came to a close, the two principal foci for government programs in the world of work were "workfare" and "welfare-to-work." Under the first concept, able-bodied recipients of cash assistance are expected to work off their checks by performing public works, generally in their local community. As a result, about thirty-five thousand people, for example, were enrolled in New York City's Work Experience (Workfare) Program in 1998, filing papers, answering telephones, and cleaning city parks. When New York City's mayor Rudolph Giuliani first took office in 1993, he was adamant that anyone who received an assistance check would have to work. His long-term goal was "to end welfare by the end of this century completely." In 1998 Mayor Giuliani brought Jason Turner from Wisconsin to head New York's Human Resources Administration and implement a welfare-to-work program. As his first symbolic act, Turner promptly converted the city's Income Maintenance Centers to Job Centers. The change, however, was to be more than cosmetic. "The Human Resources Administration is now a business organization," Turner wrote in his first memorandum to staff, "and our mission is to move our participants to self-sufficiency [welfare-to-work] through employment" (District Council 1998: 4). As one observer wrote, "Turner harbors an almost mystical belief in the power of work—not just as a source of income, but also as a redemptive force that can treat depression, order lives and stem moral disintegration" (DeParle 1998: 54). Perhaps New York was only echoing the earlier ideology of Franklin Roosevelt and Harry Hopkins.

Punitive as some of the mandates of the 1996 federal law may appear, they have put forth a notion that intergenerational dependence can be ended and have set in motion both restrictive and enabling provisions to move a large number of Americans from welfare to work. Even if buoyed by a strong economy, achieving the goals of this legislation may be difficult, and many casualties can be predicted. However, since the 1996 act is the law of the land, social workers and the organized profession cannot afford to stay above the fray. We have something to contribute. As Iversen (1998: 552) wisely suggests, "occupational social workers should apply systematically the specialized knowledge and skills they have accumulated in workplace practice to practice in welfare-to-work and similar work-program settings." As we look at occupational social work practice in the next chapter we must have a clear vision of what these opportunities may be and how to seize them.

Study Questions

1. In your judgment, is the "contract" between employers and their workers really "broken," or has it just been altered by changing conditions in a global economy?

2. How would you assess the advantages and disadvantages of the growing productivity of U.S. workers from the vantage point of the several participants and stakeholders in the world of work?

3. How would you evaluate the similarities and differences of the long-range, intergenerational effects of slavery versus indenture? Is this an issue that is relevant to current workers and work organizations? Explain your answer.

4. What do you perceive as the impact and implications of the continuing decline of labor union membership in the United States? Could this downward trend be reversed?

5. Some view the expanding supplemental and contingent workforce as a blessing; some, as a curse. What do you see as the trade-offs?

6. How would you evaluate the prospective impact of the Personal Responsibility and Work Opportunity Reconciliation Act of 1996 on work, workers, and work organizations?

CHAPTER 4

Social Work in the World of Work
and in Traditional Settings

Occupational Social Work

Workers are in all settings—not only in the traditional profit-making corporations that produce goods and services for sale but also in schools, hospitals, prisons, and even the military. Since workers are likely to have the host of problems that assail all human beings, we contend that to truly meet the gamut of human needs social workers also should practice under the aegis of work organizations (i.e., employers and trade unions) as well as in more traditional social agency settings.

The occupational social work (OSW) field of practice has evolved from the logic of this proposition. While often defined more expansively in Europe and abroad (United Nations 1971), in the United States OSW has been conceptualized more narrowly by most observers. Googins and Godfrey (1987: 5) characterize it as "a field of practice in which social workers attend to the human and social needs of the work community by designing and executing appropriate interventions to insure healthier individuals and environments." Professionals attending the First National Conference on Social Work Practice in Labor and Industrial Settings offered a somewhat similar explication, stating that OSW "refers to the utilization of social work expertise in meeting the needs of workers or union members, and the serving of broader organizational goals of the setting" (Akabas, Kurzman, & Kolben 1979: 5). While these definitions are useful, a more expansive definition (Kurzman 1987: 899) suggests that occupational social work constitutes "programs and services, under the auspices of labor or management, that utilize professional social workers to serve members or employees and the legitimate social welfare needs of the labor or industrial organization. It also includes the use, by a voluntary or proprietary social agency, of trained social workers to provide social welfare services or consultation to a trade union or employing organization under a specific contractual agreement."

Several points are worthy of note in this latter definition. First, the focus is on the centrality of both management and labor and the importance of serving their appropriate organizational needs, as well as those of workers—employees or members. Second, an emphasis is placed on the deployment of professionally trained social workers and on the knowledge, values, and skills they bring to this practice setting. Third, the attention here is on the auspices of the professional practice: a nontraditional, nonhuman service host setting. The implications of this final point merit further discussion.

While social workers commonly practice within settings directed by members of other professions (such as hospitals, schools, correctional facilities, and substance abuse clinics), each of these environments generally functions within the human service tradition, broadly defined. As Bakalinsky (1980) notes, the firm thread customarily binding the diverse primary and host settings in which social workers are employed is a humanistic philosophy that underscores the inherent dignity and worth of the individual. The common denominator in a capitalistic economic system that motivates employers, however, is the priority of productivity and of profits. Individuals (as workers) have an instrumental value in the context of a superordinate goal—employees are a means toward an end. Lest this issue appear directed only toward the management side of the occupational social work equation, we are reminded of the parallel dilemma when working as agents of organized labor. For example, if an approaching union election brings a staff directive to set aside program activity in order to assist in furthering the survival needs (reelection) of the union leadership—the practitioner's employer—how should the occupational social worker respond? Such are the conundrums inherent with professional practice in nontraditional settings that are outside of human service norms, folkways, and traditions (Kurzman 1988a).

As Cunningham (1994: 200) illustrates well, "It is not so much a question of the EAP counselor being at risk of becoming a tool of management by revealing the contents of client records or by using counseling sessions to steer clients in the direction of corporate goals and agendas. Rather, it is a question of having services curtailed or compromised by budgetary cutbacks, benefit restrictions, and escalating accountability forms and procedures that compete with the time needed to provide adequate service to employees." All social workers, including those in the most traditional settings, can identify with many of these prototypic organizational constraints.

Ultimately, it is impossible to ignore the historic role that employing organizations—corporations and trade unions—have played in America since the start of the industrial revolution. Work organizations are the centerpiece of the modern American experience. Work is performed by workers at the locus of work organizations. Each day, 4 million employers engage the services of almost 140 million members of the American workforce to produce the goods and services that not only meet the needs of the American people but also stimulate our trade abroad to fortify our nation's position in the world economy. As a result, private employer-supported social welfare spending reached $852 billion in 1992, rising from less than $100 billion in 1972 (Kerns 1995). Health and medical expenses claimed the largest dollar amount, with private health care expenditures continuing to exceed government health expenditures (Kerns 1997; Hoefer & Colby 1997).

Thus employers, especially for-profit corporations, are the principal engine of the American economy, with the corporate presence in social welfare rapidly growing in importance (Karger & Stoesz 2002). For-profit organizations inevitably play a powerful role, employ more people, and underwrite as much social welfare spending as the public and nonprofit sectors, which traditionally host our profession. This historic and continuing role of corporations in this country is well documented, and further evidence will show that these core institutions have been the source of much good, as well as considerable danger and exploitation (*Work in America* 1973; Stellman & Daum 1973; Page & O'Brien 1973).

With respect to American corporations' historic commitments to services for their employees, an early example usually cited is their deployment of "welfare secretaries," starting at the beginning of the twentieth century. They helped immigrants adapt to American folkways and corporate workplace demands. The motivation for their employment, however, was seen by some observers as a mix of "paternalism, philanthropy and the desire to get more out of the worker," and therefore the "welfare secretary" movement ultimately failed (Wagner, Queen, & Harper 1930: 38). Finally, during the Great Depression of the 1930s, all vestiges of what Brandes (1976) termed "welfare capitalism" collapsed under the weight of national economic decline.

With the advent of the Second World War, industrial settings returned to the philosophy that workers might be more productive if personal problems were ameliorated. Employers introduced social workers in significant numbers to help cope with war-induced manpower problems, but this commitment waned in the late 1940s when soldiers returned from abroad and workers once again became plentiful.

Although employers' behavior had given evidence during the war that they considered it good business to spend money to understand their workers' needs and to help develop, strengthen, and hold their employees, these same employers reverted to firings as a means of handling troubled workers at the end of the war, when a large civilian labor force became available. When workers are scarce, recruitment and training costs are high. When the supply of workers is excessive, recruitment and training costs decline. Social intent did not survive the employers' cost-benefit analysis, which suggested to them, in the postwar era, that the marginal cost of social work services was greater than the marginal cost of new recruitment. (Akabas & Kurzman 1982a: 210–11)

Although industry in Europe and South America employed growing numbers of occupational social workers, there was relatively little such activity in the United States during the two decades following the Second World War. Industry absorbed its prewar workforce, and the nation entered a period of economic and social laissez-faire. As the sociologist Harold Wilensky and the social worker Charles Lebeaux (1965: 163) correctly noted at the time, "Industrial social work . . . hailed for the past twenty years as a 'new frontier in social work,' simply has not materialized in America."

Modern occupational social work practice can be dated from the early 1970s. Applying Rostow's (1960) economic paradigm to social development, a successful "development of preconditions" led to a period of "take-off" in the 1970s and 1980s and a "drive to maturity" in the 1990s. At the First National Conference on Social Work Practice in Labor and Industrial Settings in 1978 (Akabas, Kurzman, & Kolben 1979) and the subsequent 1979 Wingspread Conference Meeting on Human Service Needs in the Workplace (*Meeting Human Service Needs* 1980), OSW was clearly ready to evolve and take off as an authentic field of practice.

During the 1970s the federal government enacted major legislation requiring adaptation, accommodation, and compliance by American industry. These statutes included the Hughes Act of 1970, OSHA of 1970, Rehabilitation Act of 1973, ERISA of 1974, and Pregnancy Discrimination Act of 1978. Management also was faced with new dilemmas that were having an impact on their productivity and profit, such as the rapid increase of labor force participation by women with children and by inner-city workers of color; greater job turnover and the unexpectedly high cost of training and replacement; the escalating cost of providing health and mental health fringe benefits; and government's expectation that employers comply with new statutes covering occupational safety and health, accommodation for people with disabilities, the employment rights of pregnant women workers, the protection of workers' pensions and the assurance of a drug-free workplace. The expertise of professional social workers, long demonstrated in traditional settings, took on new value to leaders of industry. Personnel, medical, training, and human resource departments were shouldering unfamiliar responsibilities for the work organization, and they had to rapidly develop and launch more progressive policies and programs. Social workers were hired to help assess and change old personnel policies, to mount new training projects, to design and implement affirmative action programs for women, minorities, and people with disabilities, to participate in corporate efforts to implement alcohol and drug education programs, to conduct out-placement counseling, to serve customers, to consult on the development of more flexible (yet cost-sensitive) fringe benefit options, and to initiate appropriate preretirement programs for the growing number of World War II veterans approaching retirement age.

Foremost among the duties held by these incoming occupational social workers, however, was the responsibility to provide counseling for employees whose work or home-based problems were affecting their job performance (Akabas 1995a; Kurzman 1992; Straussner 1989; Smith 1988). Evolving from the ephemeral occupational alcoholism programs of the late 1970s and early 1980s to become employee counseling programs by the 1990s, these emerging corporate services were entitled employee assistance programs (EAPs) (McGowan 1984; Akabas & Krauskopf 1986). As testimony to their rapid growth and institutionalization, a major national employment study found that by 1991 45 percent of full-time employees surveyed worked for firms with an EAP. In addition, the researchers estimated that approximately 76 percent of American work sites with more than a thousand employees had an EAP at that time (Blum, Martin, & Roman 1992).

While some observers envisioned EAPs as a management tool to enhance employees' productivity, others conceptualized these programs as a new worker benefit to meet management needs by preserving precious human and fiscal resources. We believe there is greater truth in the latter notion, as can be seen by the following definition (Kurzman 1993: 35) of a comprehensive EAP: "Comprehensive EAPs are free and confidential workplace entitlements that are voluntarily sponsored by employers or trade unions or jointly by both. In-house (internal) and contract (external) EAPs respond to the human service needs of workers and their families and to the corresponding agendas of the work organization."

Management's Motivation

The broader questions are, why would it be in the vested interest of employers to establish EAPs and similar work site programs? From a business perspective, how would occupational social workers contribute to the "bottom-line" of productivity and profit? To answer these questions and understand employers' investment in EAPs and similar human service programs, it is instructive to look at several contemporary workplace issues.

First, the cost of providing employees with traditional health and mental health coverage as part of their benefit package has increased and continues to do so (albeit more slowly) under managed care. A national Foster Higgins study (Freudenheim 1993) found that health benefit costs of the large and medium-size employers surveyed rose more than three times as fast as overall living costs. Specifically, they found that the average cost per employee of providing mental health and substance abuse coverage doubled between 1987 and 1992. Companies were spending about $22 billion providing therapy and counseling to employees in 1993—approximately 10 percent of employer spending on all health care (Freudenheim 1994). Surveys showed however that companies with comprehensive EAPs—which include attention to health education, fitness, and wellness—were spending about $500 less per employee in the annual cost of providing health care (Kurzman 1992: 87). As Donovan (1984: 66) stated, "the provision of mental health care and alcoholism treatment seems to contain overall health care costs because of significant reductions to the subsequent utilization of medical care." Alcohol abusers, anxious and depressed workers, and those coping with situational stress make disproportionate use of such health benefits, along with those who smoke, are overweight, and fail to exercise. Many of these costs may be contained by EAP programs of education, prevention, and early intervention (Foote 1978; Winslow 1966). One of the authors (Kurzman 1993: 38) notes:

> Managers realize that anxious and overwhelmed working mothers are applying for expensive disability coverage during times of crisis; that men who are depressed by the sadness of divorce are having more accidents, which result in increased premiums for workers' compensation; and that middle-aged daughters at work, who are caught without support in caring both for their young children and their aging parents, show higher rates of tardiness and absenteeism and may ultimately be discharged, under conditions that entitle them to six or more months of costly unemployment insurance.

Second, the cost of replacing an employee tends to be high, even when that worker does not perform an exceptionally skilled function. In addition to the cost of unemployment insurance (premiums for which may rise based on benefit utilization), most new employees need some training. For example, if the customarily good performance of a telephone operator (a common semiskilled job) sharply declines to "unsatisfactory" due to an inability to cope with the dual demands of caring for her three young children and providing for her frail, homebound in-laws, the company can dismiss her, pay the costs of her entitlements, and direct human resources to hire a replacement. However, the new worker will need weeks (on full salary) in the firm's training program before coming on duty, and the more trainees, the greater the number of trainers who need to be hired and the more space to be rented for training. Some trainees will not successfully complete the course of training. Those who do will be under the watchful eye of a supervisor for several weeks (two people doing one job) and probably will not be fully productive operators, like their predecessors, for several months. Telephone companies, like other employers, have come to realize that a referral of the original operator to the firm's EAP (an investment in a valuable human resource) may be more cost-effective than firing the old employee and hiring and training a new worker.

A third incentive for industries to establish an EAP derives from their investment in and commitment to their most highly skilled workers. In a manufacturing setting, these may be craft workers who bring unique talent and skill from abroad; in the executive chamber, they may be a handful of executives who are on the fast track, with potential to rise to the very top of the corporate ladder; in the research and development unit, they could be the newly minted Ivy League Ph.D. scientists whose creativity and sheer brilliance represent the company's future—the competitive edge in its rivalry with the competition. Designated "preferred workers" by Akabas in her study (1970), such employees have a premium value to the employer (Weiner, Akabas, & Sommer 1973). If their superb performance is impaired by the sudden death of a loved one, experimentation with a controlled substance, divorce, or paralyzing stress from coping with child-care or elder-care responsibilities, the company will place high value on getting them the professional assistance they need to return to their prior level of innovation and excellence. The firm's disproportionate investment in such "preferred workers" provides the motivation to develop a capacity to respond to their needs quickly and effectively.

Fourth, employers realize that there is a finite pool of skilled workers. With the present and prospective expansion of technology at all levels and in virtually every industry, the demand for well-educated workers with sound verbal, writing, and computational skills has increased. Such potential employees however are in limited supply, especially in the inner city where the major markets and corporate offices tend to be located. While some employers can move their plants, distribution centers, and back-office work to other settings, many large employers cannot. Banks, utilities, hospitals, universities, and local government, for example, are tied to the locations in which they serve customers and do their business. They cannot readily relocate to tap a different labor pool. Furthermore, these employers tend to need a large labor force. The three largest employers in New York City, for example, fit this profile: Verizon (formerly N.Y. Telephone and then Bell Atlantic), Columbia University, and J. P. Morgan–Chase Manhattan Bank. In this context, creating a comprehensive program of employee assistance services is seen as a good business investment.

Finally, there are a growing number of protected classes of workers, who have statutes and case law to protect them. Title 7 of the Civil Rights Act of 1964 makes it unlawful for employers to discriminate against any individual on the basis of "race, color, religion, sex, or national origin" (Singer 1995: 2149). The Age Discrimination in Employment Act of 1973 covers and protects employees as young as age forty. The Pregnancy Discrimination Act of 1978 guarantees that all pregnant women employees be treated the same as employees with any other temporary disability (Kamerman & Kahn 1987). The Americans with Disabilities Act of 1990, covering companies with as few as fifteen employees, mandates "reasonable accommodation" to the disability of a qualified applicant or worker, whether it be physical or emotional, so long as it does not cause the employer "undue hardship" (Akabas, Gates, & Galvin 1992). The Family and Medical Leave Act of 1993 guards the rights of all men and women to take job-protected unpaid leave to care for themselves or for family members. Of necessity, compliance with this and similar legislation has coaxed industry into the "people business." Social workers and similar human service professionals now are needed to do EAP counseling (casework), affirmative action and supervisory training (group work), consumer relations and community affairs work (community organization), and corporate human resource planning (policy and administration). Employers that do not build in a capacity to respond proactively to these new rules of doing business can expect lawsuits from employees and grievances from unions on a case and class-action basis. Knowing their rights, workers today frequently litigate their complaints, often at great cost to the employer in terms of money and good public relations. In sum, employers are constrained by laws, precedents, union contracts, and public expectation, making an investment in occupational social work programs of prevention simply "good business."

Labor's Incentive

In order to understand trade union motivation for establishing such programs and services one has to look through a historical lens. Many American unions started as mutual aid societies; a group of workers banded together to share risks such as ill health, unemployment, accidents, and death that would interfere with their ability to earn wages. Over the years, a service outlook replaced the sole early focus on fiscal benefits (Akabas 1984a). As these "societies" and "guilds" evolved to become trade unions, they became part of an economic, social, and political movement able to negotiate with management on behalf of their collective members. While the relationship between these unions and the organized social work profession was unstable—even adversarial during the opening decades of the twentieth century (Karger 1988)—social work "established a rapprochement with the trade union movement in the 1930s through active support of the Congress of Industrial Organizations' (CIO) organizing drives and through caring service to unemployed workers during the height of the Great Depression" (Kurzman 1987: 902).

Representing almost one-third of America's nonagricultural workers during most of the 1940s and 1950s, the union movement had clout, particularly with the Democratic party, which held the presidency for twenty years, from 1933 to 1953. The noted sociologist C. Wright Mills (1948) spoke of America's labor leaders as "the new men of power," and the CIO's political leader, Sidney Hillman, had the ear of President Roosevelt on political issues beyond the scope of management and labor relations. In fact, five days before the 1944 National Democratic Convention it is said that FDR—wanting labor's wholehearted support—insisted that before party leaders made a vice presidential recommendation (from among James Byrnes, Henry Wallace, and Harry Truman), they must "clear it with Sidney" (Josephson 1952: 619).

With the start of a progressive decline in union membership and political influence in the 1960s, organized labor found it no longer had the political access and influence it had previously enjoyed. In order to prevent unionization of their businesses, employers frequently offered comparable wages and benefits and then asked workers why they would want to spend part of their hard-earned income paying dues to a union. To some extent, unions had to deal with the effects of their own success and managements' sophisticated and concerted effort to dissuade workers in new plants from choosing unionization.

As Akabas (1977: 743) observed: "When the benefits of labor organization are available to all workers, either through collective bargaining or through employers' unilateral efforts to avoid organization, some *new enticement* must be offered to achieve union membership growth and loyalty" (emphasis added). Observers from outside the human services professions support this conclusion. As early as 1970 the prominent labor law scholars Derek Bok and John Dunlop (1970: 365) wrote: "By emphasizing new benefits and services, unions may make a fresh appeal to the unorganized—an appeal that smaller employers, at least, would find hard to emulate. In addition, a variety of benefit programs may provide opportunities for involving the members more closely in the life and affairs of the union, thus giving greater meaning to union membership."

Former UAW president Douglas Fraser agreed that labor unions should begin to offer innovative services and expand the scope of their employee assistance programs, and the labor economist Audrey Freedman (Holusha 1990: F12) stated succinctly: "Unions will have to become more social service organizations if they are to have a future."

In this context, initiating new services for members and their families is in the union's self-interest. First, providing social services and advocacy for individual members places unions at the center of furnishing a precious commodity that is difficult to secure in the marketplace, where quality services are expensive, treatment providers have long waiting lists, and care may be hard to locate or unavailable at hours convenient for single-parent and dual-career families (Googins 1991; Landy 1960). Offering personal social services at the union (or under its sponsorship) is an incentive to join the union (in an agency shop) or to affiliate with an existing union by "signing on" during a membership drive or campaign for certification. Indeed, if labor expects to expand by organizing the service, communications, and technology sectors, where women are heavily represented, unions will need to recognize women's disproportionate responsibility for child and elder care and establish member assistance programs (MAPs) to respond to their family-based needs (Akabas 1984b). Second, when unions find it hard to win a major increase in wages, they may choose to negotiate a new fringe benefit. Management has the incentive of the potential deductibility of such expenditures against corporate taxes and sometimes the lower political visibility of a benefit contribution rather than an equivalent increment in wages. (Similarly, for workers, it is a benefit that passes outside the purview of income taxation.) Management also is increasingly aware that a union member assistance program, operating in concert with a managed care intermediary, may gradually help to reduce the contractual cost of health care, and employers therefore may be receptive to funding of a labor-management sponsored program as an instrument of health benefit cost containment.

A third motivation for labor's development of member assistance programs is the pragmatic need to win grievances. For example, when management cites workers (i.e., union members) for cause and initiates their suspension or discharge, the union generally files a grievance to protest management's action. Such protests may evolve into binding arbitration by an independent and impartial third party. If management can document the worker's inability to follow established work site routines, maintain appropriate workplace relationships, or demonstrate adequate job performance, there may be little the union can do to protect such a member from discipline or discharge (Neff 1985). However, if a professional social worker from the union's member assistance program can testify at the arbitration hearing that the union business agent agrees to (1) an administrative referral of the member to the MAP, (2) placing him on short-term disability while he undergoes treatment for an emotional disorder, (3) insisting that he follow the plan of individual and group treatment that the MAP's licensed social worker has prescribed, (4) advocating for his return to work only when the member has fully complied with the prescribed program of rehabilitation, and (5) respecting the right of the MAP professional to decide if and when to issue a "fitness for duty" recommendation to the independent arbitrator, then the opportunity for labor to win the arbitration on behalf of its member may be greatly enhanced (Molloy & Burmeister 1989; Antoniades & Bellinger 1983; Molloy & Kurzman 1993). The union's ability to protect its members by preserving their jobs may thereby become a significant latent function of a professionally staffed member assistance program. Since a core duty of a labor union is to protect its members, preserve their rights to employment (even during periods of impairment), and ensure that their wages, benefits, and seniority are shielded from unilateral actions by management, social work services have a pragmatic value for the foresighted trade union.

In this spirit, a member assistance program that protects members' jobs, responds to their personal and family crises, and advocates effectively for individual entitlements is likely to win the loyalty of union members toward their leaders. And while profits may be the way corporate executives ensure the continued support of their shareholders and directors, in a labor union, where leaders depend on the support of their members for reelection, loyalty is the coin of the realm. A labor leader who has established a MAP that is able to save members' jobs, restore workers' mental health and sobriety at times of personal crisis, and preserve families and marriages during episodes of life cycle change and stress—such an enlightened union leader is likely to secure members' loyalty and to win reelection.

As a result, we should not be surprised that an important AFL-CIO labor leader (Perlis 1977: 31–33) wrote in support of a social work–specific "human contract" for the American workplace: "This human contract, developed by labor and management . . . should concern itself with those personal and family problems which are not covered by the union contract. . . . These areas of human concern . . . [which] impact upon the well-being of the troubled worker can be strong enough to cause absenteeism, turnover, in-plant disruption, poor morale, and the loss of productive capacity. . . . [Therefore] what every joint union-management committee needs . . . is a professional trained in industrial social work."

Despite Perlis's recommendation, such programs have not grown in number during recent decades, in part due to the increased tension between management and labor that makes support for such initiatives more difficult to achieve. Union membership has been in steady decline, and labor has been simply fighting for survival in the private sector due to corporate cutbacks, globalization, downsizing, outsourcing, contracting, and promotion of the "casual workforce." These realities have been exacerbated in many unionized sectors of the economy by aggressive management activity to achieve union deauthorization and decertification (Scott & Arnold 2003). In addition, instead of having the advantages associated with being unitary and monolithic, organized labor in effect is merely a loose confederation of grassroots locals and district councils that come together as sixty-eight national (and international) unions under the banner of the AFL-CIO (Murray 1998).[1]

Consequently, the situation of trade unions in America today is a classic case of "bad news and good news." On the one hand, the overall percentage of the American workforce holding union membership has been in steady decline, falling to 12.9 percent in 2003. Moreover, union membership has declined to 8.2 percent for private sector workers (U.S. Department of Labor 2004). Globalization has hindered unions' efforts to stabilize their membership base as companies close unionized factories and move more work overseas. The nation's recent explosion in jobs has been concentrated in industries where unions traditionally are the weakest (small business, finance, high technology), while job losses have been greatest in sectors

---

[1] There are also about twelve independent unions, such as the United Mine Workers of America, the Brotherhood of Locomotive Engineers, and the United Transportation Union.

where unions are strongest (steel, auto, and textile). Moreover, the fastest-growing cities—such as Atlanta, Dallas, Miami, Houston, and Phoenix—historically have the lowest percentage of workers in unions.

On the other hand, the union movement has been rejuvenated since John Sweeney took the helm of the AFL-CIO in 1995. Sweeney has reemphasized organizing, restored a public visibility to labor and labor issues, built up a multimillion-dollar AFL-CIO strike fund, and was instrumental in achieving a favorable settlement in the 1997 UPS strike (see chap. 3). Union membership nationwide rose faster in 1999 than at any time in the previous two decades, with growth coming not just among government workers but also in the less represented private sector. To increase its political clout, Sweeney created a novel organization in 2003 called Working America, designed for nonunion workers who agree with the labor movement on issues such as increasing the minimum wage and promoting occupational safety and want to campaign alongside labor on those issues.

Among notable recent political victories for the union movement were the organizing of 74,000 home health aides in Los Angeles; 5,200 textile workers in North Carolina; 10,000 passenger and gate agents at U.S. Airways; and 58,000 schoolteachers, secretaries, and cafeteria workers in Puerto Rico (Greenhouse 1999a, 2000; "A New Day," 1999). Despite an overall membership decline, unions also remain strong in the public sector, representing 44 percent of federal, state, and local government employees in 1990, and among all professional and technical workers in America, the figure is more than 50 percent (Tambor 1995). In an encyclical titled "On Human Work" (1981), Pope John Paul II called trade unions "a mouthpiece for the struggle for social justice," a description apropos of labor's historic, symbolic, and continuing role in America. Lawrence Root (2000: 15) sums up the current situation well: "Despite their declining proportion, organized labor continues to be a significant part of the social and economic landscape and represents an organized, visible voice for an important part of the workforce. . . . Also, unions set standards which influence the practices of others. Non-union employers often match union pay and benefits in order to attract employees and avoid future unionization. In this way the impact of unions and their policies extend[s] beyond their specific worksites."

Labor and Management Examples

Occupational social work practice—in both labor and management settings—provides an exceptional opportunity to illustrate the effectiveness of the social work profession's conceptual framework. The generalist practice method, person-in-environment focus, ecological model, prevention orientation, and empowerment perspective have a goodness-of-fit with the setting, population, and auspices. Similarly, work organizations are powerful players, enabling occupational social workers to influence policy and develop resources on behalf of workers and their families. These realities can best be illustrated by providing examples of occupational social workers' policy and practice interventions.

CASE EXAMPLE

By 1985 Local 1199, the Drug, Hospital, and Health Care Employees Union (now, 1199: National Health and Human Service Employees Union, SEIU, AFL-CIO) was the largest among three unions in New York City representing home care workers employed by Medicaid-funded vendor agencies. Known locally as the "conscience of the labor movement" because of the union's long history of organizing oppressed health and hospital workers and lifting them out of poverty, Local 1199 is a progressive but very independent labor organization, then unaffiliated with any national or international union or with the umbrella AFL-CIO. The union's Home Care Division represented about twenty-one thousand home health aides and attendants, predominantly African-American and Latina women, caring for the frail homebound elderly and disabled. On average, they earned about $7,000 a year. They had no sick leave, out-patient health benefits, job security, or opportunity for education or advancement. They were truly the "working poor."

In 1985 Local 1199 agreed to engage in a collaborative three-year research and program development project with the Hunter College School of Social Work of the City University of New York to accomplish two goals: provide data as a foundation for more effective collective bargaining, legislative action, and public education, and consider the development of a union-based social service (member assistance) program to help home care workers gain access to needed health and social services (Donovan, Kurzman, & Rotman 1993: 581). Social work faculty, along with a doctoral student, drew a random and stratified sample of 404 home health workers (union members). The data gathered from interviews with them showed that their median annual salary for the previous year was approximately $6,000 and that their median household income (from all sources) was just $8,000.

(continued)

(Noteworthy, the weighted average poverty threshold for nonfarm familles of three people in 1985 was $8,573 [Social Security Bulletin 2002].) Moreover, the insurance plan in their collective bargaining agreement covered only hospitalization; they had to pay out-of-pocket from their net (disposable) income for all medical, dental, prescription, optical, and laboratory services and care.

Based on the social work profession's historic commitment to both the provision of responsive social services and to advocacy for progressive social change, the social work faculty consultants recommended a two-prong venture to the union leadership (Donovan 1987, 1989a, 1989b). First, a Campaign for Justice would be launched (jointly with a sister trade union that represented other New York home care workers) under the banner of a newly formed New York Labor Coalition for Home Care Workers. Using the data assembled by the school of social work, the coalition devised a strategy of legislative and political action using sophisticated media advertising to educate the public, "good government" organizations, and elected officials about the importance of home care work and the need to provide decent wages and benefits for this cadre of workers. Over a two-year period, considerable public support was enlisted, including endorsements from key political figures and influential religious and community leaders. Armed now with hard data and strong public support, in early 1988 the union reached general agreement with management on the terms of a new two-year contract that raised wages by 53 percent and provided, for the first time, a full range of basic health benefits to all home care workers (Donovan, Kurzman, & Rotman 1993).

Second, the union leadership recognized their members' need for a union-sponsored member assistance program to respond to workers' crises in the areas of health, housing, personal stress, and family emergencies. The survey showed that the need was immediate and could not wait for further data analysis or the outcome of collective bargaining (Roberts-DeGennaro, Laranzola, & Phillips 1986). Local 1199 leadership agreed to hire a trained social worker ahead of schedule to provide crisis intervention and short-term casework service in the fall of 1986 and to expand the MAP the following year by providing stipends for the field placement of two graduate social work students. By the end of the second year, more than five hundred members had been seen individually by this social work staff. The MAP soon after was institutionalized by the union, and it now employs five full-time MSWs. In short, Donovan, Kurzman, & Rotman (1993: 584) conclude: "The union was able to accomplish two important goals by engaging the help of a school of social work. First, the academic base for research provided the independence and credibility necessary for research data to be persuasively used in a campaign of public education and legislative action. Second, the development of a professional member assistance program helped union leadership respond to the needs of their home care members in a service arena outside their own expertise."

Occupational social work provides a goodness-of-fit for generalist policy and practice intervention in management settings as well. In 1983 the new, innovation-oriented president of Hunter College (a large public institution of higher education in New York City with twenty thousand students) noted that personal and organizational problems seemed to impair the ability of the college workforce to focus on work and to work together as well as she had anticipated and had experienced in other settings. She also was committed to her reputation as being "people oriented" in her management style—a leader who could inspire loyalty, organizational cohesiveness, and productivity by meeting the often unrecognized and unmet needs of workers, supervisors, and middle managers. In this organizational context, she asked her deans and vice-presidents to come forward with initiatives that she might implement to respond to the unmet personal and professional needs of the faculty and staff of the college.

The School of Social Work responded with the idea that she should launch a comprehensive employee assistance program to serve all employees of the college, as well as members of their immediate families. The EAP would be conceptualized as a new and free, professional, confidential, on-site employee benefit. Staffed and directed by members of the social work faculty, and further supported by stipended second-year graduate students, the EAP would be "an earned entitlement, universally available to all participants in the workforce without cost and in a familiar environment—the world of work" (Kurzman 1987: 900). In Kahn's sense (1973), the proposed EAP would not offer stigmatized "case services"; instead, its programs and services would be developed as social utilities of the workplace—on tap, as needed, for the work institution itself and for all workforce participants and their families. Now, more than twenty years (and four college presidents) later, the Hunter College EAP is well established and fully funded in the permanent budget of the college. Leaders of the several labor unions representing faculty, skilled trades, and support staff meet quarterly around the table, with equivalent representatives from management of the college, as an EAP labor-management advisory committee. They help to set policy and to decide the focus for practice in the months ahead. The members—each representing a key college constituency—interpret the program and services to their own constituents, reaffirming the authenticity of the program and confirming its genuine commitment to confidentiality. Members also bring the interests, needs, and concerns of their colleagues and of their work settings to the table, enabling EAP staff to maintain a connection and a responsiveness to both the gatekeepers and the "quiet voices" of the academic and nonacademic units of the organization.

Given the high cost of mental health care in the community, the minimal coverage for such outpatient services in the college benefits package, and the long wait to access such care at more moderate cost at community-based agencies, the faculty and staff are very grateful for this new entitlement. They also are appreciative that Hunter remains the only college among the nineteen of the City University of New York where management has voluntarily chosen to establish and permanently support a supplementary and universal EAP entitlement.

The Hunter College EAP also serves latent functions for the School of Social Work. Cognizant that the school's primary mission is graduate social work education, the EAP is a fieldwork site each year for three second-year students; indeed, it is the most prestigious and sought after placement at the school. The EAP also serves as a "social agency" where teaching faculty volunteer to carry cases to hone, maintain, and refine their practice skills. In addition, managing the employee assistance program, which serves the entire college (faculty, support staff, maintenance workers, and senior management) gives prestige and clout to the dean and to the school. After all, the social work–sponsored EAP performs a critical function by serving the entire workforce and in often helping to solve vexing problems for the work organization.

Management's ability, for example, to discharge workers whose behaviors are perceived as disrupting the productivity of work units, who abuse the rules of absence or lateness, or who have become prone to error or poor productivity are all increasingly circumscribed by laws and regulations. In addition, an increasing number of classes of employees (older workers, women workers, workers of color, workers with physical or emotional disabilities) are protected by specific federal and state laws. Furthermore, employers such as the college can be publicly and financially sanctioned if they fail to comply with legislation mandating a drug-free workplace, standards of occupational health and safety, proper pension protection, and mandated family and medical leave options. Most work organizations now require in-house expertise in order to comply with these new regulations and to assist protected classes of employees to function more effectively, knowing that such employees may not easily be subject to discharge. Finally, virtually all nonexecutive managerial employees of the college are represented either by a local of the American Federation of Teachers (faculty and middle management) or a local of the American Federation of State, County, and Municipal Employees (custodial and support staff). These powerful labor unions make it difficult for managers to discharge an employee. Moreover, after a relatively short period of time, most nonexecutive employees are protected either by tenure or by permanent civil service status. Considering these realities, the usefulness of an EAP becomes apparent.

The stability and success of Local 1199's member assistance program and Hunter College's employee assistance program are associated with their ability to respond to the legitimate vested interests—the manifest and latent needs—of the work organization and its constituencies. With the modest assist of these social work programs, the college and the union have found it much easier to meet their organizational goals and to achieve organizational stability. Like individuals, these work organizations have "survival needs," that is, a need to coexist with the multiple internal and external forces that constantly impinge upon them. In this sense, these institutions are adaptive organisms that must learn to create a homeostatic relationship with an ever-changing environment so that they can continue to be competitive in the marketplace and maintain stability as one planet in the orbit of a larger solar system (Kurzman 1977).

Comparison with Social Work in More Traditional Settings

Occupational social workers need to understand well the current policy and practice issues in the world of work. As we move here to a discussion of more traditional social work—to contrast and compare the two—we would argue that social work practitioners in all settings need to appreciate the significance of work (of its presence and its absence) in the lives of each one of their clients. Indeed, work is the focal activity of an American labor force of approximately 140 million people, a force that increases at a rate of approximately 3 million people a year. For workers, employment performs many functions, including the provision of financial rewards, opportunities for the expenditure of time and energy, intrinsically meaningful life experiences, supplemental social interactions, and status and respect.

Contrary to popular opinion, Americans (men and women) are spending more time at work now and are more productive at work than ever before. The average adult worker now puts in almost eighty more paid hours a year (or about two weeks) than he or she did twenty years ago. "Americans are now working longer for pay than even the notoriously industrious Japanese, who are currently putting in about as many hours as Americans did in 1980" (Reich 2000: 112). A UN study reported that Americans worked 137 hours (or about three and a half weeks) more a year than Japanese workers (Greenhouse 2001a: A6). According to the U.S. Bureau of Labor Statistics, growth in productivity (a measure of the hourly output of goods and services per worker) was at a record 4.3 percent overall in 2000, the strongest in seventeen years (quoted in Brick 2001). While the good news is that American companies have become more productive, the bad news is that jobs and earnings have become less secure, and wages and benefits of production workers have eroded (Osterman 2000). If social workers are concerned about their clients' wish "to make a living" and "to make a life" they will need to focus on the reality that their clients face: it is often harder than ever to do both.

In fact, this classic division between "home" and "work" is not useful anymore. Twenty-five years ago Kanter (1977: 8) pointed out the idea that "work life and family life constitute two separate and non-overlapping worlds . . . and can be studied independently" is a mythical notion. Neither is a complete, closed, autonomous system. Clients perform task functions at home and often maintain warm and supportive friendships at the workplace (Sandler & Gray 1999). In her 1997 study, the sociologist Arlie Hochschild found that often work has become a form of "home" and home has become "work." In her aptly titled book *Home Away from Home*, Janet Woititz (1987) noted that it is not uncommon to hear workers describe their workplace relationships as "we're just like family" or to state "I spend more time with them than with my family at home."

Today, for nearly four out of five American couples (compared to only one out of five in 1950), both partners are in the labor force, with women working nearly as many hours for pay as men (Hunter 1999: 38–39). Economists note that it is unique to Americans that they continue to increase their working hours while hours are declining in other industrialized nations, suggesting that this phenomenon has a lot to do with the American psyche and with American culture. If Rachel Carson (1962) could imply that "we are what we eat," perhaps then it also is fair to suggest that "we are what we do—for a living." Traditional social workers ignore these realities and these data at their own peril.

Employment and Unemployment in Perspective

The federal government initiated its first commitment to stimulate and underwrite employment during Pres. Franklin D. Roosevelt's first term, at the peak of the Great Depression. Roosevelt acted because he was deeply concerned about the micro and macro consequences of profound and prolonged unemployment. At the end of the Second World War, President Truman and the U.S. Congress restated this ideology and pledge upon passage of the Full Employment Act, which declared that creating useful employment opportunities was the continuing policy and responsibility of the federal government (Garraty 1986). The commitment was reaffirmed by Congress in 1978 with passage of the Humphrey-Hawkins Full Employment Act, which set an unemployment rate of just 3 percent as the national goal (Karger & Stoesz 2002: 126).

Economists consider a 3 percent rate of unemployment to merely be frictional unemployment, which is considered unavoidable (even desirable) in a free nation that has labor mobility, open markets, and a dynamic economy. Frictional unemployment takes into account time spent between jobs, seasonal fluctuations, and the inevitable shift of capital among markets here and abroad. In contrast, cyclical unemployment occurs when economic activity declines and unemployment rises as a result. Downward trends in the business cycle (such as a recession) create joblessness of greater magnitude than the widely accepted levels that constitute frictional unemployment. Even more serious for most workers and their families is the phenomenon of structural unemployment that Sherraden (1985: 403) refers to as "deeper and longer—lasting maladjustments in the labor market" resulting from major shifts in the nation's economy that accompany automation, cybernetics, "capital flight," and changes in the technical skills required by employers. Sometimes referred to as technical unemployment, such fundamental and pervasive structural alterations in employers' options or needs simply make some workers' wages too high or skills obsolete, and as the British would say, many workers "become redundant" (Murray 1998: 170).

Finally, when the decline of labor market demand is not merely cyclical but deep and persistent the nation may experience chronic unemployment. Current monetary and fiscal policy serve to mitigate against the likelihood of such cyclical fluctuations becoming chronic—as they did during the Great Depression. If the job market, however, ultimately cannot absorb most of those who want to work, even as nontraditional or contingent workers, such a deficiency in labor market adaptability and demand can trigger chronic unemployment.

Practice Implications

Social workers practicing in more traditional settings also need to understand these employment realities because they are important in the lives of their clients. At a family service agency or at a community mental health clinic we naturally ask at intake about clients' presenting problems and then about their families. We want to know about their marital status, children, family dynamics, conflicts, and satisfactions. We also may inquire about their housing, neighborhood, recreational and social activity, religious affiliation, physical health, and even their hobbies. We often construct an ecomap or a family genogram. But if we are simply going to pursue such a line of inquiry, however sound and appropriate, what messages are we sending to our clients about the significance and centrality of their work? How will we evaluate the role that work (or the lack thereof) may play in the life of our clients as we form a biopsychosocial assessment and develop a plan of professional intervention.

In hospital social work settings, where discharge planning usually is a central social work function, one similarly needs to assess the supports and risks that will be present in the family, home, and community when a patient is ready for discharge. If our patient is a breadwinner, however, wouldn't we also need to know about his or her job in order to evaluate when (and if) the patient can return to work and, if so, what advocacy and supports may be needed from the union, job modifications requested of the supervisor, and changes in benefit coverage initiated by human resources? Social workers in prison, parole, and probation settings have learned that two of the best predictors of client recidivism are offenders' disinterest in education and training and their lack of job skills and motivation for employment. Since structure, peer relationships, income, and the potential for greater self-esteem are inherent in work, how could social workers in correctional settings practice effectively without a central (if not primary) focus with their clients on education and employment? The reciprocal link between joblessness and crime in fact was confirmed by a study of the Economic Policy Institute, which showed a relationship similar to what Brenner (1973) had found (see Chap. 2) for mental hospital admissions (Herbert 2000).

Most social workers would agree that in doing therapeutic work with adolescent and latency-age children, not to discuss school would be negligent. After all, children spend a great deal of time (and expend a lot of physical and psychological energy) in school settings in their preparation for the forthcoming demands of the world of work. What, then, would be the rationale for not discussing work just as extensively with adult clients? For this reason, in most settings "tell me about your family" should be followed (or preceded) by "tell me about your work."

Public Supports and Constraints

One of the seldom-discussed yet influential traditions in America is our preoccupation with individualism, admiration for private initiatives, and preference for local problem solving. Unlike virtually all the other industrialized countries of the world, the United States tends to avoid the formation of national public policies and services whenever a private or local initiative can be envisioned. The historian Arthur Schlesinger (1956: 57) observed that Pres. Calvin Coolidge spoke with no exaggeration (and much public praise) when he said, "If the Federal Government should go out of existence, the common run of people would not detect the difference in the affairs of their daily life for a considerable length of time." However, when the Great Depression began, just five years later, Americans noticed a difference in a short length of time. The federal government had virtually no policies or programs in place to cushion the blow of unemployment.

President Coolidge was not alone in his opinion and his preference. As late as 1929 the American Federation of Labor (AFL) was in agreement with politicians and employers in opposing government-sponsored unemployment insurance—already an established practice in most European countries. Samuel Gompers, the AFL's longtime leader, merely wanted his members to get "a fair day's wage for a fair day's work." He repeatedly denounced unemployment insurance as a "socialist idea" and considered such a program to be "inadmissible in the United States" (Kennedy 1999: 25).

The eventual passage of the Family and Medical Leave Act of 1993 provides a good template for current discussion. With successful models already well established in Europe and a rapid increase of women at work, pressure for a government-supported child care program for working families had bipartisan support in the country during President Nixon's first term in office (1968–72). In a 1969 message to Congress, Nixon himself had remarked (quoted in Hunter 1971: 51): "So critical is the matter of early growth that we must make a national commitment to providing all American children an opportunity for healthful and stimulating development during the first five years of life."

Two years later, however, when Congress passed a bill to initiate a modest program to support child care for working families, Nixon vetoed the legislation. He stated that the intent was "overshadowed by the fiscal irresponsibility, administrative unworkability and the family-weakening implications" of the child care centers that the legislation envisioned. The president went on to say that, "given the limited resources of the federal budget, and the growing demands upon the federal taxpayer, the expenditure of $2 billion in a program whose effectiveness has yet to be demonstrated cannot be justified . . . ; and the legislation, *ex nihilo,* would just be creating a new army of bureaucrats." Finally, and perhaps most significantly, the president concluded his message by stating (Rosenthal 1971: 20): "For the Federal Government to plunge headlong financially into supporting child development would commit the vast moral authority of the National Government to the side of communal approaches to child rearing over and against the family-centered approach."

Nineteen years later, Pres. George H. W. Bush, despite his professed intention to move women "from welfare to work," followed suit by vetoing a family and medical leave act, although it involved *no cost* to the government. He stated that its provisions, such as guaranteed family and medical leave for employees (without pay) to care for newborn babies and ill family members, "would build inflexibility into corporate decision-making"; therefore, "while such benefits should be offered, they should be *voluntarily* provided, or negotiated *privately* between employers and employees" (emphasis added). In the supportive words of Rep. Cass Ballenger (R-NC), "Any mandate undermines the voluntary, flexible and creative benefit system currently in place in this country" (Holmes 1990).

Three years later, Pres. Bill Clinton signed a family and medical leave act similar to the one President Bush had rejected—twenty-two years after President Nixon's 1971 veto. The 1993 legislation enabled millions of Americans to care for their families while being assured job security at minimal cost to employers (Hooper-Briar & Seck 1995: 1543). However, child care for working families remained largely a private matter. Some large employers, such as Ford Motor Company, J. C. Penney, IBM, and AT&T have offered such benefits voluntarily or as a result of successful collective bargaining by their unions; however, they are clearly the exception, not the rule. As the president of a prominent advocacy group recently noted (Greenhouse 2001b), we are still the only major nation "to address a major social problem—child care—through the private sector rather than through a public solution."

Social work practitioners in all settings must understand the dilemmas that this reality poses for the working families who constitute the overwhelming majority of their clients. In what Reich (2000) terms the "pre-employment era" in America, extended families and local communities came to the aid of individuals if they needed help, whether it was raising a barn, looking in on an aging mother, or caring for a sick child. In the present "postemployment era" there is less sense of community. Relatives may not live nearby; churches and other local communal institutions may not see this role as their function; and coworkers may be strangers rather than lifelong friends. More than 20 million Americans, roughly one-sixth of the workforce, change their jobs each year, half of them involuntarily (Foster & Schore 1990); indeed, recent government data show that, between the ages of eighteen and thirty-two, the average individual in the United States will work for 8.6 different employers (U.S. Department of Labor 1998). The changing (and unwritten) work contract between companies and their employees prevalent in the world of work today, notes one observer, replaces the promise of lifetime employment to loyal employees with that of simply a lifetime of employability (Tobin 1993). Therefore, an individual's sense of connection with his or her coworkers and their families, increasingly as a contingent worker, is likely to be more fragmented and more fragile.

Many men and women, especially office and factory workers, have been used to shopping together at lunch or going for a beer after work, bowling in a union or company league on Wednesday nights, heading over to the Elks Club on Friday evenings, and socializing as families on the weekends. They followed the maturation of one another's children as they took first communion, graduated high school (perhaps college), got their first job, married, and had children. There was a sense of community, stability, and support. When emergencies occurred, they cared about and therefore covered for one another. Contingencies were accommodated and the unexpected was managed, for example, by swapping shifts in response to emergencies such as child or elder care. In studying the behavior of employees in one rather traditional corporation, a sociologist found that friendships with coworkers were stronger than with people outside work; their "parenting" of subordinates at work was often more satisfying than their real parenting at home. She even found coworkers to be more helpful in coping with traumas, such as the death of a parent, than was their family or their religious congregation (Hochschild 1997). In the new world of work, the question is: how will we fill this gap?

Given the dominance in America today of dual career (or single-parent) families, the uncertainty of any measure of job security, more independent contracting, and a diminished sense of "community," an understandable urgency for the public provision of supports for working families has peaked. But the response has not been commensurate with the need. Why then is it so persistently difficult to get Americans and their elected leaders to support what Jansson (2001: 4) and Reich (2002: 115) refer to as "social investments"? Virtually all other modern industrialized nations see merit and value in making such universal public investments, especially in their children, who, of course, are the country's next generation of parents and workers. Why was Congress not able to override the Bush and Nixon vetoes: modest first steps to recognize the country's need for family leave and child care?

The primary concern was less fiscal than ideological. More than two hundred years after the Declaration of Independence was written, Americans continue to place such a high value on personal freedom, independence, and individual autonomy that the failure to win widespread political support for governmental investments may be more than a matter of political party, war, unemployment, interest rates, or inflation. In good times and bad, the resistance, even opposition, involves our values, folkways, and national culture. It is not just a matter of what we can afford but also what we will accept. The presidential vetoes of innovative "social investment" legislation are perhaps eloquent reminders of why we as a nation are unwilling to formulate or to fund a comprehensive health, family, or child care policy—indeed a coherent social policy of any kind in these arenas. Our country's reluctance to develop and finance government-sponsored social programs, unless at least loosely based on an insurance principle (Social Security, unemployment insurance, workers' compensation) or means-testing (public assistance, Medicaid, food stamps) is not accidental. In many ways, it is an artifact of our history and evolving culture.

Instead of moving in the direction of reformulating entitlements or initiating universal social investments, the United States continues to move toward asking individuals to take more personal responsibility for their family needs and to pursue all work opportunities. "Workfare programs" have in fact been a feature of the welfare landscape since the 1967 welfare amendments known as the Work Incentive Program (WIN). Under WIN regulations, work requirements became mandatory for most of the unemployed, and AFDC recipients who were deemed employable and yet refused to work could be terminated from relief. Workfare precepts were reinforced in 1988 when they became the conceptual backbone of the Family Support Act.

Cosmic change was foreshadowed, however, by President Clinton's 1992 campaign promise that, if elected, he would "end welfare as we know it." Passage of the Personal Responsibility and Work Opportunity Reconciliation Act of 1996 translated that pledge into public policy. The federal government's welfare commitment to poor people, in place since 1935, was ended (see Chap. 3). The concept of entitlement was rescinded; federally earmarked categorical programs were replaced by block grants; and a five-year lifetime limit was placed on the receipt of financial assistance (Dickinson 1997; Abramovitz 1997).

Philosophically central to this monumentally significant new legislation were its many provisions to force adult recipients (mostly mothers) to move from welfare to work (Hasenfeld 2000). The new law, for example, (1) required all recipients to find work within two years, (2) prohibited a single parent with a child older than age five from claiming lack of child care as a reason for not working, (3) mandated that recipients with no dependents start working part-time after they had received food stamps for three months, and (4) penalized states unless 25 percent of all families receiving aid were engaged in work at least twenty hours per week by 1997 (50 percent by 2002). As a result of these mandates (and the aid of a booming economy), the number of people on welfare in America fell from 12.2 million in August 1996 to 7.3 million in August 1999. President Clinton could claim that by mid-1999 the proportion of welfare recipients who were working was four times as high as when he took office in January 1993 (Pear 1999a, 1999b).

President Clinton's promise to "end welfare as we know it" appeared to many to be a code phrase for "moving people from welfare to work." Perhaps this was true. In 1996 the president signed the new requirements into law on August 22, and by September 15, the *New York Times* noted that IBM, Lockheed Martin, Anderson Consulting, and Electronic Data Systems all were competing for state welfare-to-work training contracts (Bernstein 1996). In New York City, Mayor Rudolph Giuliani vowed that he would end welfare entirely by the year 2000 by forcing all recipients to take a job. "From the welfare capital of America," he said proudly, "we will become the work capital of America. . . . We will be the place to come to relearn the work ethic that made America and New York City great" (Giuliani 1998). Early studies would seem to confirm Mayor Giuliani's promises and President Clinton's data. Mandatory, broad-coverage welfare-to-work programs seemed capable in good economic times of moving into employment a significant proportion of welfare recipients who would not have done so on their own (Gueron & Pauly 1991).

The larger question involves whether the states can meet the several new federal mandates for all recipients within five years with jobs that will lift them out of poverty and into self-sufficiency. While many supporters of the 1996 welfare reform law suggest it has been successful because of the number of mothers who have taken paid jobs, the equation is not so simple. As Maiden (2001: 153) observes, "In their enthusiasm they fail to point out that a vast majority of these mothers and their children are still poor." Many former welfare recipients find their new jobs are only temporary, part-time, or at the minimum wage, with no benefits (Bluestone & Rose 1997). They frequently find themselves locked into service positions in the secondary labor market, defined by Piore (1977) as being characterized by low wages, poor working conditions, harsh and often arbitrary discipline, and little opportunity for advancement. Such jobs will have little success in boosting people out of poverty. Many experts feel the trick of welfare reform and mandatory employment is to catapult recipients beyond the secondary and into the primary labor market where there are better wages, health benefits, job security, and chances for advancement. Jared Bernstein (1999: 4), an economist and social worker with the Economic Policy Institute, suggests that we should "use this opportunity to construct a viable alternative to the current policy, one that does not simply link welfare to work, but does so by strengthening the earnings potential of low-wage workers. . . . Low wage times shrinking hours equals working poverty. And that's what I believe is the best we can expect of welfare reform as it is currently conceived: to turn the welfare poor into the working poor." As Hasenfeld (2000: 198) suggests, "What the majority of the poor need is not welfare reform, but a reform of low wage work."

Occupational Issues

Writing about occupational social work more than twenty years ago, the authors stressed that this new field of practice's location in the workplace under the auspices of work organizations provided its distinctive identity (Kurzman & Akabas 1981). Working primarily in employee or member assistance program settings, occupational social workers were stationed, in Bertha Reynolds's words (1975), at a "natural outpost" where more than 100 million Americans then spent a major portion of their adult life. In Carol Meyer's terms (1976: 189), there is an advantage to social workers being at the "crossroads of life," since it is where "the practitioner meets the citizen." During the gradual evolution of occupational social work over the past two decades, the focus on program location and service auspices continue to hold great significance in any thoughtful conceptualization of the field.

However, as Mor Barak (2000b: 205, 208) notes, occupational social work practice today refers much more broadly "to the need for social work intervention not only with workers in the workplace but also with individuals and groups at the point of entry to, or exit from, the world of work, and with those who are temporarily or chronically unemployed. . . . The main element in the field's recent evolution has been the move away from defining it by its practice location . . . to defining it by its practice mission."

There is good reason for this shift. Its impetus derives not only from the appropriate pragmatism of responding to changing need but also from the profession's idealism, embodied in its commitment to social justice. In this context, social workers need to respond not only to changes taking place with the family, in the community, and at the workplace (i.e., pragmatism) but also to their ethical obligations in this nontraditional arena (i.e., idealism). This latter proposition requires further discussion.

To be ethical practitioners, social workers must be virtuous (e.g., honest and respectful) and also must understand their duty (e.g., to refrain from prohibited intervention on the one hand and to carry out their responsibilities on the other). As Jonsen and Hellegers (1976) note, the third ethical obligation is the most abstract and difficult to fulfill: pursuing the "common good" in order to promote social justice. In a compelling discourse, the philosopher John Rawls (1971) proposes a theory of distributive justice. To achieve the "common good," he suggests that the greatest resources should go to the most disadvantaged. "All goods are to be distributed equally," Rawls (1971: 62) suggests, "unless an unequal distribution . . . is to the advantage of the least favored." In effect, Rawls offers a theory of equity rather than a theory of equality. There are practical implications. "In a society that places certain portions of the population at a competitive disadvantage for no reason or fault of their own, such a theory underscores the need to ensure fair and equitable distribution of scarce resources in the context of pervasive social inequality. If one accepts Rawls's proposition, one must look at human services practice in the workplace not only through the lens of its professional practitioners, but in the context of the institutional arrangements in which they are employed" (Kurzman 1998: 556).

One could argue therefore that while EAPs (and other work site services) continue to be important loci for professional social work practice, the profession must explore other institutional arrangements as well. In Iversen's (1998: 556) terms, a "systematic application of specialized occupational social work knowledge and skills to job retention among work group constituents would refocus practice on the employment needs of poor people, thereby furthering the mission of the profession to increase equality and social justice." In the spirit of advocating for social justice, a greater concern for the unmet needs of the rising tide of contingent workers, permatemps, freelancers, and dislocated workers—variously estimated in 1996 to constitute a tenth to a third of the civilian labor force—would be warranted (Bluestone & Rose 1997: 60). Although the increasing and involuntary membership of white managers and professionals in this contingent workforce has gained the most attention of the media and politicians, one must not overlook the large and persistent number of women, older workers, racial minorities, and people with disabilities who continue to be forced to accept these work arrangements (Barker & Christensen 1998).

We are reminded of the Lynds' (1929) classic study of Middletown (Muncie, Indiana) in the 1920s. They found that the principal factors that distinguished the "working class" from the "business class" were insecurity, instability, and marginality of employment, with their consequent disturbance in the rhythms and conditions of life. The business class, they noted, was "virtually never subjected to interruptions of this kind" (55), while among the working class these realities were a recurring theme. The business class of the past two decades in America has been ruthless about cost cutting, streamlining, and reorganizing. As a result, surgical downsizing has become a fact of life for many workers. Even as unemployment has clung to historic lows, there has been no real job security for anybody (Tulgan 2001). Although Democratic presidential candidate Al Gore accurately touted the creation of "22 million new jobs and the greatest prosperity ever" during his eight years as vice president (1992–2000), as well as a decline in the official unemployment rate from 7.3 to 3.9 percent, these statements did not speak to the quality of these new jobs or to the change in median incomes of the working and middle class (Stevenson 2000). Indeed, as economic historians have noted, after adjusting for inflation, median family incomes for ordinary workers during those eight years hadn't budged. A major report (Mishel et al. 1999: 4) summarized the facts well. "The booming economy has thus far failed to lift the economic prospects of middle-class workers beyond where they were before the last recession. . . . Despite their substantial contribution to the growing economy, wages for these workers have been stagnant." Meanwhile, total executive compensation during this period rose from an average of $1.8 million to an average of $12 million—an increase of more than 600 percent—resulting in compensation packages that averaged 419 times the earnings of a typical worker (Reich 2000: 74–75). Following Rawls's (1971) conceptualization of distributive justice, one might conclude that an authentic question for America is whether there can be *real* prosperity unless there is *shared* prosperity.

The quality of much of the "new employment" merits closer examination. The number of temporary jobs, for example, doubled between 1982 and 1989, and doubled again between 1990 and 1997 (Merrifield 1999: 41). Microsoft, a leading employer during this period, expanded its workforce primarily through the creation of "nonstandard jobs" and the use of "permatemps" rather than through direct employment. Most such new employment opportunities involved the extension of short-term contracts with workers through private temporary staffing agencies. Many such temps had worked at Microsoft for five years or more, receiving promotions, supervising staff, even becoming project managers. When several of these long-term temps filed a federal lawsuit against Microsoft, the Ninth Circuit of the U.S. Court of Appeals (sitting as a full court) ruled in favor of these plaintiffs. The justices said these independent contractors (temporary workers) were in fact "common-law employees" since they worked on the Microsoft campus, were supervised by corporate managers, and used company equipment, just like all other members of the Microsoft workforce. Hence, these "permanent temporary workers" were entitled to participate in Microsoft's lucrative discount stock purchase and 401(k) plans (in which Microsoft provided a 50 percent match), just like those who were considered employees (Greenhouse 1998a: D6).

In order to respond therefore to John Rawls's exhortation for the primacy of equity as a step toward social justice, occupational social workers increasingly will need to expand their practice domain to focus on what Iversen (1998: 561) terms "the full spectrum of individuals' work situations." This reformulation would include the unemployed, dislocated, marginally employed, working poor, and the growing new population of welfare-to-work mothers. While retaining a commitment to those who enjoy reasonably stable employment, social work must serve and advocate for the growing number of individuals who are outside or at the margins of the world of work.

It is at this juncture that we discover competing values. At times, employer goals, such as increased productivity and profit maximization, may not be entirely congruent with worker needs. Yet neither can exist without the other: Workers need jobs, and organizations need a workforce. The professional challenge is to recognize not only the competing values but also the symbiotic relationship here, and to discover an equilibrium that optimizes the legitimate common interest of both parties. Occupational social work expertise is not in promoting profit maximization but in helping work organizations (management and labor) meet the needs of individuals, groups, and communities in the world of work—and, reciprocally, in recognizing their mutual vested interest in doing so.

Inherent Tensions

The competing values framework's focus on our role and function leads us organically to a discussion of the tensions intrinsic to this field of practice. Labor and management's adversarial relationship, corporate whistle blowing opportunities, our duty to protect client confidentiality, and the omnipresent and often voracious demands of for-profit organizations are among the issues that occupational social workers frequently must cope with in labor-management settings.

Professional social workers perform many functions as staff of employing organizations. They conduct employee training, oversee affirmative action programs, manage member and employee benefit systems, direct corporate giving programs, supervise disability management units, provide supportive services to labor-based legal services programs, coordinate corporate managed care functions, serve as consultants to human resource managers, and design and implement preretirement programs— in addition to establishing, staffing, and directing employee assistance programs (Akabas & Kurzman 1982a: 199–204). Staffing labor or management-based EAPs is the occupational social worker's best-known and currently most prevalent function.

When occupational social workers have direct, firsthand knowledge that illegalities or abuses are taking place that damage workers and their communities, what responsibility do they have to "go public" if these activities persist? At what point do social workers' commitments to protect the rights of sexually harassed workers, ensure clean water for communities that are secretly being polluted by their employers, and expose the quiet segregation of employees of color take precedence over their commitment to confidentiality and loyalty to their employer? When, if ever, should they "blow the whistle"?

There is a paucity of discussion on the issue of whistle-blowing in the social work literature in general and even less in the books and journals on occupational social work practice. The earliest authoritative article on the subject was written in the mid-1980s by Harold Lewis, a prominent ethicist in the profession. Lewis (1985: 11) stated: "Standing up for one's principles can be an isolating, depressing and career destroying experience. Usually, deciding to challenge a practice on ethical grounds can result in considerable cost to the challenger. Yet, we need people courageous enough and committed enough to blow the whistle when such action is indicated."

Although the term "whistle-blowing" does not appear in the NASW Code of Ethics (1999), indirect references are made to this option in several sections of the current code (see Standards 2.09–2.11). Social work's preeminent ethicist today (Reamer 1998: 142–43, 146) notes: "There are times when social workers' efforts to discourage and prevent unethical behavior do not succeed. In such cases, a social worker must consider whether to expose the unethical behavior to those in a position to address it. . . . Such actions, often referred to as "whistle-blowing," are among the most challenging faced by social workers. . . . On occasion, whistle blowers are themselves suspect; their motives may be questioned and their reputations sullied."

Hence, a decision to blow the whistle must be made with great prudence (Reamer 1992b: 69, 2002: 8). "Deciding whether to blow the whistle must be approached deliberately and cautiously. Human service professionals first should carefully consider the severity of the harm and misconduct involved; the quality of the evidence of wrongdoing; the effect of the decision on colleagues and the setting involved; the whistle-blower's motives . . . ; and the viability of alternative, intermediate courses of action" (Reamer 2001: 186–87).

In the current environment, many major national corporations (for whom we might well work, performing one or more of the occupational social work functions noted above) are being found in serious violation of the law and engaged in cover-up activities to hide these unlawful acts from government, corporate stakeholders, and the general public. As an employee, would we be willing to blow the whistle if we had knowledge of such behavior? Similarly, major labor unions (including ones that employ social workers in member assistance programs) have been found to be conducting their elections illegally and spending members' dues fraudulently. If we had evidence of this, would we be willing to speak out, knowing that there would be consequences for doing so? "There is a vast difference between the troublesome and the troubled worker," adds Akabas (1984a: 27). "A whistle blower may be troublesome but not necessarily troubled." If intermediate efforts prove unsuccessful, it takes both caution and confidence to blow the whistle successfully, even though it may be an ethical mandate. Moreover, in the pursuit of profit, corporations (including those that employ occupational social workers) often are not merely opposed to the unionization of their labor force but may be actively involved in illegal antiunion activities. Some such employer activities violate existing statutes, regulations, or administrative law rulings. Knowledge of such activity may create a conundrum for social work staff who are employed in a training unit, EAP, or affirmative action department.

Such moral dilemmas, however, are not only present in settings where we are working under management auspices. The ambivalent relationship between social work and organized labor, for example, is a well-documented matter of record (Straussner & Phillips 1988; Karger 1988). Social workers' opposition to labor's central weapon, the strike, refusal to support labor's enmity toward strikebreakers (scabs), and early employment as "welfare secretaries" by many of the most solidly antiunion corporations created a rift between the parties during the first two decades of the twentieth century. Not until the 1930s did an authentic reconciliation between organized labor and the social profession take place. At that juncture, "[p]rominent social workers, such as Jane Addams, supported the garment workers in building their unions; Harry Hopkins sided with workers at every turn, seeing them (not the corporations) as America's heroes; and Harry Lurie led the National Conference on Social Welfare to support Roosevelt's New Deal, as well as the right of workers to organize and bargain with their employers. . . . Most important, social workers themselves were joining labor unions, or organizing their own locals when none were present in the voluntary sector" (Molloy & Kurzman 1993: 47).

Under the banner of the Association of Federation Social Workers (AFSW), social work staff conducted the first strike in the profession in 1934 (Fisher 1980), and sixty years later, Tambor (1995) found that about one-fourth of the social work labor force had become union members, mostly in public sector agencies. Today, "the majority of social workers acknowledge that unions perform an important function in the profession," notes Reamer (1998: 198), "by helping maintain worker morale and, ultimately, promoting working conditions that enhance social workers' ability to meet clients' needs." Since 1968 the NASW *Standards for Social Work Personnel Practice* (1991) have affirmed the right of social work employees to bargain collectively with respect to wages and working conditions, and the 1996 NASW *Code of Ethics* formally addressed professional social workers' right to form and participate in trade unions (Reamer 1998: 198). While occupational social workers sometimes have to decide how to deal with the "union busting" activities of their corporate employers, it is important to note that fierce opposition to unionization (and to militant action where unions are present) is no less an issue in public and nonprofit social work settings (Karger 1989; Tambor 1994; Peters & Masaoka 2000).

An additional inherent tension involves the tradeoffs between internal and external EAPs. Since more occupational social workers work in employee assistance programs than in any other workplace setting, this issue highlights a major tension. In-house (internal) programs predominated during the early years of EAP growth. Many employers, and some labor unions, hired or redeployed specific employees (often to their medical or personnel departments) to provide EAP services to the staff and their families. As EAPs became more prevalent and expanded their functions during the 1980s and 1990s, employers tended to contract out for these services through purchase of service arrangements. While initially family service agencies and community mental health centers were the principal external providers, soon private firms, owned by licensed mental health providers, were formed to compete for a portion of this profitable market. Employers then had a choice between establishing their own internal programs or purchasing these services from a nonprofit or proprietary external provider on a contractual basis (Fleisher & Kaplan 1988; Cunningham 1994; Blum & Roman 1987).

The rapid growth and current predominance of such external EAP programs may not be difficult to understand. As Googins and Godfrey (1987: 121) have noted, "Whereas the indigenous [internal] program may rely on one or two individuals, the contracted program can provide a greater array of skills and treatment resources. Consequently, the services of the larger treatment staff can be channeled to meet the particular needs of the troubled employee or even organizational needs; . . . the contracted design [also] allows the smaller company to take advantage of an array of services without having to pay for full-time [in-house] staff."

Spitzer and Favorini (1993: 353) add that "in most cases, the external EAP is in a better position than is the internal EAP to provide a broad range of comprehensive services, such as twenty-four-hour emergency coverage; wellness programs; consultation on regulations for a drug-free workplace; resources for dependent care; and, increasingly, managed mental health care." Studies also indicate that external programs show a significantly higher rate of employee self-referral and an increased client perception of confidentiality (Straussner 1988; Hartwell et al. 1996; Blair 1987). It should be no surprise, therefore, that a national probability sample of sixty-four hundred private, nonagricultural work sites with fifty or more full-time employees found that EAP services are much more likely to be provided by external contractors (81 percent) than by internal providers and at an offsite location (83 percent) than on the work site premises.

The professional implications for the curtailment of in-house EAP programs should be examined. Harlow's (1987) study and Straussner's research (1988) found that internal EAPs had three times more referrals from supervisors than the external programs, greater accessibility to potential clients, higher employee visibility, better outreach and services to substance abusing workers, and greater utilization by employees who were people of color. Akabas and Krauskopf (1986: 31) add that, because they are on site, internal programs can provide "rapid feedback to the organization when systemic difficulties develop." As Polaroid Corporation's former EAP director notes, in-house managers develop an ability to "sense the environment" (Miller 1977). As one external social work provider (Filipowicz 1979: 20) admits: "The in-house program creates a mechanism through which intervention can be made quickly and appropriately at the point of breakdown in the employees' performance. The counseling professional, because he has knowledge of and contact with the industrial community and its unique character, is able to facilitate a solution that is immediate and meaningful to the employee. This allows the professional located within the organization a clear advantage over the practitioner in the community agency who is isolated from the employee's work environment and lacks familiarity with the milieu, management, and groups with whom the employee must interact." And it is not surprising that Straussner (1988) found, in her survey of EAPs, that only in-house programs saw advocacy as one of their responsibilities.

The final tension to consider is present for occupational social workers in all settings, not just for those who staff employee or member assistance programs. The auspices of our employment (and hence of our professional services) here are outside the public and nonprofit sectors in which we customarily are employed. Of necessity, employers' primary goals will be productivity and profit. As Bakalinsky (1980) opined, the core strain evolves as one of "people versus profits," and the central conceptual question for occupationally based practitioners becomes, whose agent are we? "The world of work lacks norms of professional behavior and confidentiality that we hold as our basic professional responsibility," notes Akabas (1983: 139). "We always walk a tightrope there, and must be mindful, in the extreme, of protecting individual confidentiality, recognizing that work institutions are not concerned primarily with human well-being."

In this context, it is essential that our definition of occupational social work and the scope of our client-centered focus take these powerful realities into account. Moreover, we need to focus on work issues, work-related practice, and workplace policies that reflect the subdominant values of due process, pluralism, and social justice. Our focal point therefore must include not only "workers and their families but others who wish to prepare for, enter, return to, and retire from the work world as well. The need for youth employment training, personnel and guidance services, sheltered workshops, union upgrading programs, dislocated worker services, vocational rehabilitation projects, and welfare-to-work opportunities [must be] core concerns for the occupational social work practitioner today" (Kurzman 2000: 159).

"Ethical mandates in professions like social work," observe Briar and Vinet (1985: 352), "require a social change focus as an integral part of practice." Addressing an inherent professional tension, which may be endemic to proprietary settings, occupational social workers must be mindful of Bakalinsky's cautions if their practice is to prove progressive. As Bombyk (1995: 1940) notes, "when seeking both incremental and fundamental social change, progressive social workers [must be] wary of capitalism's tendency to put profits before human needs." As social workers first, we must remind ourselves of the profession's dual commitment to function and to cause, to social service and to social change, and ensure that our practice within work organizations meets the mandate to fulfill both functions.

Opportunities abound to realize these twin outcomes. Understanding work cultures and the relationship of work organizations to the broader society will effectively open up new options. Work-sensitive practitioners will be in an ideal position to develop new social services and to promote progressive social change, thus fulfilling a covenant of the social work profession.

Study Questions

1. The authors point out the potential value dilemmas and conundrums when working under the auspices of employers and unions rather than public or voluntary agencies. Would you agree or disagree with their observations and their positions on this question?

2. Support here is given to the concept of a "comprehensive employee assistance program" model. Do you agree with this conceptualization or not? Support your position.

3. A theme of this chapter is that occupational social workers frequently have an excellent opportunity to provide social service and to promote organizational change. In the union (Local 1199) case example provided, do you feel that such an outcome was—or was not—achieved?

4. Critics of occupational social work practice sometimes say that EAPs simply duplicate services available in the community and deflect resources from the impoverished and unemployed. How would you respond to this argument?

5. What would you say are both the merits and dilemmas posed by the increasing rate of productivity in America today?

6. In the past thirty-five years, two U.S. presidents have vetoed bipartisan legislation that would have promoted government-supported child care programs for working families. In what ways would you agree or disagree with the position of the presidents on this issue?

7. What are your views on the relative advantages and disadvantages of the current emphasis on "welfare-to-work" in this country?

CHAPTER 5

Distinctive Presenting Problems

We have described the historical and conceptual background for the development of occupational social work and have contrasted this field with the more traditional activities of social workers. In the remainder of the book we hone in on the special nature of social work in the workplace. This chapter reviews the presenting problems that the professional can expect to encounter that are unique to the field of practice. The reader will observe that though the specifics may differ and may require a new knowledge base, the skills the social worker brings to problem assessment and problem solving remain relatively unchanged.

When an employer begins recruiting workers, human beings answer the call. They bring their expert knowledge, skills, abilities, and experiences that are relevant to the particular job, and they bring all the usual, individual personal issues and problems that are typical of the human condition. In many cases, the result is a gap between the employer's expectations and the employee's needs. The employer's interest is primarily in productivity. How can this particular person fill the demands of the job to maximize the outcome in relation to the work performed? This question focuses on the skill of the individual and his or her functional fit in relation to the tasks, routines, relationships, and physical environment of the job. It reflects the employer's conviction that if the skill and experiential match is good, the individual will perform with commitment and competence. This faith on the part of the employing organization all too often ignores the individuality of the job occupant. It assumes that work and the rest of life are separate and divisible. It trusts that if this is not so, the individual will make it so out of a sense of responsibility and obligation that is part of the employment "contract."

But for the individual the question is more personal. He or she is likely to ask, first, "how can I gain entry into the world of work?" And then, "how can performance on this job contribute to my quality of life and general well-being and that of my family?" The implications of this difference in goals are significant. Increasingly, research suggests that the individual's aim is for balance between work and family, between income and leisure, between self-determination and community acceptance. Although different individuals may place themselves at different points in this formulation, each has a point of indifference in relation to more work, more income, more self-determination as compared to the alternative. The day when the male householder accepted total responsibility for family income and exchanged it for a reciprocated lifetime commitment to a job and an employer are long past, on both sides of the relationship. Mutual obligation has been replaced by the concept of the disposable worker. The incongruity, however, has not been fully recognized and is the grist for policy reexamination and often individual discontent on a regular basis. Additionally, as a society we have recognized the important role that the world of work plays in achieving equity throughout the population. With this has come an understanding that there may be organizational practice and policy issues in the world of work that place certain individuals "at risk" and preclude the participation of, or do not assure fair treatment to, others such as immigrants, the unskilled, people with disabilities, gay men and lesbians, people of color, and women.

In short, all is not well in the world of work nor in the outcomes that result from participating in that world. This should not surprise the reader who recognizes, as do Bargal and Schmid (1992: 5), that "[e]nvironments tend to change much more rapidly than organizations." But their caution is important, "Performance gaps and inability to adjust to external change can threaten organizational activity and survival." For the world of work, the gap between our best intent in relation to human needs and our shortfall in fulfilling this intent represents an ideal arena for a contribution by occupational social work with its target of both individual and organization and its modus operandi as running the gamut from individual counseling to advocacy and an active social change agenda (Abramovitz 1998; Csiernik 1998; Witkin 1998). The operative question is, what are the problems that the interaction of individuals and work organizations activate? This chapter deals with these issues, going from the micro to the macro. We look first at the problems that seem to come from individual needs, for example, those where the fit between the individual and work itself is the problem or those resulting from efforts of the individual to secure a viable balance between his or her work demands and family needs. Individual counseling and direct service intervention often can mitigate these problems. Then, we move on to those problems that repeat themselves throughout particular organizations such as harassment or discrimination. There may be a need for practice and policy initiatives to achieve an inclusive workplace in which all participants experience comfort and support (Mor Barak 2004). Finally, we consider those issues that appear generic throughout society regardless of workplace, such as the increasing gap between the rich and the poor. These may require advocacy and social policy initiatives that lead to the enactment and enforcement of new legislation in order to respond to situations and policies that deny economic self-sufficiency and feelings of self-worth among disadvantaged and oppressed groups.

Presenting Problems for Individuals with Work Responsibilities and Conflicting Family Needs

Perhaps nowhere is change more evident than in the demographic composition of the labor force. The change has been from an almost exclusively white male terrain at the midcentury point into a multicultural, dual gender, multiracial landscape with great diversity in sexual orientation, family structure, physical and mental condition, and attachment to dependents' needs. Yet the structure of the employment relationship, as exemplified by the length and timing of the workday and the components of the benefit system, has changed relatively little in the same period. This lack of synchronization in rates of change has caused significant individual problems among the employed population, differently at different occupational levels or in different work organizations, and among those with different personal and family characteristics, but pervasive among a majority of employed people. It helps explain the high levels of stress and the sense of feeling undervalued in the work relationship reported by so many workers today.

CASE EXAMPLE: JAN, A TROUBLED WORKER

Jan comes to you in your role as an EAP counselor, having been sent by her supervisor because of deterioration in her work performance. She is in serious job jeopardy. She tells you that she is so worried about her family that she can scarcely get to work, much less perform well.

Jan indicates that her mother, who is here from China on a six-month visitor's visa, has a health problem and she (Jan) wants to get a permanent

(*continued*)

visa extension for her. During the interview you learn that Jan's mother was here on a visit at which time she became ill, was hospitalized, found to have cancer, and received surgical intervention and aftercare. She has now been discharged, but the doctor indicates that it would be desirable for her to be checked every three months for the next year, and if any recurrence is found, she should be placed on a chemotherapy regime. Although her visitor's visa is up, Jan is unwilling to send her mother back to China because she knows she cannot get the necessary care there.

Jan's husband is fearful that they are harboring an illegal alien. Since he and Jan are legal residents but not yet citizens, he is afraid their own future application for citizenship will be at risk. They have been fighting regularly about this, and Jan's husband insists that if she does not send her mother back, he will go to the Immigration and Naturalization Service (INS) himself to see that she is sent back.

What are the issues in this case? What can you do to help Jan? In what order? What do you have to know about the law to provide appropriate service?

Or consider the situation of an individual dealing with work responsibilities who experiences conflicting family needs. These might include child care concerns, ongoing elder care requirements, demands surrounding the health of a family member, or conflict issues with either a spouse or other relatives (Akabas 1990). These issues arise out of the tremendous changes in demographics over the last decades. Examples are abundant and the trends so well known as to require no verification. The increased employment of women sixteen and over is perhaps the most startling, having gone from a participation rate of 39 percent in 1967 to a 57.4 percent rate in 1999. Related to this has been the employment of mothers, which increased 54 percent between 1970 and 1993 (Secret et al. 1998; Kamerman & Kahn 1995), particularly those with preschool children who now account for 54 percent of employed mothers. Given the precipitous rise in divorce over the same period, many working mothers are single-parent households, although even male single-parent households have increased perceptibly (McCroskey & Scharlach 1993).

Accompanying these trends has been substantial immigration and extreme levels of family mobility. Both have removed many young couples from their support systems, a trend compounded by the rise in dual-worker families. Forced by economic necessity to migrate from their countries of origin, move from their family location within the United States, or seek two paychecks to survive, these families often experience conflict over who should work, where, and for how long. The most recent trend has been in reports that fathers express increased interest in being available to families and regard work demands that interfere with family needs as a quality of life issue (Clark 2000). This is probably related not just to dual working parents but also to the fact that marriages are entered into at later ages and childrearing occurs at a more mature age, for many, than would have been so just a few decades earlier. The result appears to be an increased interest and sense of responsibility among fathers, reflected in the fact that, in reports of employees' concerns, men are no longer immune to work/family conflicts. Additional pressures on the family come from the other end of the age spectrum. As life expectancy increases, making the fastest-growing age cohort those over eighty-five, the number of fragile elderly who require family attention increases significantly, adding to the burden of working members (Guralnik et al. 1988; Manton et al. 1993). Thus one observes a simultaneous change in the nature of work and in family patterns. Families, without social support, with more members working and working longer hours, come face-to-face with work changes that make employment less secure and more stressful and demanding than ever before. The impact of these contradictory trends is summarized well by Carnoy (1999: 422) who notes that "with increased competition in the globalized economy and the rapidly rising capacity to operate in global time to enhance productivity, the ideal worker is one who never sleeps, never consumes, never has children, and never spends time socializing outside the workplace."

If this is the lay of the land, it seems inevitable that family problems will arise, particularly in a workplace that has people working longer hours than ever before and more hours than workers in any other of the industrialized countries, and all this in a nation that lacks a public system of child, elder, or health care. The problem is compounded, furthermore, by what countless observers have noted, namely that workplace policies designed to respond to the concerns about family/work balance all appear to be balanced in favor of workplace productivity rather than worker and family well-being (Lambert 1993; Glass & Estes 1997; Medjuck et al. 1998; Carnoy 1999; Akabas 2000). Consequently, it is rarely those who are most in need of supportive family policies who are the target of even those initiatives. Consider, for example, the Family and Medical Leave Act of 1993, designed to provide job protection for up to twelve weeks of leave to allow working family members to take care of themselves or their ill relatives. Eligibility is contingent on having been employed for at least one year. No pay is provided for the leave, and the employer must have at least fifty workers within a seventy-five-mile radius to come under the law's jurisdiction. These conditions effectively eliminate protection for those most in need—the poor and disadvantaged, often single-parent head of family, workers who are least likely to have been working for the same employer for the requisite time period, are unlikely to be able to afford unpaid leave, and who, even if the income could be sacrificed, are likely to be uncovered by the law because they hold positions in the secondary labor market made up of contingent workers or those who work mostly for small employers, that is, those with under fifty unskilled, low-paid workers as their pool of employees.

As has been correctly observed, the policy goal is to maintain the workforce, not to assure the well-being of the employee. Thus an unmitigated strain, and disproportionately on the most disadvantaged among them, occurs for workers who seek to retain employment and be available for familial caretaking roles. This strain manifests itself in numerous ways. Child care arrangements may be inadequate but settled on because they are all that is available (Akabas 1984b). Carnoy (1999) has even suggested that the work demands interfere with the family's responsibility as a learning institution and may result in parents having less capacity to contribute to the process that will make their children productive in the flexible, knowledge-intensive economy of the future. The problems are magnified when the child requiring care has special needs, where a host of other dilemmas present themselves, including the need for health care coverage that may make parents "indentured" in a job to protect the health care coverage. The problem presents itself when remaining in that job restricts the parent/worker's labor market mobility and, therefore, his or her ability to find a better job that can improve earning capacity or working conditions. Taking care of a family member under such circumstances contradicts the employee's work interests (Freedman et al. 1995).

Yet another arena causing work/family tension is involved with elder care. Advances in medical technology have lengthened the life expectancy of Americans. The fact that the cohort of the over-eighty-five fragile elderly is increasing proportionately faster than any other group in the population, like the impact of many other demographic developments, creates a burden that falls on employed people who are expected to assume responsibility, in this case for these older family members. Satisfactory elder care arrangements can be illusive, and the often long-distance nature of these needs sometimes causes particular strife for the working couple. Noteworthy is that all these family-related problems vary by employees' positions in the life cycle, their ethnicity, their income levels, and many other characteristics (Fredriksen & Scharlach 1999; Lechner 1993). Whether the family/work balance is compromised by ongoing care needs or specific health crises of the child, the elder, or workers themselves, the presenting problem is consistent. There exists a social expectation that these issues will be solved within the family unit. This places particular stress on the working mothers, daughters, and daughters-in-law (Medjuck et al. 1998; Lechner & Sasaki 1995). The observable outcomes of this unrecognized and unsupported value of women's home labor is absenteeism, lateness, compromised careers, physical fatigue, financial and emotional strain, and loss of the contributions that affected workers could make to the productivity of the work organization (Fredriksen & Scharlach 1999).

Individuals Not Meeting Work Responsibilities

The converse of the problems experienced in the family because of workplace responsibilities is the difficulty experienced by the workplace because of the problems individuals bring to the workplace based on their personal experience or nonwork obligations. These problems are the issues reflected in the beginnings of occupational social work. They take many forms. A primary focus is on performance problems resulting from substance abuse. A majority of current users and abusers of legal and illegal substances are employed. It is estimated that 60 percent of those who report use of illicit drugs in the prior month and more than 70 percent of heavy drinkers are working (Hanson 1993; Dusenbury 1999). To the extent that their substance abuse affects the functional capacity of these individuals to perform their assigned work or results, as is often documented, in excessive absenteeism, more costly medical care, and accident or injury to themselves or others in the workplace, the abuse is a serious concern to employers (Hoffmann & Larison 1999). Not surprisingly, therefore, employers seek a drug-free workplace, and this has been supported by both legislation, such as the Hughes Act of 1970 and the Drug Free Workplace Act of 1988, and by regulations issued by the federal government, particularly those from the Department of Transportation, that view workers in safety-sensitive jobs who abuse substances as a significant target for intervention.

There is little agreement about the causes of substance abuse. The medical model would argue for a genetic predisposition of an individual to a negative reaction to alcohol and other drugs that, once activated, moves the person inexorably toward addiction. But others, while they may grant that predisposition exists, are convinced that it may be exacerbated by other aspects of the individual's environment, psychological or social state.

Consider the following presenting problem.

BART, A TROUBLESOME WORKER

You are the EAP counselor for a large shipping firm that does a consider-able amount of hauling for the government. One of the truckers, Bart, comes in to see you. He tells you that he is on leave because of the fact that he dislocated his right shoulder several weeks ago and cannot drive the heavy rig to which he is assigned. He tells you he is very depressed and wants your help in getting back to work, any work. He tells you that he feels discriminated against. Most of the guys who are truckers and are injured get some kind of light duty, but none has been offered to him. He thinks it's because he is a Muslim, and the truckers and their supervisors are what he sees as a tight clique of Irish and Italian Catholics.

You smell a heavy odor of liquor, and he seems to be quite unsteady. You ask him if he has been drinking and he says yes, but it is only because he is so bored without work and he has to do something. He assures you that if he could get back to work, drinking would not be a problem. He notes that, after all, drinking is against his religion and he has never been involved with liquor before.

What are the issues in this situation? Are any laws involved? Do you have any legal responsibility? What can you do in this situation? How would you order your response?

Actual or perceived discrimination has been a contributory cause to the occurrence of an alcohol problem for Bart. Thus the workplace does not emerge blameless (Fine, Akabas, & Bellinger 1982). In other situations there may be a workplace culture that encourages drinking or that creates sufficient stress so that vulnerable individuals seek self-medication. In all these circumstances, the workplace may be viewed as contributory under a biopsychosocial explanation. But whatever the cause, the impact, which interferes with performance, is usually identified by a supervisor. The dys-functional behavior frequently places the individual in job jeopardy, which even with positive intervention, may not assure continued employ-ment. In this context, prevention and abstinence become superior choices. Noting that the workplace is the ideal location for early detection of peo-ple with "unhealthy life styles," in cooperation with employers and trade unions, social workers have invested significant energy not only to treat-ing the addicted person but also in trying to help employees understand the consequences of substance abuse and the means of its avoidance

(Richmond et al. 2000). If the experience of drug testing for new job applicants is used to measure their impact, these efforts have clarified employer expectations for those seeking work. After a decade in which an increasing number of employers, including some smaller firms, have instituted preemployment drug testing, numerous studies indicate that fewer and fewer job seekers test positive for the use of illicit substances.

It is not just substance abuse, however, that impairs one's condition sufficiently to cause difficulty meeting work responsibilities. Others face an obsolescence of skills when jobs change. This has been a particular problem for older workers, recognized by Congress in the passage of the Age Discrimination in Employment Act of 1967, which forbids differential, discriminatory employment practices against those over forty. If workers have not kept refreshed in their abilities and the employer has not upgraded their skills in contemplation of the new developments, performance suffers, creating serious problems for the individual. In those circumstances or when the work itself is a poor reflection of the interests, knowledge, and abilities of the job occupant, the mismatch increases the stress and insecurity the worker is likely to experience. Because work is so important to one's identity and sense of self-worth, these issues may place individuals' physical and mental health at risk and constrain their ability to meet job requirements.

Many other members of the workforce experience a diminution in their physical or mental capacity from other causes, particularly the onset of disability. As Akabas has noted elsewhere (Akabas & Bikson 2001), despite the fact that disability represents a high-cost item to employers whose motivation in most other circumstances is profit focused, few in the workplace other than workers with disabilities seem engaged with these causes of job jeopardy. The usual experience of workers whose disabilities are sufficiently debilitating to cause lost time is instructive. If the cause was an accident or illness resulting from employment, workers' compensation payments are likely to begin within a week of onset. If the lost time results from causes not related to work, short-term disability payments might be provided (by law in New York, New Jersey, California, Hawaii, and Rhode Island, often in unionized settings within the collective bargaining agreement and not infrequently by choice among large corporate employers). Rarely, however, does the workplace contact such an employee to ask what could help return the person to work. A pervasive claim in the employment sector is that any contact might be intrusive, and despite the requirements of the 1990 Americans with Disabilities Act (ADA), there is a belief that someone has to be "100 percent" to manage the demands of competitive employment. Lack of education, information, and understanding may immobilize everyone from dealing effectively with this presenting problem.

The rational response for workers experiencing the onset of disability is to covet benefits. They may be determined to overcome their disability but still experience fear, anger, deterioration of self-image, sense of loss and vulnerability, and a host of other negatives with regard to their problem. Questions arise: "Will the people at work care? Will I ever be able to work again? Will I be rewarded for my years of loyal service by accommodation? How am I going to make it financially? How can I best protect myself and my family?" As time elapses between the occurrence of the disabling condition and empathetic contact from the workplace, a productive worker turns into an unemployed person with a disability seeking some measure of financial security. The scenario imagined is, "They do not want me back to work. They are paying me to stay home. I better get the message—hold on to these disability payments since they are the only thing between me and financial ruin. I guess I really am disabled." Thus is created the "disability mindset," which would cause a person to adopt a disability mentality, unable to risk work for fear of losing benefit coverage.

The threat to job retention and, therefore, to economic well-being represented by disability has been recognized in the income maintenance provisions of Social Security Disability Insurance (SSDI). Employed people who develop a disability that negatively affects their capacity to perform a major life function (e.g., work) and that is expected to last more than a year or end in death, and who are unable to earn the amount considered representative of "substantial gainful employment" are entitled to draw SSDI benefits. Many opt for this alternative. But people with disabilities, employed or seeking entry to the workplace, prefer employment to drawing benefits (Sellers 1999; Akabas & Gates 1993). In this, as other issues presented in this section, the workplace carries a major causative share in creating the presenting problem. One of the responsibilities facing work organizations, particularly since the enactment of the ADA, is to find a means of accommodating to the job maintenance or new employment of people with disabilities. This, like the other presenting problems discussed, offers an opportunity for the social worker in or outside the workplace who is carrying out an assessment of an individual to bring awareness of the importance of work into the clinical dialogue and to be knowledgeable about the many presenting problems related to the workplace that can help explain the adjustment difficulties being experienced by the individual. Armed with this understanding, the professional can assist the worker in being able to devise strategies that may remedy the problem. Systems can be put in place that have the potential for fulfilling human needs, meeting legislative mandates, containing costs, and increasing productivity (Akabas, Gates, & Galvin 1992; Akabas & Gates 1993).

Workplace Action Placing Individuals "at Risk" Concerning Continued Employment

To serve working people who experience problems maintaining their work role, it is imperative that the social worker understand the many ways in which the action of the employer can disrupt the well-being of the most committed and competent employee. Gone are the days, for example, when employers offered an unwritten agreement of lifetime employment as the reward for loyalty and productive performance. Nor have unions, which historically provided a relatively strong voice for attention to workers' rights, been able to insure such protections. The rise of global competition, decline of the manufacturing sector, expansion of part-time and contingent work, and development of a hostile legal and legislative environment have combined to make it difficult for unions to organize and maintain their power in the collective bargaining situation, leaving more and more workers without representation. From representing 35 percent of the labor force in the 1950s, unions, by 2003, had only 12.9 percent of all wage and salary workers as their members, totaling 15.8 million workers (AFL-CIO n.d.). Thus plant closing, downsizing, and rightsizing have become accepted, even rewarded, corporate actions, although they are merely euphemisms for creating job insecurity. The vast majority of labor force participants will not only hold numerous jobs but will also occupy at least three different career tracks during their working lives and are likely to experience periods of unemployment that will threaten their mental health (Brenner 1973).

In this fast-changing world of the global market place, the knowledge worker (a term commonly used to describe the rapidly increasing number of workers who depend on brains and education rather than brawn or physical skill to meet job requirements) learns that the only job tenure assurance available is to embody skills that are at the frontier of current technology. The strategy for many workers has become specifically limiting one's tenure on a job to achieve varied experience and to build extensive work-related networks of potential support. In the recent period, marked as it has been by unprecedented demand for labor and intimations of shortages of those with required skills, a plan for regularly changing jobs could be viewed as feasible protection against dismissal. But this moment of high employment has fizzled, and the issue of job displacement has begun to reoccur. It suggests that everyone may suffer from what has been for the unskilled and disadvantaged a regular event. Few things are more frightening than finding one's employment at risk. If we gain self-respect, a means of organizing our day, social contacts, financial well-being, and a sense of accomplishment from work, then it is safe to assume that we lose all that in the face of unemployment (Maurer 1981). And as brief periods of displacement turn into long-term unemployment, the resilience of workers declines. They begin to wallow in self-blame as an explanation for their status, leaving them subject to depression and dependence. Social workers seeking to serve individuals cannot ignore the severe impact that results from job loss. For many facing these issues, as well as those who are exiting the labor force, these detachments represent serious personal problems that require attention from those professionals who have specialized training to serve workers and their needs.

But it is not just redundancy that causes an individual's attachment to the labor force to be "at risk." Relocation, too, has its negative consequences, even when it represents a promotion for the worker. The disruption such a move represents for a family unit is huge. Friendships are interrupted; children's school ties are in turmoil; working spouses find themselves thrown into unemployment; housing, religious affiliation, and even food and service suppliers have to be renegotiated. This all occurs at a time when the worker him- or herself is settling in to a new and often more demanding job situation and has less time than usual to devote to family needs. It represents a major stress on what may be a fragile family system. Marital discord, domestic violence, children with behavioral issues, spouses with disrupted careers, and older adults who find their usual elder care in disarray are all predictable problems on the relocation agenda.

Perhaps the greatest risk for workers, however, is jobs for which the pay is inadequate to meet a family's basic needs. In the 1960s Liebow's research uncovered the finding that many African American men, whose income assured only poverty for their family, would leave their family in discouragement to start a new unit elsewhere, hoping to be more successful. Lerner (1980) has pointed out that workers whose earnings place their families in poverty engage in self-blame. In America, where everyone has a chance to succeed (so the myth goes), the less-than-successful come to believe that it is their fault that their families lack basic necessities. They suffer from what Lerner refers to as "surplus powerlessness," a sense in which they conclude that they are incapable of getting anything right, so not only do they "fail" at their jobs but the spillover affects their marital situation in a self-fulfilling prophecy of incompetence. The stress of this scenario results in mental health problems (Schore & Atkin 1993) with their concomitant impact on productivity. The presenting problem may be low wages that place the economic well-being of the worker and family at risk, a situation in which the employer contributes to the cause and experiences the result of the shortfall. Risk to the employee ultimately results in risk to the employer. There are the millions of working poor for whom economic self-sufficiency is difficult to achieve as Ehrenreich (2002) so dramatically described in her book *Nickel and Dimed,* in which she records her experience holding four low-paid, relatively unskilled jobs in various locations throughout the United States. Because of the shared nature of these problems, occupational social workers are presented with a great opportunity to provide leadership or assistance to help solve employers' problems by working as advocates for the economically disadvantaged employee (Akabas & Kurzman 1982b; Mudrick 1991; Mor Barak & Tynan 1993). This advocacy must extend beyond the organizational system to the economy as a whole, where issues of economic and social justice can be dealt with in a more comprehensive manner. For example, it may be appropriate for more social agencies to involve their clients in voter registration and education drives. Such action would be in keeping with the extraordinary social worker, social policy strategy team of Richard Cloward and Frances Piven, who were the primary organizers of the Motor Voter movement that reached fruition in the passage of the National Voter Registration Act of 1993. That bill required states to offer on-the-spot voter registration at various government agencies. It realized its dramatic potential in 1995, the first full year after implementation, when 11 million people either newly registered to vote or corrected their voting addresses, reportedly, "the largest single increase in voter registration since the practice of registration was established" (Motor Voter n.d.). This opportunity to empower agency clients to participate in the political process might be a productive counterbalance to the "learned helplessness" that too often afflicts those who find themselves overwhelmed by the problems of daily living.

The Fallout of Unsupportive Workplace Cultures

Two important certainties exist in tandem, namely the knowledge that achieving high levels of productivity requires dedicated effort, available only when workers feel valued, and the fact that workplaces frequently ignore the needs of workers despite this knowledge. The short-term thinking of most of American industry leaves little time for attention to the longer-run payoffs stemming from providing a caring environment for employees. The result is the creation of many presenting problems among the labor force participants because they perceive the culture as unsupportive. Prime among these is the feeling of being undervalued, harassed, and not fitting in, of suffering severe stress, particularly by being discriminated against in the distribution of the rewards of the workplace. Unfortunately, this lack of attention is reinforced by a societal culture that values different people differently. If one is a person of color, or a woman, or gay or lesbian, or has a disability, there are likely to be subtle (and not so subtle) messages from the workplace culture that marginalize the person because of his or her difference from the long-preferred male, white, Protestant, married prototype of the "ideal" worker.

Consider this presenting problem.

TINKO, AN UNPRODUCTIVE WORKER

Tinko is in charge of payroll at a large hospital. She has felt respected. As she has aged, she has felt very comfortable because she is valued, as is the usual situation in her Asian culture. She has been employed there for thirty-five years. A new comptroller has been employed who is half Tinko's age and has changed everything. Without consulting with Tinko, he has made significant changes in the payroll procedure and Tinko now feels like a clerk. She has talked with her friends about how little respect the comptroller has for her and that at her age she is not accustomed to being treated like that. Tinko becomes more and more withdrawn. Then she starts missing work. A previously reliable worker becomes a problem worker.

What is happening? Does she have a discrimination complaint? What could have been done to avoid the situation? If you are an EAP counselor, what can you do about it?

In 1998 the Equal Employment Opportunity Commission (EEOC) received almost eighty thousand complaints alleging discrimination based on race, gender, condition of disability, age, national origin, religion, and equal pay, in that order, and state human rights commissions recorded many more such claims (U.S. Equal Employment Opportunity Commission 1999). Achieving an inclusive workplace, where all participants experience comfort and support and respect for diversity, remains a work in progress for the American labor market.

This is not a problem created by the workplace alone. We are a society that is marked by racism, sexism, homophobia, ageism, and many other prejudices. Most institutions today recognize the gains to be realized from diversity but struggle, not entirely successfully, to rid themselves of the obstacles to its achievement. Gummer (1998) has suggested that true diversity is not just a matter of accepting that discrimination is bad and then seeking fairness by including differences and expecting everyone to behave similarly (in line with existing culture). Nor is it a matter of including varied populations and leaving them, in their own niche, to take care of their own customers, markets, or individuals seeking services. Rather, diversity is a matter of inclusiveness, of organizational learning and effectiveness, where we learn from each other and end up doing better because we understand more, consider more, and are enriched by differences among us. This is a model that is fulfilled by very few major employers, and the human cost is enormous. Spalter-Roth and Deitch (1999: 476) report: "Without inclusive policies, many workers may experience downward mobility with each new job. . . . Without continued support for policies that promote gender and race equality, workplace practices such as downsizing, right sizing, and outsourcing, which promote job instability, will continue to reinforce queues that result in inequalities in reemployment, occupational mobility, and earnings each time workers apply for jobs during their lifetimes."

Other kinds of problems that result from lack of organizational inclusiveness are also of concern here. One example is cited by Hopkins (1997), who found that African American women are least likely of any group to perceive supervisors as supportive. She explains this using social identity theory, suggesting that these women view supervisors, who are usually white and male, as outside their own identity and, therefore, unlikely to be helpful. As a result, despite the supervisors' appointed role of helping troubled workers, employees who do not feel a strong identification with particular supervisors are unlikely to try to utilize them as a supportive resource. Thus the supervisor cannot function in what has become a key role, of lending the kind of support that keeps workers motivated and, therefore, productive. Lack of trust, the by-product of a culture that has settled for symbolic diversity and is incomplete in achieving inclusiveness, places a drag on productivity. It may manifest itself in problems such as stress reactions, lack of confidence in management, or poor coworker teamwork, but it is important to recognize that these presenting problems are only the tip of the proverbial iceberg and the unseen seven-eighths is accounted for by the dysfunctional results of an unsupportive culture.

Unsupportive workplace cultures are evident not only in their inability to embrace inclusiveness but also in their inattention to issues of health and safety and in their general climate. For many years, the labor force participation rate of older men has been declining. This has been attributed to the fact that many have done demanding physical tasks that cannot be performed by their aging bodies, causing them to drop out of the labor force. Certainly, one of the major reasons for early retirement is poor health, and for some this can be traced back to work demands. This, however, may be a time-limited problem because technology, globalization, and international competition have effectively eliminated most of the jobs that led to these outcomes and have shifted employment in the United States into less hazardous endeavors. But as jobs change, so, too, do the means of protecting employees from the wear and tear that work has caused to many individuals. The example of carpal tunnel syndrome leaps to mind. Almost unknown several decades ago, this repetitive motion injury, resulting from such work as daylong data input, has become the scourge of today's office workers. Strategies and equipment exist for combating this and most other work-related health and injury problems. Many studies show that ergonomic safety is cost effective in the long run; in fact, recent findings suggest that workplaces have begun to be responsive to these possibilities as a direct result of the high price attached to workers' compensation coverage in many states (Conway & Svenson 1998). It simply becomes too costly to ignore safety considerations, particularly if the specific task has come under surveillance by the Occupational Safety and Health Administration (OSHA) (Krueger 2000). The arguments posed against regulation, however, are instructive. Employer representatives, such as the National Association of Manufacturers and the Chamber of Commerce, make the claim that OSHA robs workers of income because the money employers spend on meeting the requirements of safety regulations reduces their ability to pay higher wages. In short, the intimation is that the choice is between what employers regard as "excessive" safety precautions and employee income. In this scenario, many workers fall back on a sense of their own invulnerability and are apt to opt for wage increases (which they may never see). Unions have been outspoken in pressing the demand for safety, suspecting that increases in cost are probably passed on to consumers rather than being allowed to interfere with profits or wages. Where this is not the case, however, work environments continue to endanger workers' security, again putting the presenting problem at the door of the employer community. This does not imply that all, or even most, workplaces pursue unsafe strategies, but it does suggest that social workers need to be aggressive in ferreting out the underlying policy issues involved in presenting problems and attend to those issues at the same time that they help workers meet what appear to be their more immediate needs. (See chap. 6 for suggestions concerning systemic approaches to solving problems.)

Societal Issues Requiring Workplace Response

The workplace is the opportunity system where much of the power and many of the rewards of American society are distributed. If the profession of social work accepts, as its mandate, assisting disadvantaged and oppressed groups toward economic self-sufficiency, it is at the workplace, and with the forces of labor and management, that much of the work must be done. The workplace is not necessarily a welcoming or supportive environment for people of difference. Despite legislative encouragement and organizational pronouncements supporting current diversity and the immigration that assures future diversity, data indicate that the recruitment and retention policies of most employing organizations combine to cause disparate impact on the incomes and prospects of many groups seeking entry into the world of work. Social policy, at the same time, has become more and more focused on work as a responsibility of all citizens. The safety net has been reduced in its coverage over time and in relation to the level of support offered to different disadvantaged populations. In the face of these developments, the need to enter and succeed in the American workplace becomes ever more vital, yet the possibility of doing so becomes ever more illusive.

Consider the situation in relation to many immigrants. Although they immigrate for many reasons, they all come to America, in part, in search of economic betterment. Employment, therefore, is a chief target. In fact, migration accounts for more than 20 percent of new labor market entrants every year (Kossoudji & Cobb-Clark 1996). For those who come as unauthorized workers, however, this is a difficult path. The Immigration Reform and Control Act of 1988 was designed to protect legal workers from the supposed competition of undocumented job seekers. Though employing them is illegal under the law, employers are all too willing to hire them as a cheap source of labor. Many undocumented workers, therefore, secure jobs, but their employment is accompanied by constant fear of discovery. This becomes a basis for inexcusable exploitation. For example, Wal-Mart was cited recently by the INS for using a cleaning contractor for its stores that hired undocumented workers and paid them less than minimum wage and no overtime despite requiring them to work seven days a week. Should the undocumented workers try to organize into a union, employers respond by threatening to call in the INS to deport them. Thus they face the acculturation complexities of any immigrant population, and in addition the law has armed employers with a weapon of intimidation that undermines any opportunity for empowerment among these new residents (Bacon 2000).

Gender and racial bias constitute another explanation for groups that experience broad scale inequity in the labor market. For example, the gender and racial gap in median weekly earnings is wide (Bielby 2000; Beggs 1995). Controlling for differences of education, experience, and other factors that have been correlated with differences in earnings, studies confirm the constancy of the gap that keeps white males, doing the same or comparable work, earning more than all other population groupings such as women and people of color. But because the gap is a result of deeply held beliefs and their consequent expression in institutionalized discriminatory behavior, it has proven to be a stable force in the labor market. Employers continue to express their preference for white males by violating "rational" economic behavior, that is, by paying them at a wage rate that is higher than their marginal productivity for their labor and awarding them the best jobs and the speediest promotions. Observers note that although women must "prove themselves" on the job to be considered for promotion, white males are promoted on their "future promise." Such institutional sexism and racism have been found to exist to a lesser degree in proportion to the percent of federal public sector employment in an industry (Beggs 1995). In other words, the greater the level of federal government involvement in the economics within an industry, the lower we would expect the levels of race and gender inequality to be. This suggests several strategies for dealing with labor market inequity. Prime among the solution sets has been for the discriminated to gravitate to those geographic areas, industries, and jobs where the economic force of government is felt most. This offers those groups some power over the triple threat of glass ceiling, glass walls, and sticky floors—that is, levels of employment they can see but cannot reach; job clusters they can observe but to which they cannot gain entry, thus finding themselves in job ghettos where employment offers little if any advancement because of an abbreviated promotional ladder. Similar difficulties face those who are gay or lesbian.

Nor can the needs of the welfare population that policy prods toward work be resolved without input at the workplace. Many of those pressed by new legal requirements to gain employment because of time-limited eligibility for welfare coverage are products of an inferior educational system that gave them no skills to compete in the world of work that depends on technical knowledge and computer ability to even enter that world. The same problems are experienced by teenagers who see no future for themselves and too often drop out of school, making them even less prepared for the high-tech environment of the workplace. In short, the disadvantaged, oppressed "club" probably includes the majority of present and would-be workers to a greater or lesser extent. There is a disconnect in the labor market activities between public policy and private behavior. A more efficient economy is required for the pie to expand sufficiently to take up the labor supply of all the disenfranchised groups and to raise workers out of poverty. This depends very much on the action of employers, as Kossek and colleagues have observed (1997: 89): "But over the long run, employers will lose if more and more workers have low wages and little or no job security. Employer strategies that invest in workers' education, knowledge and skills, and family well-being, and that provide greater employment protection and opportunity to develop on the job, are not merely socially responsible actions to enhance the employability of the working poor. These strategies enable all employees to contribute more effectively to the bottom line, which ultimately benefits business."

The litany of problems that can be placed at the door of the workplace are even more extensive than this review would suggest, but they do not necessarily reflect evil intent or even careless lack of concern. Rather, we suggest the cause is an inability to recognize mutual interests. Empirical evidence indicates, time and again, that there is a significant correlation between employee well-being and organizational productivity. Whether the explanatory model has been provided by Maslow (1954) who contends that we cannot do our creative best—self-actualize—until all our more basic needs are met or Herzberg et al. (1959) who insist that we must take care of the hygiene factors that stand in the way of achievement before we can move toward the motivating factors that encourage achievement is less relevant than the fact that there are conditions and situations within the power of employers and trade union to change, and it is in their self-interest to do so. Both groups can prosper only in an expanding, globally competitive economy. The highest level of marginal productivity from every worker and potential worker is understood to maximize the gross national product and the profitability of individual enterprises. Everyone benefits when the total pie is expanded. The goal is to find those changes that might reduce the level of problems that human beings experience in gaining entry to or being in the workplace, which impede both their contribution to the economy and their sense of self-worth. This will initiate the necessary conditions under which mutual interests can be pursued in the achievement of prosperity.

Where does this leave social workers who, by professional code of ethics, are dedicated to social justice? As these presenting problems are dumped at the social worker's door, whether in EAPs and MAPs or in clinical settings of agencies and private practice offices, the professional response is challenging. While it remains for the next chapter to explore possible problem-solving strategies, let it be noted that attacking these issues individual by individual is an unlikely formula for success. Institutional achievement of inclusiveness, attention to safety, creation of a management that inspires confidence and trust, all beckon. Such a vision requires complex organizational change—and yet it has been said that the only human beings who enjoy change are wet babies. To move an organizational focus to securing self-esteem, self-worth, and equity for employees on all levels requires creating a truly diverse, inclusive, safe, and caring work environment. Required are executive commitment and modeling, mentoring, offering support to all; initiating, participating in, and supporting training that promotes diversity; facilitating communication channels where constructive discussion can take place; and being ever alert to one's own behavior and that of others. The question is " how can a social worker, internal to the workplace or in some external relationship to it, help the system achieve these responses?"

Too often social workers in the workplace have settled for a narrow definition of role. They have attended to individual problems rather than integrating their practice into organizational or community needs. Yet there is a vast population uncomfortable with their position in or seeking entry into the world of work. Arguing that "human rights are integral to social work's mission," Witkin (1998) suggests that we reframe problems in relation to the ways in which they violate human rights so that "new areas and means of intervention become available, and new sources of support can be mobilized." Witkin concludes his discussion with a quotation from Eleanor Roosevelt, which seems as relevant today as when she uttered it. "Where, after all, do universal human rights begin? In small places close to home—so close and so small that they cannot be seen on any maps of the world. Yet they are the world of the individual person; the neighborhood he lives in; the school or college he attends; *the factory, farm, or office where he works.* Such are the places where every man, woman, and child seeks equal justice, equal opportunity, equal dignity without discrimination" (200, emphasis added).

This is the challenge for the occupational social worker who would choose to deal with the presenting problems observed in and about the world of work. Social workers are in a position to identify, understand, and interpret to the greater society the needs that must be met to achieve this outcome. In the next chapter we describe some of the actions that may start the professional on the way.

Study Questions

1. What are the differences in the employer and employee perspective on the desired outcome of employment; how do these differences affect behavior? Can mutual interests be identified and promoted? How?
2. What recent changes in demography and social forces have occurred in the workplace and how would you evaluate the adequacy of the response by the workplace to these changes? Can you suggest policies or programs to improve compatibility between work and family needs?
3. The authors differentiate between problems caused by workers' personal lives and those problems that reflect a significant causal contribution from the workplace. Do you agree with this differentiation? What different approaches to problem resolution are suggested by this causal differentiation?
4. Some believe that educating low-income clients about their rights and helping them register to vote is an empowerment strategy, while others view such actions as manipulation of vulnerable people. What do you think of the strategy as an attack on poverty per se or client empowerment and promotion of policy change?
5. What arguments can be made to support the concept that a supportive workplace culture increases productivity? Do you agree? Why or why not?

CHAPTER 6

Delivery Systems

Conceptual Dimensions and Structures

Many constituencies are involved in the world of work, each of which has different interests and expectations in the development and support of services from the workplace. Managers and their investors have a primary interest in productive employees who contribute to the organizations' bottom line. They have devised services and benefit programs to encourage the productive cooperation of workers that will maximize the corporate profit goal (Lambert 1993; Root 1993a; Wallen 2002). Unions seek membership loyalty as a primary outcome. They bargain for contract coverage of benefits and services directed toward meeting those human needs that they evaluate will foster loyalty (Hiatt & Jackson 1997). Workers seek an environment that will provide fairness and security and be supportive of their own development and that of their family members. The likelihood that employees will maintain good attendance records and report satisfaction on the job has been found to increase when these needs are met (Casner-Lotto 2000; Gullason 2000). Society, by the social policy it initiates, as evidenced by TANF's welfare-to-work initiative, the Ticket to Work, and Work Incentives Improvement Act of 1999 designed to return Social Security Disability Insurance recipients to active labor force participation and other legislatively inspired programs, has given notice that it expects every adult to produce. It places responsibility on the world of work to provide a nondiscriminatory environment in work organizations—as evidenced by such legislation as title 7 of the Civil Rights Act of 1964, ADA, ADEA, and the Fair Labor Standards Act—that rewards the producers by providing standards of wages, hours, and working conditions that fulfill minimum human needs. All these interests and related goals combine to promote the potential of social work in the workplace as an obvious instrument for achieving these varied, desired outcomes. The issue of attention in this chapter is to discern what systems, based on what concepts and structures, have been created to deliver on this potential.

Not surprisingly, as one surveys the landscape, many alternative patterns appear. Immediately following the terrorist events of September 11, workplace social service delivery systems seemed to increase significantly in their importance. Employers everywhere called on EAPs to carry out trauma debriefings among their employees. Unions, too, understood the importance of helping members cope so that they could continue to function in the workplace. The expectation was that intervention would minimize both the fright experienced by their employees/members and the negative impact of that fright on their mental well-being and, therefore, productivity. This heavy demand for EAP/MAP organizational services was short lived. As things settled down and life returned to a semblance of order, the brisk demand for trauma debriefing services diminished, and without that "case finding" mechanism the demand for counseling at the workplace diminished accordingly. But a principle had been established. Work organizations need to be able to respond to crisis conditions, and social service delivery at the workplace provides a viable mechanism for such a response. New settings joined the ranks of those that offer social services to meet individual and organizational needs that are apparent in the workplace.

Employers and unions can build internal responses, in which they hire the staff expertise necessary to create in-house systems to meet the needs of their employees/members. EAPS and MAPS, as well as family/work initiatives and union education programs, are some by-products of this approach. At the other extreme, work organizations can depend solely on community resources to meet the needs of their employees/members, surmising that the needs of their own population are not very different from those of most people and, therefore, the needs can be met through the same channels that other community residents use. This circumstance is rare and likely to be most typical of small employers. Intermediate between these polar positions, the combinations are countless in which the employer or union creates an internal response (e.g., hires an EAP contract supervisor), who, in turn, organizes coordination with the varied services available within the organization and from the general community. Providing financial contributions to community day care and elder care programs, as well as awarding purchase of service contracts to health care and counseling service providers, are the result of a mixed internal-external handling of the needs of the target population. Coordination with risk management, internally, and health care resources, externally, constitutes yet another example of the continuum available (Rosenthal &

Olsheski 1999). This kind of interrelationship between work organizations and community resources can be initiated by either party. It is, for example, as likely that a family service agency will solicit a contract to provide counseling to the employees of a particular employer or members of a specific union as the other way around, that is, that the employer or union initiates a request for a program proposal from an organization that may contract for services in a local labor market or may be a national syndicate that offers service anywhere in the country and even worldwide. The largest of such external providers is estimated to oversee EAP services to more than 60 million lives, including workers and their dependents. Nor does provision of direct service cover the gamut of possibilities. Social workers and their agencies/consulting services may be asked to assist with making decisions and administering corporate social responsibility programs, affirmative action and training initiatives, disability management efforts, and other human resource management functions including the managed care of benefit packages.

Occupational Social Welfare System

Definitions often prove useful in understanding turf. Early in the development of social welfare, Titmuss, (1968) a leading social welfare theorist, identified that alongside the well-recognized public and voluntary social welfare systems stands a little acknowledged but vital third entity that he called the occupational welfare system. This sector is made up of trade union and employer responses to social welfare needs of labor force participants and their dependents. Weiner and colleagues (1971), in laying out the field of practice of social work and the workplace, defined the occupational social welfare system as the combination of benefits and services that accrue to an individual in his or her status as worker or as a dependent of someone in that status. Later, Googins and Godfrey (1987) extended the definition to include the sponsoring organization and the community at large, defining occupational social welfare as a field of practice in which social workers attend to human and social needs of the work community by designing and executing interventions to insure healthier individuals and environments. This expansion gives the practitioner liberty not only to consider the needs of individuals but also to attend to the construction of a systems approach to organizational as well as individual issues. Googins and Davidson (1993: 479) actually advocate, "If the EAP is to continue to be relevant to the changing corporate climate, it may realize its mission better by shifting from an individual to an organizational focus." Newer concepts of workplace programs view them from a value-added perspective, that is, focused on the question of in what way can the provider of service add value to the employing organization (not just the individual) by the activity in which it engages (Kaufman and Guerra 2002; Peters 1999). Such a perspective may, for example, manage disability programs designed to accelerate the return to work of employees experiencing compensable accidents and injuries in the workplace, thereby reducing the compensation and replacement costs (Orbach 2001; Gates, Taler, & Akabas 1989).

All these definitions have similar characteristics. They are consistent in their auspices, namely management and labor, and in their target population, specifically workers/members (and sometimes their dependents). The elements of programs and benefits are more variable, which allows for innovation and creativity in system design or for passing responsibility on to the community, depending on the program sponsor's organizational culture, mission, and specific programmatic goals. For example, if labor force recruitment and retention are the objectives, the employer will build an organizational culture that (1) announces concern for employees in its mission statement, (2) encourages supervisory support that is sensitive and flexible in response to presenting problems, and (3) develops a benefit package that meets needs under varying family circumstances (Warren & Johnson 1995). Such an employer will have an internal system that might include paid leave for family emergencies, gym membership, or a host of other components that help distinguish the organization from other workplaces to attract and achieve commitment of the individual to the firm. Alternatively, the employer can leave employees to depend on the community system if its culture, for instance, views child care as a family/mother's obligation or considers workers as interchangeable parts, easily recruited and requiring minimal training to function effectively within the organizational setting.

Wherever the work organization falls on this spectrum, it is the occupational social welfare system that represents the resource base for responding to the needs of employees/members and their dependents. Naturally, the system has evolved over years, if for no other reason than that needs change. In recent years significant changes have occurred in the composition of the labor force and in the nature of the economy. A key, though by no means sole, example of this has been the great increase in the proportion of women in the workforce and the accompanying range of issues that come when you hire workers but get human beings, particularly those from unaccustomed labor pools (Karuntzos et al. 1998). In response, many enlightened American businesses and unions have moved from a traditional, management-driven model focused on work processes to the new paradigm of employee participation focused on employees' priorities (Casner-Lotto 2000). Balancing work and family issues, for both male and female employees, has risen in importance, and workplace life course programs have been identified as one way of mitigating the strain of work on families (Brayfield 1995; Warren & Johnson 1995). In many situations this has led to a life cycle approach to service and benefit development, offering something for everybody, from school tuition payment for the new recruits, vouchers to cover the costs of child care and adoption for growing families, and improved retirement pensions and part-time work options to meet the interests of older but valued workers.

Whether a workplace offers any program, and the differences among such programs, have significant income distribution implications. As Ozawa (1985) has pointed out, the benefit and service package represents income to those who receive it or at least services that they may need and for which they do not have to pay, thereby positively affecting their standard of living by leaving them with more disposable income for the purchase of other goods and services that they may desire. Since these benefits and services are more usual in large firms, which are more likely than smaller ones to pay a living wage, the benefits serve as an additional income distribution to the haves over the have-nots. Furthermore, since the cost of the benefits are deductible to the employer, providing benefits and services to employees reduces profits and, therefore, the taxes that might be paid by the firm, consequently limiting the funds received by the government that can be allocated to provide public services to the already poor.

The income redistribution impact of the benefit and service package becomes even more apparent when applied to the global economy. Recent demands by labor and human rights representatives that overseas sites of American manufacturing companies provide decent wages and working conditions to their foreign employees are emblematic of this concern about the channeling of business profits to those who are already rich. Cheap goods, manufactured under below-standard working conditions and wages, place additional downward pressure on the compensation of the lowest-paid workers in the United States. These workers are some of the social work profession's likely targets of services. Noting that social work practice has always been influenced by the events in the greater economy, Reisch and Gorin (2001: 19) suggest, "In the 21st century, social work will be shaped by the new global economy and the growing gap between high and low wages, permanent and temporary employment." With the framing issues so relevant to the workplace, it is no wonder that the conceptual basis and structures of the workplace service delivery system have been affected extensively as national and international economic conditions change (Lambert 1999).

Employee and Member Assistance Programs

There is almost universal understanding in the world of work today that if you have a personal or family problem, one of the resources to which you can turn is the employee assistance program or, in the case of union members, the member assistance program. Yet these programs represent a fast-changing response that itself is barely a few decades old. Although welfare capitalism and its concern with employee well-being (albeit in the interest of high productivity) harks back to the nineteenth century, its manifestation as EAPs and MAPs (hereafter referred to as EAPs to cover programs sponsored by either auspice) dates to the 1970s. EAPs started as a corporate or union acknowledgment of alcoholism among workers. Programs that became available in large business or labor settings were offered as an in-house service to employees of specific work organizations to help them deal with their substance abuse problems and to retain their employment. Since then, these initiatives have changed in response to a cacophony of voices representing disagreements concerning the appropriate location, service package, target population, program goal, and underlying values. An important determinant of the structure has been how the organization defines the mission of its EAP (Davidson & Herlihy 1999). Most of those that have seen it as a place for illness and for problem-focused attention to performance issues have relegated this limited role to an off-site structure. Those that view it as a place where one receives help without hassle for solutions to everyday challenges have found their turf to be more expansive. In general, the more expansive the coverage, the more likely the services are to have some in-house dimension and some coordination with other in-house activities (e.g., EEOC, training, or disability management) as well as with purchased services and other community resources. In addition to social workers, who have been the dominant professional group, a variety of different professionals and recovering people have staffed these efforts, including psychiatrists, psychologists, vocational counselors, and certified alcoholism counselors.

There is a spectrum of conflicting attitudes regarding the delivery of social and mental health services through the workplace. Some view service delivery as a tool to manipulate workers to put all else aside to meet the demands of their employers (Bakalinsky 1980; Lambert 1993). This position suggests that provision of services reduces workers' need to join unions and empower themselves. It hypothesizes that services such as child care resources are provided as a device to assure that parents/ employees are not distracted from their main responsibility of being productive workers. Other commentators suggest more benign motivation, including opportunities to offer a public image that is appealing to customers and employees alike, a chance to gain competitive advantage by being able to recruit and retain the most able employee pool, willingness to provide preventive services in the hope that the more costly curative efforts can be avoided, and a desire to assure a more even playing field for all employees by offering help to reduce the problems some workers (perhaps more likely women and those of color) face. Some view an in-house location as the only means of assuring a coordinated, systems approach to service. They cite the importance of cooperation between different units to assure cost-effective, universal service delivery. Others insist on external programs because they believe they better protect confidentiality, which they view as one of the most important criteria for evaluating services. Some consider the abuse of alcohol and other substances as the guiding programmatic goal, while others believe the program focus should be broad based, meeting the varied needs of diverse populations and organizational actors (Csiernik 1999; Kurzman 1993).

Increasingly, societal pressures have favored those latter alternatives, causing the auspices to broaden their attention to include a full-service approach to the generalized social and psychological needs of workers and even beyond, to view the organization as well as the individual as the client of attention (Googins & Davidson 1993). This has led to many program innovations under the auspices of EAPs. Sprang and her colleagues (1999: 109), for example, report on a parenting-at-work option under EAP sponsorship that allows new mothers to bring their infants to work, thereby combining high-quality child care with reduced absenteeism and early return to work of vital, productive workers. These researchers report that the mothers viewed the program as a "great advantage to them and the babies" and indicated increased job satisfaction and commitment to the employer as the outcome. In helping employees meet elder care responsibilities, Lechner and Sasaki (1995: 105) describe programs that offer "seminars on work and family issues, resource and referral advice, dependent care assistance plans (employee sets aside nontaxable wages to use within the year for dependent care expenses), and some type of flexible work schedule." The authors note that these are all fairly inexpensive initiatives that can be easily implemented.

Direct service innovations such as single-session group interventions to deal with employee stress have been introduced by other EAPs and have proven beneficial in improving teamwork and helping achieve organizational change as well (Gladstone & Reynolds 1997). Many enhanced interventions are targeted at the special needs of particular groups. For example, Karuntzos and her colleagues (1998) report on extensive enrichments directed specifically at EAP services to respond more effectively to the needs of women and ethnic/racial minority employees. These include hiring and better training for specialized EAP counselors, revising supervisory training, coordinating with focused community resources, revising materials describing EAP services and the content of outreach seminars, and paying particular attention to diversity issues.

Even the interventions in response to alcohol and substance abuse among employees have been reevaluated in light of the evolving nature of the employee assistance programs. Considering that the roots of EAPs are in alcoholism treatment efforts closely related to Alcoholics Anonymous and that AA is dedicated to total abstinence, it is noteworthy that the *Employee Assistance Handbook* (Oher 1999) includes a chapter titled "Brief Interventions and Moderation Approaches for Preventing Alcohol Problems." The author (Bruhnsen 1999) reports on an intense effort by the EAP at the University of Michigan to deal with an often-overlooked problem, namely those whose drinking behavior is predictive of, but has not yet reached, the level of severe alcohol problems requiring specialized treatment. In a harm-reduction approach, the university developed a cognitive-behavioral initiative based on self-control training (as compared with the disease model of alcohol abuse, which argues that complete abstinence is the only possible response). Using education and behavioral modification, the approach allows clients an array of options that provides the individual with choices more in keeping with a strengths perspective and an empowerment model. The value of the moderation approach is its preventive character, thereby reducing the cost and length of intervention and increasing the value added by the EAP to the organization and the productivity of its workforce through a combination of early case finding and brief intervention.

A digression may be of value here. For workers in employing organizations that are required, because of the organization's status as a federal contractor, to certify that the workplace is drug-free, abstinence from drugs is an absolute necessity. It is important to remind ourselves, however, that there is a moralistic assumption to abstinence as an outcome and although it may be the best goal, it is probably not realistic for a majority of those abusing substances. This is a disease (or choice) characterized by recidivism. One of the principles guiding social workers is to meet the client where he or she is and proceed in a pragmatic, incremental, nonjudgmental manner. Reducing harm can be a worthwhile personal and public health objective. It is in keeping with a social justice agenda that accepts that everyone (including anyone who may abuse substances) is entitled to decide the extent to which he or she chooses to limit use (Brocato and Wagner 2003). As Marlatt and Witkiewitz (2002: 869) have observed, "Zero tolerance, the requirement of absolute abstinence promoted by traditional programs, may hinder individuals who are wanting to decrease the risks associated with heavy drinking, but do not want to quit drinking completely."

Admittedly, this is a controversial approach, but that is so, perhaps, because of its newness as a perspective. There are those who see harm reduction as an act of colluding with clients to avoid the presenting problem. As Denning (2000) points out, however, for many individuals driven from treatment programs by the demand for absolute abstinence, their lives are worse than before they sought therapy. The harm-reduction approach can be seen as a step approach with abstinence as the ideal end goal. It has an advantage in that it prevents unnecessary stigma. It prioritizes ameliorating the physical, social, and economic harms associated with drug use, makes eliminating use a secondary (but not unsought) priority, and is consistent with NASW's policy statement (2000). For the social worker practicing in the world of work or with clients who are employed, understanding this radical but value-neutral approach and applying it appropriately may bring a new degree of effectiveness to practice.

While the foregoing are merely examples of the direction of EAPs, an important conclusion can be drawn. EAPs, as an evolving workplace program, are faced with an important dilemma, which is now being debated by the Council on Accreditation for Children and Family Services. There is a safe road for EAPs to travel, based on an approach under which EAPs follow the traditional path. They view their role as the diagnosis and treatment of alcohol and substance abuse problems or under a broader brush, though still an individually focused approach, they undertake the assessment of and intervention in solely those problems that interfere with the individual worker's job performance. There are many who believe the effectiveness of EAPs is assured by this undiluted focus on intervention based on job performance criteria and largely connected to substance abuse as the causative agent. In these circumstances, the EAP has tight, if perhaps unduly self-contained boundaries, that threaten no one's turf and appear to be without risk. It is true that such EAPs can enunciate their goal and measure their achievements. The authors suggest, however, that this paradigm might be identified as the "wimp" model of EAP development. The question arises as to whether or not their achievements are sufficient to warrant their continuation. In today's world, as allocation of corporate resources grows increasingly competitive, this model is threatened with oblivion as it struggles unsuccessfully to overcome the corporate strategy to downsize or to contract out any service that does not offer a clear and significant contribution to the bottom line. The wimp model has such modest outcomes that it may find it difficult to claim significant value added to the organization. It also fails to fulfill the promise implied by the continuum of social work practice, ranging from the micro to the macro, with its full array of professional skills, particularly those of negotiation, advocacy, and activism in the interest of social justice. It confirms what Leiter and Wahlen (1996: 18) have observed: "Even when effective, individually focused interventions may do little more than enable people to tolerate poorly managed situations."

Alternatively, EAPs can recognize that "[t]he expanded EAP has become accepted as a means to attract and retain good employees" (Orbach 2001). This organizationally focused alternative is based on a proactive, ecological approach in which the EAP becomes a corporate assistance program (Maloof, Governale, & Berman 1997) and systems change agent. Making the focus both the individual and the organization, all the while taking account of the environment, is a winning strategy that provides support for a claim of high value added. Under these conditions the EAP professional looks through many lenses—for example, the work/family lens, the disability lens, the affirmative action lens—in order not only to help individuals but also to analyze presenting problems, identify employee concerns to management, and point out the impact of the work environment on individuals. This recommended advocacy model has a goal in which "social workers can take the initiative in moving occupational social work from being a mechanism of social control to one of active social change in order to enhance workplace wellness" (Csiernik 1998: 37). Such an approach allows the EAP to become a consultant to corporate management or the union and to serve as a bridge between the community and the employer/union. It responds to the public expectation that business should exist not just to make money but also to promote societal values (Kaufman & Guerra 2002).

Many new opportunities emerge from such a positioning of the EAP. One of the authors was involved recently in considering how employers could be enlisted in efforts to improve the employment opportunities for consumers with mental health conditions. Given changes in medication that improve functional capacity, government policy developments that require work outcomes, and their own sense of empowerment to normalize their lives by participating in the all-American "game" of work, people with mental health conditions can, want to, and indeed are expected to work (Steele & Berman 2001). Yet their unemployment rate continues at the unacceptably high level of approximately 85 percent, caused largely by the fact that the consumers of mental health services are excluded from the world of work by a scenario of fear and stigma within employing organizations (Gabriel 2000). Research has shown that people with mental health conditions succeed in the workplace to the extent that they are appropriately accommodated in relation to task, routine, relationships, and work environment and to the degree that they have natural supports from supervisors and others in the workplace (Gates 2000). A search for an ally in responding to the unemployment levels among people with mental health conditions brings one to alight on EAP personnel and wonder in what way they could be the source of natural supports at the workplace while at the same time assisting employers with meeting the mandates of the ADA.

A survey among EAPs that was designed to identify the overlap between their customary activities and the needs of people with mental health conditions who seek employment confirmed that EAP staff customarily carry out many functions necessary to support the employment and to assist in job retention of people with mental health conditions. These functions include disability management–related services such as coordination with other departments or with unions around policies and practices that affect their clients, training for supervisors, and coordination with providers working with clients to support people in work. It also includes facilitating return to work in cases of disability leave, managing cases of disability particularly around consultation concerning needed accommodation, helping clients with disclosure, providing education to the work group, and follow-up with supervisors after EAP interventions (Akabas & Gates 2002). But the good news of EAPs' potential skill to help resolve the unemployment rate among people with serious and persistent mental health conditions is followed, unfortunately, by the bad news that EAP staff participating in the study did not believe that they had the authority to advocate for employment opportunities. In short, they did not feel imbedded in the system sufficiently to be able to influence its operation at least in relation to policy determining recruitment and hiring, if not job maintenance, of people with mental health conditions.

Although this is but one example of an EAP shortfall and the accompanying dilemma encountered by EAPs, it is symptomatic of the perplexing complications faced by social workers in many situations. Some of the reluctance uncovered in the survey reflects the numerous conflicting forces identified in chapter 4. But the cautious attitude is reinforced by severe time demands on an overworked EAP staff who may recognize the opportunity and need represented by the vision of a broad mission for EAPs, yet cannot overcome the real pressure represented by a goal-measured performance evaluation and external managed care arrangements (Austrian 1998). (The issues involved in managed care are discussed later in this chapter.)

Specialized Programs in the Workplace

Nonetheless, EAP staffers have shown great creativity in program development. The provision of social services in the workplace acts as an ongoing needs assessment process. The presenting problems and related issues that are brought forth as one attends to the requests for help from individuals in the workforce signal the gaps in service delivery. Some gaps identify needs to which the workplace should respond. They warrant social work attention because no one else is paying attention to them, and while they extend the boundaries of the specific workplace program, they are close enough to the usual roles and responsibilities of social workers so that the knowledge base is sufficient for such professional undertakings to enjoy organizational credibility and acceptance. The foregoing has been replete with examples of this kind of activity, but yet another example of the direction of social work service in the workplace may be in order.

The intent of most workplace programs is to enhance the well-being of the labor force in the interest of productivity. Many avenues are available for accomplishing this goal besides offering mental health services focused on individual counseling. As the place where individuals spend more waking hours than any other, the workplace serves as the ultimate developmental institution, following the early influence of family and school. Educational initiatives that allow employees to learn skills that can help make them more flexible and more likely to achieve promotion are significant aids to meeting both the staffing needs of the employer and the fulfillment of the personal aspirations of the employee. Serving similar dual needs are courses that help develop conflict resolution skills and improve the capacity of workers to negotiate with each other and to develop their aptitude to participate in team activities. Benefits accrue to both the organization's productivity and individuals' well-being as workers gain proficiency in offering support to each other and in establishing an organizational culture of mutual respect, one that nurtures human growth and development and embraces change.

Educational initiatives that expand one's understanding of what contributes to well-being are an approach to achieve the desired outcome. Such initiatives pay attention to issues and turf that can add value to the organization, tend to be unclaimed by other departments, and perhaps most important, are within the professional competence of social work practitioners. High among such interventions are health promotion programs. Gebhardt and Crump (1990: 262) claim that "growth of work site health promotion programs has partially resulted from the belief than an organization should take some responsibility for the welfare of its valuable resource, the worker." The authors note that the increasingly sedentary lifestyle of American adults contributes to disease that, in turn accounts for absenteeism, high medical costs, turnover, increased workplace injuries and high workers' compensation costs, anxiety and depression, and self-reports of low morale. Among the possible program responses can be initiatives that increase awareness of health issues, such as health fairs, screening sessions, and educational classes; efforts that provide specific activity such as back strengthening exercises; and more generalized interventions that create healthy environments, such as cafeterias that serve healthy meals and on-site gyms that allow for regular exercise.

What marks all these efforts is a twofold approach to practice. First, the social worker must operate out of a strengths perspective and view individual clients as depositories of ability untapped but available for growth and problem solving. Second, professionals must utilize an ecosystems approach to service delivery, viewing understanding of individuals as resulting not just from individual insight but also as fed by clarity around the organizational context in which the individual must operate. This requires that social workers define their turf as the total organization and the systems beyond its boundaries. Connections with other units within the workplace provide the basis for such contextual understanding. Working out of an EAP framework, social workers are in position to use their direct contact with employees and their cross-unit interaction with organizational representatives as practice opportunities. Such opportunities challenge social workers and require commitment to a broad arena of practice utilizing program development and prevention skills and knowledge (Akabas & Farrell 1993).

Some of these efforts can be achieved through a modest redefinition of social work's own professional boundaries. But other issues arise for which coordination with other units within the workplace is essential. This kind of activity arises because, although the knowledge base and expertise may not be within social work, the total initiative would be enriched by social work participation or because whoever has elected to pay attention to the issue recognizes the value of a social work contribution and invites participation. Involvement of this kind falls under interdisciplinary collaboration, different in the workplace because the colleagues may be EEO officers, lawyers, or risk managers rather than the accustomed human service partners, but similar to work in more traditional settings because the effort requires the same listening skills, attention to building trust, negotiation, and advocacy ability that characterize all interprofessional practice.

CASE EXAMPLES

Imagine successive women coming to talk with an EAP social worker about how difficult they find it to relate to their male supervisors who seem to make constant requests for overtime work, which they find both unreasonable and impossible to refuse. The women know they are dependent on these supervisors for outstanding performance evaluations if they want to achieve partnership status in the consulting firm for which they work. The women's reported difficulties place the firm's diversity initiatives at risk and raise the possibility that they may bring suits against the company for discrimination because the supervisors are insensitive to the strains of overtime on working mothers.

Or consider the dilemma of an EAP social worker who, through clients' sharing confidential information, becomes aware that several employees are victims of domestic abuse. There is a threat to the safety of the women and their coworkers posed by the possibility that the spouses or intimate partners will follow their wives or significant others into the workplace. If the situation "explodes," the social worker may be blamed for not sharing a warning with the firm's security service.

Or assume a stream of workers conveying their feelings of stress over their fear of being unable to handle the changing technology. They indicate that they believe that once the new procedures are in place, they will be displaced by younger, more highly educated personnel, and they are angry that their years of loyal service and commitment to the organization are going unrecognized. It is apparent to all of them that they need additional knowledge and skill but no indication has been forthcoming that the organization will supply any training. The social worker is aware of the elevated level of anxiety as the employees are scrambling to find community college courses that may help prepare them for the imminent changeover. The stress of working, going to school, and meeting personal responsibilities

(continued)

has most of them so upset that they have developed many, potentially costly, somatic complaints. This is happening at a time when the rising cost of the experience-rated health care benefit is the subject of a special internal task force led by the benefits director.

Each of these situations is identified in the normal course of EAP practice with individuals. Each may require attention beyond the specific responsibility and expertise of the particular EAP social worker, yet each has systemic implications that the social worker cannot afford to ignore. Collaboration across departments seems a natural route to allow the social worker to participate in problem solving. Management style may be the cause of the women's difficulties, but changing it is beyond what could be initiated by the EAP alone. An alliance, however, with the EEO officer, who is charged with achieving diversity and protecting the organization from suits by discontent employees who feel they are being discriminated against or believe their rights have been violated, might result in some effective organizational response. Perhaps with involvement of the director of training, the three could fashion an educational program that would help insensitive supervisors understand the negative impact of their management style. The workplace is, after all, the tertiary educational institution, following school and family (Eichner 1973).

Without exposing the confidential reports of the abused women, data that benchmark the efforts of other organizations to support the safety of their employees and protect them and the organization from workplace spillover of domestic abuse can be used to raise the need for strategic planning to avoid unexpected violence (Urban & Bennett 1999; Johnson & Indvik 1999). The social worker, while offering confidential in-house counseling, can provide information publicly concerning the prevalence and outcome of domestic violence and can raise the generic issue of internal security. Interdisciplinary collaboration with the security director can evolve a protective plan for the victimized employees of the firm and their coworkers. Such planning recognizes that "the workplace is not a world unto itself," as battered women make their way into the workplace with their problems of absenteeism, lateness, embarrassment, depression, and debilitating injuries (Johnson & Indvik 1999). It is the social worker's contribution to identify the need and facilitate a response.

An even greater degree of prevention is involved in the example of the stress experienced by the workers fearful that they may be facing technological displacement. Here the interests of the medical, benefits, and risk management departments, at least, are involved. A combination of responses is obviously required. Health promotion may be one way to go, allowing workers time to pursue stress reduction. The benefits manager may want to consider a trade-off between dollars for health care and those supporting education and training, believing that skill and its accompanying returned sense of control and empowerment will reduce stress as much as, or more than, stress reduction exercises. The risk manager may suggest finding ways to retire the workers involved, believing that instead of retraining, replacing the aging with new, younger workers is best for the business entity. Into this maelstrom, the EAP worker can arrive to negotiate, coordinate, and facilitate the response. The parties will have to work toward a balance under which the needs of employees, the firm, and the community can all draw on the expertise of an interdisciplinary team in achieving an effective plan that does not cause a sympathetic morale problem among other workers or violate legal requirements for a nondiscriminatory workplace.

Organizational Change Initiatives

The environment for social work and the workplace is clearly in a state of flux, related in many ways to the chaotic internal and external environmental conditions experienced by the world of work. In these environments, change is inevitable, but effective change is not guaranteed. An approach to change starts with the realization that rarely is change welcomed. Although existing circumstances may be painful and disruptive, they are at least known. It is the unknown and its companion, the unexpected, that most people and organizations seek to avoid. It is not unusual, however, that the accomplishment of change is essential to organizational survival. Under these circumstances change can be expected to penetrate all levels, the individual, the organization, and the community. Social work skill and knowledge can help every level to weather change and maximize the benefit from it. Recent practice provides many relevant examples, a case in point being the downsizing and need for reorganization that has plagued so many organizations.

When downsizing is contemplated, an assessment of the situation should be undertaken before the actual event. Social workers participating in such planning can suggest a range of responses to mitigate the impact of downsizing on personnel. The most obvious, if at all possible, is the sharing of honest, precise, and specific information with participants at all levels. People are likely to accept even unpleasant decisions when they participate and feel that they are being treated fairly (Kim &

Mauborgne 1997). Nevertheless, almost all individual organizational actors are likely to find downsizing personally stressful. At the individual level, almost equal amounts, albeit different types, of attention are required by those who are released and those who survive the downsizing. The social worker can provide emotional support for individuals who are released, but very quickly their need for practical help in understanding their benefits, deciding on their preferred career path, organizing their job search, securing baby-sitting services, and other mundane but essential coverage so that they can be available for job interviews will outweigh their psychological counseling requirements. Although employers sometimes provide these services in-house during a period between notice of dismissal and its actual occurrence, most workplaces seek physical separation from the released employee at the earliest possible moment. This has led to the development of outplacement organizations, frequently staffed by social workers, that contract with businesses to perform these tasks for dislocated workers. They provide desk space and reception and telephone services off site to the former employee, while the former employer bears the cost, and thereby help discharged employees have both the location and support they need to secure alternative employment.

But being a survivor of a major downsizing effort does not leave one unscathed. Confidence in management and one's sense of job security may decline; team efforts may be disrupted; guilt may develop concerning those who have lost their jobs, all of which are likely to cause discomfort among those who remain (Buhler 2003; Allen et al. 2001). If their productivity is to be maintained, their morale will need attention. This takes the professional into the realm of mezzo practice. Attention to the organization as client and a response that engages all participants in community building is an approach that social workers are well equipped to orchestrate. Both individual support and organizational activities that convey a message that the organization understands the pain being experienced and wants employees to know they are valued will be essential. Here, too, communication takes on added importance. Participants will place a premium on full and open information and will feel reassured when they know where the organization is heading and what is expected of each of them. In essence, the social worker must help the corporation renew its culture and regain commitment from those who will continue to perform its work.

Depending on the size of the community in relation to the extent of the downsizing, there may be a need to deal with the impact of change on a macro level. During the 1980s when plant closing after plant closing in the rust belt destroyed local communities, anger was appropriately placed at the door of businesses that literally as well as figuratively "folded their tents and escaped into the night." As a result, plant-closing legislation, namely the Worker Adjustment and Retraining Notification Act of 1988, was enacted requiring ninety days' notice before such action could be taken. The message of that legislation should not be lost on businesses undergoing significant downsizing. The impact of severe downsizing extends far beyond plant walls, and the firm that values its customers and its public image will attend to how its behavior is likely to be viewed by the communities in which it operates. Here again social work guidance can be instructive. What kinds of community-based services will be needed by those who have been let go? What information do community planners need to prepare their service delivery systems? Is there a way the company can help sustain the community's capacity to respond? What liaisons should be created? How should the organization position itself with relation to the community?

These questions call on the range of skill, knowledge, and values of social work applied to the work setting. Although downsizing as an example may have negative connotations to some, causing discomfort to the professional who would prefer not to be identified with such an issue, that would be an unfortunate misinterpretation. Good social work in these circumstances should be based on a strengths perspective, responding to the potential and opportunity inherent in change situations, and can be preventive in outcome if strategy is well planned and well implemented. Many examples of change could be offered that might appear more positive yet would meet the same resistance to change, for example, a plan to open an on-site day care center at the workplace. There would be those who fear it as a distraction for workers, a cost center that would take resources away from what they view as more immediate priorities, a possible source of risk of liability, a path that favors some employees and their needs over others, a benefit that reduces the choices open to parents and immobilizes them from job changes because they are loath to disrupt the child care arrangements of their offspring, an initiative that undermines the community's services, and on and on. Regardless of the issue, the suggestion here is that social work participation can help to make change a positive force at all levels of intervention at the workplace (Hopkins & Hyde 2002). The largest obstacle confronting the social worker who would be a "corporate assistant" in the change process is the inherent fear that change inspires in most humans. Perhaps no one in the corporate environment is better equipped to guide an institution through the process of dealing with fear than a trusted social worker using the professional facilitation skills inherent in good practice.

Managed Care

Despite the clear potential of EAPs that are internal to or maintain close relations with a given workplace to serve the organization in a multiplicity of roles, countervailing trends have gradually but consistently narrowed attention, with the result that many workplace services are provided only through large, external, national organizations that handle services for many employers simultaneously. Such a contractual EAP can provide a menu of choices from which a particular business or union selects and contracts for a specific package of the offerings available. Obviously a workplace vantage is a good location from which to provide services to those involved in the world of work, but it is also possible to deliver such services from a private practice position.

One of the intervening variables in the delivery of services to workers through the auspices of the employer, the trade union, or jointly between them has been the growth of managed care. It has both expanded and restricted the potential services and delivery team. In its simplest definition, managed care is merely "any of a variety of mechanisms designed to contain health care costs by assuring that people get the health care they need and do not get health services they do not need" (Friedman, personal communication 2001). Its connection with EAPs is complex. Often mental health care is delivered as a carve-out from the total health care package. This results in moving at least the ongoing counseling, a significant portion of the EAP function, to the control of the insurance company selected to cover the mental health care costs. Managing insured behavioral health care, once the employee/worker is referred, is done by a managed care administrator operating a specialized, criteria-based, computerized system that reviews the needs of each worker and makes referrals to a pool of providers within a scenario of options that focuses the treatment on the most necessary and short term. The operation of managed care involves a network of many private practitioners, day treatment clinics, substance abuse providers, and inpatient facilities that constitute a panel of service providers from which entitled employees may choose or have selected for them a treatment source. Most behavioral health managed care companies engage in a careful screening of those whom they admit to these panels and contract fees with them that are less than customary charges. An underlying assumption is that the quality of care will be maintained as the cost is contained (Langman-Dorwart et al. 1992).

As Austrian (1998: 321) notes, there is some concern, however, "that these [referral] decisions are often made by people who do not know the client, who do not have training in mental health or substance-abuse treatment, and whose main concern is cost containment." Additionally, practitioners delivering these services rarely have direct ties back to the workplace so that an important dimension of service, one that involves the workplace in a systems approach to care and problem resolution, is often lacking. Where workplaces provide a liaison to the EAP that can make the necessary connections, however, and the private practitioners or other network participants are alerted to this avenue, the systems approach is not lost and the managed care representative may improve service by holding the treating professional accountable for quality, timely service. This may also offer a wider array of options than an internal EAP in relation to the characteristics of providers.

Under managed care, some EAPs have evolved into gatekeepers of behavioral health care, and indications are that private practitioners comprise most of the providers to which individuals find themselves referred under the managed care systems. These providers have been recruited and reviewed by personnel working for the managed care company. They have met established criteria for professional training, license, and experience and have agreed to accept the treatment guidelines, billing, and reporting practices and payment schedule of the company on whose panel they agree to serve. The process then involves individuals whose employer has contracted with the EAP for behavioral health services. Such individuals call the EAP requesting care and are screened by a case manager who performs triage under a preestablished computerized decision tree and then either refers the individual to a specific provider or offers the names of several providers from the panel whom the case manager believes will be able to appropriately treat the individual seeking care. In either situation, the selected provider will see the individual and develop a treatment plan for which authorization will be sought from the managed care representative. Most authorizations are for a limited number of sessions (or if triaged to an inpatient facility for a specific, usually brief, number of days), after which the provider either discharges the individual or seeks reauthorization for continuing treatment.

Nothing is inherently wrong with managed care, despite serious complaints about it from many social workers (Barnes 1991). It is merely an attempt to see that people receive the care they need and do not receive (and, therefore, save companies from having to pay for) care that is not needed (Asch & Abelson 1993). Furthermore, the choices of caregivers available through managed care are probably superior to the ones individuals might find for themselves. Most people find professional services through recommendations from family or friends who are no better qualified, and often far less qualified, than the managed care company to make that selection. Difficulties arise in managed care situations when the monitoring is excessive, making it hard for the practitioner to build an in-depth relationship with the consumer of service, when the negotiated price is so low that panel members are available to accept referrals only at relatively inconvenient times when they cannot fill their hours with better-paying clients, or when the panel lacks the diversity necessary to match some individually requested characteristic of the therapist such as geographic location, language ability, or national origin. For most workers and their dependents with more serious mental health conditions, managed care probably offers faster and more extensive access to treatment facilities than might be available without the managed care company serving as an intermediary.

Quite another issue than satisfying the individual needs of the insured individual makes the replacement of EAPs with a system of private practice/managed care provision of service problematic, namely the distance, both actual and conceptual, between the workplace and the provider of care. The initial EAPs were in-house and as such were part of the same system as the workers whom they served. The staff knew the work situation, the supervisor, and the culture of the organization and had the relationships necessary to negotiate helpful accommodations for individuals as they sought to resolve substance abuse and other problems that impeded their ability to meet the required performance standards on the job. If that accommodation required negotiation with the union, the representatives were near at hand. A cooperative spirit existed in the interest of maintaining or returning to work an individual with a problem. The private provider on the panel of the managed care company has no such connection. In fact, a particular worker may be the only employee of the contracting employer that the provider ever serves. With a large panel in place, and many employer contracts, the behavioral health care system that has replaced the in-house EAP may use literally hundreds of providers and make little or no effort to channel those seeking care to particular providers based on the employer of record. As a result, the provider has no knowledge of the workplace system. In fact, there is no requirement that the provider understand the workplace as a criteria for joining a panel, even though all the referrals to the panel providers emanate from a workplace connection. The customary lack of concern about an individual's work experience and environment that pervades the mental health field in general is all too often equally evident in the attitude, behavior, and practice activities of the managed care panel provider. The powerful connection with the workplace that made the EAP effective in helping workers regardless of presenting problem has been lost. Additionally, external EAP providers and their managed care intermediaries rarely gather case data to move toward cause-based action that can create human resource policy change in a positive direction. This is something their internally based predecessors often accomplished.

These losses have been compounded by another development on the managed care scene, namely the structural nature of the system. Earlier in the development of EAPs, many family service agencies and independent contractors developed service delivery systems in response to a corporate or union search for external services. These small contractors were usually local in nature and could be intimately involved with the companies or unions with which they contracted. Informal relationships developed that made service delivery and problem solving easy and responsive to changing needs despite their external location. Over the last decade, contractual EAPs and their related managed care companies have become mammoth operations, often with headquarters in some distant city, to which access is a function of e-mail and other computerized systems. Clearly, social work in the world of work may be losing what has been its greatest strength, that is, in Bertha Reynolds's words (1975), "stationing itself in the natural life space of its clients." The work ahead is to convince both unions and corporations that the maximum effectiveness of workplace practice requires not just the person-in-environment model but being at those crossroads, namely at the workplace or in contact with the workplace.

The Interrelatedness of Community Services and Clients as Workers and the Workplace

None of this should suggest that the impact of social work in the workplace is confined to the workplace. The workplace has not been, nor will it ever be, the major provider of the services required by the 140 million working Americans and their dependents. Workers are both the financial supporters and the predominant customers of most community services. The community and its social and health services are a vital part of the service delivery network to workers and even more so to dependents of active workers and to those who move to retirement status.

Alternatively, the community system cannot function at maximum effectiveness without workplace ties. The not-for-profit sector looks to the workplace for more than financial support and customers. Many social agencies are dependent on the workplace if they are to provide adequate services to their clients. It is the pro bono work of law firms that supplies many of the legal services to indigent populations. School mentoring programs and Big Brothers and Big Sisters support efforts would be all but impossible without volunteers from the world of work who share their time and experience. The operations of many agencies depend for their advice and board leadership on the commitments of corporate executives. Cooperative educational initiatives, welfare-to-work programs and vocational rehabilitation efforts for people with disabilities all depend on internships and ultimately employment from the world of work. It is vital, therefore, that bridges be constructed to help fulfill the mutual interests and needs of the workplace for the community and the community for the workplace. Once again, it is difficult to imagine a better prepared representative on either side of this equation than a social worker with good knowledge and skill in community organizing.

There are many operational examples of this mutuality. The largest single source of support for local community services is the United Way. This federation of agencies is largely a fund-raising vehicle that focuses on the workplace as a major avenue for financial support. Participating agencies agree not to approach the workplace directly on an individual basis. Campaigns are organized in most workplaces, using committees of workers to canvass their coworkers for donations. In unionized settings, the United Way fund often has a paid liaison to a workplace who is assigned to work within a union office and who takes an important role both in making referrals for service and by serving on its allocation committee. In this way the workplace not only determines how much is raised in support of community activities, but how and for whom that money is spent (Brilliant & Rice 1988).

The heavy demand from employed people for child care and elder care services represents yet another dimension of overlap. Workplace EAPs provide information and referral services themselves, or workplaces and unions may contract for work/life information and referral services, but ultimately workers are referred to the community's programs by these specialized purveyors of counseling. For example, the Ford Foundation provides its employees with vouchers (in amounts inversely related to wages) for the purchase of community child care services, the result of its own thorough evaluation of the existing options for best meeting the recognized need of workers for such services. Meanwhile, the workplace provides the more than eight hundred apprenticeship and other on-the-job training programs that support the career path development for millions of American workers who are referred to specific workplaces by the community vocational programs to which they turn to improve their employment potential (U.S. Department of Labor 2000).

Select Examples of the Vital Connections

In a perfect world, all social workers would be alert to the work-related needs of those who seek their services. All community resources would be accessible to anyone who might need service. All workplaces would cooperate in financing community service needs, and effective communication channels would make everyone knowledgeable concerning how to find, secure, or deliver appropriate services responsive to presenting problems and assessed needs. A mere enumeration of these conditions and circumstances is evidence of the fact that we do not have a perfect world. The question then arises as to what are the ingredients of programs that tend to help move toward a more "perfect" world with regard to service delivery. The closing portion of this chapter describes a few model programs and tries to deduce the basis for their achievements.

At Mount Sinai Hospital in New York City, the hospital, as provider of psychiatric services and as employer of a large, relatively unskilled labor force has built a program based on these dual roles. The outpatient mental health clinic provides services directed at vocational outcomes for its consumer population. Lack of any or at least of recent employment experience was identified by social work staff as a major obstacle in achieving placement. In conversations with human resource personnel at the hospital, social workers became aware of how difficult it was for the hospital to fill certain jobs, ranging from laundry and maintenance spots to various semiskilled technician positions. Several causes were identified including the hospital's geographic location, which made it difficult to reach for residents from certain city locations, the 24/7 nature of hospital operation that required personnel at relatively undesired working hours, and the fact that many openings were for unskilled jobs that had a high turnover rate resulting in a constant demand for such workers. These circumstances did not present obstacles to the clinic's patients who lived in the neighborhood, were often interested in only part-time work and were, therefore, available at odd hours, and who viewed any work as a step up on the ladder to employment. An internship program was established, funded by New York State Vocational Educational Services for Individuals with Disabilities (VESID), under which the clinic assessed the employment readiness of its consumers and assigned them to various VESID-funded "internships" combining each consumer's interests and abilities with the hospital's needs. These assignments served as training experiences for the individuals, which developed their skills and offered recent references for their résumés. The "interns" came to represent a pool of pretrained individuals the hospital could draw on for filling jobs on a permanent basis, good jobs that included benefits and union representation. The backup services available from the clinic's therapists, who understood the work environment and the culture of the workplace, and the funding from the state agency, which gained the successful placement of people with disabilities that its mission mandates, assured the success of this supported employment endeavor. All parties benefited from the bridges created between the treatment community and the workplace.

There are similar situations where the service delivery system and the employer and union are not so closely allied. The Family Service Agency in Norfolk, Virginia, was called upon by the U.S. Navy to help it meet the needs of its employees, young seamen. The scenario involved the seamen's newly formed families who were far from home and without the usual supports that might be available upon the arrival of a new baby. A frequent situation found the seamen leaving pregnant wives behind when they shipped out for a six-month rotation of sea duty and coming home to find a baby commanding the attention of their young, inexperienced spouses. Like any father whose work takes him away from home for an extended period and who then tries to reassert his position on return, these men found themselves in conflict situations that they had difficulty understanding. Child and spouse abuse were sometimes the result. The needs assessment carried out by the Norfolk Family Service Agency identified the need for support groups for left-behind spouses, parenting skill training, family counseling, and locations to provide respite care for children of returning seamen so that couples could have an uninterrupted opportunity to renew their relationships. This information became the basis for Family Service Centers provided by most service branches today (Harris 1993).

Another take on the significance of working well with community resources is evident in a motivational group initiative established by the Personal Services Unit (PSU, a MAP) of the Health and Welfare Plan of District Council 37, American Federation of State, County, and Municipal Employees, AFL-CIO. The PSU regularly received referrals from shop stewards of workers who were in job jeopardy because of substance abuse problems. Given the recidivism involved in substance abuse, members often ran out of benefit coverage for appropriate treatment. Community service organizations were unwilling to accept referrals of uncovered workers and were also unwilling to accept any responsibility for the fact that prior treatment had not proved effective in dealing with the problem. PSU managers decided they needed to make better use of community services for this population. They conceived a program under which workers needing treatment for substance abuse were placed in a prereferral motivational group to assess their readiness for making use of their limited treatment benefit. Attendance at group sessions became a prerequisite to referral to a treatment resource as the PSU negotiated with treatment facilities for a better working relationship. As a result of the prescreening, the community resources agreed to assume responsibility for treatment when problems reoccurred, and workers were able to gain the treatment they needed from community resources.

Conclusion

There are practice skills that become evident as one reviews the varied initiatives described throughout this chapter. Perhaps first and foremost is the importance of a work assessment. A model based on research at the Center for Social Policy and Practice in the Workplace at Columbia University offers a useful guide (Akabas & Gates, in review). The paradigm is based on a misspelling of the word "tree," namely TRRE. It suggests the importance of understanding the individual's specific job from the vantage of *task* requirements, *routine* prerequisites, *relationships* involved, and *environment* at the workplace. The work assessment requires the social worker to evaluate how, if at all, the presenting problem (or problems) is influenced by aspects of the job and how changes in the job might alleviate the presenting problem. In this assessment the social worker can learn what about the individual might be changed but also what in the system might change to be responsive to the individual's needs or the needs of many individuals. Prevention should inform the planning process, clarifying the ways in which risks can be reduced and hosts can be strengthened. Moving to the systems level may involve the professional in advocacy skills that rest on a clear understanding not only of the presenting situation but also of the target for advocacy and the basis, in action, law, or social justice, for the social worker's intervention (McGowan 1995). Although negotiation is the recommended stance for achieving results, confrontation may be necessary within the world of work or with the community on behalf of world of work interests.

As the professional in the world of work moves from the individual to the system and the community as a focus of activity, the ability to work in an interdisciplinary environment becomes essential. Knowledge of what others can bring to a situation strengthens not only the potential of their contribution but also the achievement of the outcome sought since often the social worker's role is to facilitate a team effort. Social workers operating at this level of need are challenged to have extensive awareness of the richness of community resources and knowledge of how to use community organizing skills to foster a partnership between them and the world of work. In short, practice in this field requires the professional to go outside the proverbial box, using a full array of knowledge and skills that, although perhaps not unique to social work, are more typical of the professionally trained social worker than of any other professional. The next chapter provides a conceptual and practice example of this holistic view around the problem of disability, an issue that is pervasive in all workplaces and that requires, for appropriate resolution, coordination with many actors both within the world of work and in the greater community.

Study Questions

1. What might the components be of a life cycle approach to services and benefits in the workplace? Can you identify a program response that would be particularly relevant for each age/life status cohort?
2. There is ongoing debate between those who favor a focused, target-specific EAP and those who favor a more activist approach. Which do you support and why?
3. Given that substance abuse is a condition characterized by recidivism, there are those who support a harm-reduction approach on the way to abstinence. Could you advise an employer to maintain at work someone whom you knew was actively abusing substances? Why or why not? What factors might influence your decision?
4. Managed care has its supporters and detractors. Which view seems to provide the most convincing arguments for you and why? What are the advantages and disadvantages you see in a managed care behavioral health system?
5. What do you see as the interrelationships between the workplace and the community service system? Who benefits from this connectedness and in what ways?

CHAPTER 7

Disability as a Metaphor for World of Work Practice

Disability is a pervasive concern in our society. In the previous chapter we describe the presenting problems that tend to assert themselves in the world of work. Here we use one such problem, namely disability, as an issue to demonstrate the holistic, systemic approach in practice development in the world of work. We also explore the role of the community in relation to the world of work's problem solving potential.

There are many definitions of disability based on biological, legal, and social criteria. The World Health Organization (1976) considers disability to be the result of an impairment or abnormality of body structure, appearance, organ, or system functioning. The shortfall in functional performance or activity is the disability, whereas a handicap is the disadvantage that results because the environment is unresponsive. The Americans with Disability Act of 1990 on the other hand defines disability in relation to functional capacity, that is, disability is an impairment that results in limitation in a major life activity such as dressing, walking, eating, communicating, or working; having a history of such an impairment; or being perceived as having such an impairment. The Social Security Act defines disability (in relation to eligibility for Social Security Disability Insurance payments) as the inability to engage in substantial gainful employment any place in the economy, specifically inability to earn more than five hundred dollars per month after deducting for work-related expenses. Under such a definition, the status of being blind is not a disability while being blind and unable to earn a sum equal to the substantial gainful employment rate qualifies as a disability. To complicate the situation further, state workers' compensation and disability laws and insurance disability policies are likely to offer different specifications for eligibility for payment based on a finding of disability and to differ by each state and insurance company. Distinctions are made, as well, between temporary and permanent disability and between partial and total disability and every combination thereof. For Social Security Disability Insurance recipients, for example, their disability must be expected to last for more than a year or end in death, meaning that the disability must be fairly permanent and total. Yet under new legislation, the Ticket to Work and Work Incentives Improvement Act of 1999, these "permanently disabled" individuals are the target of return-to-work efforts and are encouraged to access a "ticket to work" that will make them eligible for a rehabilitation program, the provider of which is only paid when the individual returns to work, thereby making the disability somewhat less than permanent.

Disability, in other words, is in the eyes of the beholder.

Disability is an important civil rights issue because of the stigma and discrimination that sometimes follow the existence of a disability. Visible differences are disabilities when the observers who view the differences perceive them as a limitation. Individuals with such visible differences have a disability by social construction because, despite the individual's successful adaptation that overcomes the limitation, the mere existence of the perceived difference defines the person, in social terms, as being disabled. Many people who are blind or hearing or cognitively impaired, experiencing mental health problems, or with limited mobility may be labeled disabled by social construction despite their impressive functional capacity and successful accommodation to their functional limitation.

It is almost impossible for a family to be untouched by the issue of disability. A child may be born with a congenital disability, or an adult family member through accident or the onset of illness may develop a disability, or an elderly relative may experience disability as a result of the diminished capacity caused by the aging process. In an era in which it is estimated that workers are likely to be caring for more parents than children, the likelihood that disability will effect the family of every worker at some time during his or her working years is extremely high. The estimate that 47 million Americans have an impairment that causes limitations in some major life activity merely confirms this reality (LaPlante 1991).

For the world of work, an encounter with disability comes in many guises. When a worker is hired, family members are not screened for disabling conditions. The new hire may be in perfect health yet have one or more dependents with a serious disability that may have an impact on the employer's health care costs or the consistency of the employee's availability for work. For example, the largest single cost of employer-provided psychiatric care involves care to adolescent dependents. Workers themselves may experience the onset of disability in the course of employment. Sometimes the disability grows out of a work-connected accident or illness. When that occurs, a workers' compensation claim is filed against the employer. Many organizations have established disability management initiatives to deal with these work-related incidents (Gates, Taler, & Akabas 1989). Of course, disability is not solely a result of work-connected events. Sometimes disabilities resulting from other causes are included as well. Car, motorcycle, or boating accidents and their concomitant long-term or permanent disabilities are commonplace among employees. The problem of breast or other cancer may involve even young working adults. As the workforce ages, and we all know the speed with which that is occurring among the baby boomers who are now in their fifth or sixth decade of life, the incidence of disability from causes unconnected to work will become more frequent and is likely to be progressively serious in its outcome. The stresses of the kinetically changing work world have generated mental health and substance abuse problems in large numbers, some of which are severely disabling. By law and public policy, furthermore, employing organizations are being pressured to add people with disabilities to their employee rosters. In short, the variety and causes of disabling conditions with workplace consequences are almost unlimited (Asch & Mudrick 1995).

Disability is a major cost item for many employers. It results in absenteeism and uncertainty of the labor supply, which are known to interfere with scheduling, productivity, and profitability for the employing organization. Needs for accommodation can raise issues within the work group that effect morale and cause conflict among workers (Akabas & Gates 1997). It can increase the dollars that must be devoted to health and other insurance coverage. Because it has been the basis for discrimination in employment, there are now legal mandates in the Americans with Disabilities Act of 1990 and other federal regulations for work organizations concerning how to respond to disability among applicants and employees. Violation of these requirements can result in costly court battles. Disability is also the issue among workers that, according to union executives, commands the largest share of their daily attention and generates a significant number of grievances (Mudrick 1991; Hopkins 1997).

Consider the following presenting problem.

CASE EXAMPLE: JOHN, A WORKER FACING TROUBLE

John, a warehouse worker, has a long history with the company. In his early fifties, he comes to you as the EAP director for advice. He has been diagnosed with progressive bone cancer but does not want anyone to know

(*continued*)

except you. He is receiving medication, and the doctors have told him that although his physical strength will be reduced, he should be able to live for a long time despite the cancer and that his main life restriction at this time is not to lift weights of more than twenty pounds.

You have an excellent relationship with the human resource director, and on other occasions you have been able to ask for reassignment of an individual, indicating that you have convincing evidence for its need, without having to expose any specific information. Can you do so for John and on what basis? What laws would be relevant?

Imagine that you succeed and that John remains in the warehouse but work is reassigned so he does largely clerical work and his coworkers pick up the slack in the heavy lifting. They complain to the union. A call comes from the HR director that she is sending the union rep down to see you and that all she has told him is that the reassignment was made at your request based on information you did not share but that the HR director regarded as reliable because of your past history.

How do you handle the union representative? Are your actions limited in any way by law? If yes, which actions and in what way? What would your responsibility be if you were the union representative?

The inclusion of people with disabilities in the workforce has an important positive impact as well. It is an opportunity to increase labor force diversity and can lead to improved understanding of the needs of and communication with a wide variety of consumers (Mor Barak 2000a). An appropriate response to an employee with a disability can demonstrate, in real terms, the caring attitude of management, encouraging loyalty, commitment, and productivity from all employees. Disability among employees creates the circumstances for the introduction of a systemic approach to an issue that can set a pattern for improved human resource management and can have an impact on controlling not only its costs but health care expenses in general. Pursuit of these outcomes can involve the organization in many boundary-bridging activities that result in varied contacts with community practitioners and policy advocates. They provide opportunity for interest-driven corporate philanthropy, allowing an employer to contribute to agencies that provide community services to people with disabilities while at the same time arranging support for a community organization that can serve the needs of the employing organization (Marx 1996). Disability training can provide an exemplary subject for improving supervisory skills and understanding (Akabas 1995b; Akabas & Gates 1993).

The pervasiveness of disability means that there are many ways in which it affects the workplace and all of these create streams of activity for the social worker, whether in the workplace, related to the workplace, seeking to establish a relationship to the workplace, or in a community agency serving a worker or an employed person's dependent. In handling these issues, a social worker can work internally within the workplace, from the workplace out into the community, and from the community back into the workplace. Equally likely are the opportunities disability presents to gain support of the workplace for community endeavors. Because of this wide range of potential interaction, the disability issue represents an excellent analog for examining the interconnections between workplace and community in both the policy and practice arenas. The remainder of this chapter is devoted to exploring these possibilities, starting first with the internal world of the employing organization and then looking externally at how the professional practicing in the community can be involved by the workplace, can involve the workplace, or can look for support of community activities by making a connection to the world of work.

Internal Roles for the Social Worker

Clearly, employees either arrive at the workplace with a disability connection or disability is an event waiting to happen to each employee or within each employee's family. Thus disability may present in the workplace with varying scenarios—an individual employee like John seeking counseling from the EAP concerning strategy for negotiating a job accommodation under the ADA, questions from a task force considering policy around elder care, a supervisor requesting leave to attend to the needs of a sick mother under FMLA, the health care costs involved in the birth of an employee's special needs child, requests from a community psychiatric rehabilitation program for a corporate donation or a job opportunity for one of its clients (Akabas & Gates 1993). Yet, in most work organizations, responsibility for disability as an issue is unassigned. It is both everyone's business and no one's business, making it turf for social workers to take a leadership role. It certainly represents turf appropriate to a social work agenda (like work/family issues, affirmative recruitment, preretirement planning, facilitating teamwork, and numerous other organizational concerns) and one for which social workers are, or should be, trained to respond (Weiner, Akabas, & Sommer 1973).

First, disability is a practice concern calling for direct service. Disability may be disruptive of work, family relationships, other aspects of living, or all three. A worker may need health care advice, work accommodation, or assistance in communicating needs. Second, disability is an issue of workplace policy. A systematic response to disability issues requires the involvement of many different units including risk management, the usual department for workers' compensation coverage; medical, where the determination of return-to-work readiness is made for those who lose time from work because of disability; legal counsel, who determines the application of requests for Family and Medical Leave Act coverage; and the comptroller's office, which tracks the costs of various disability income maintenance programs, to name just a few. Where a union is present, the issue may be dealt with in the collective bargaining agreement, making disability a concern for industrial relations. Further, disability warrants program development attention. Following appropriate needs assessment, the social worker might determine the need to facilitate a support group for employees who are parents of children with disabilities or to organize employees into a volunteer corps to provide friendly visiting to retired homebound pensioners. Each of these disability related programmatic responses represents a solution familiar to social workers and provides an option for professional attention and the opportunity to serve as a change agent in an employment system where a vacuum exists in service coverage (Black 1994). But disability is only a metaphor. Using another issue, such as work/family tensions, the reader could engage in a similar analysis leading to individual service, policy, and program development solution sets.

Direct Practice

Underlying any action by the social worker should be awareness of his or her own response to disability as well as knowledge of the various laws that might influence choices of action. Too often disability is seen as a biological issue that should be dealt with in relation to the options in a medical model (Fine and Asch 1988). Social workers are accustomed to serving as part of a team that looks at the "problem" of disability and the "opportunity" to fix it. While certainly one would want to make all possible medical care available, one would be outdated and inappropriate to decide to deal with disability as a medical issue alone (Mackelprang & Salsgiver 1996). People with disabilities have positioned themselves as an oppressed minority for whom disability is just one of their many personal characteristics, albeit the one on which society may focus to treat them as incapacitated and dependent (Shapiro 1993; Hockenberry 1995). For several decades now there has been increasing understanding of disability as a social construct and the responsibility for dealing with disability not as a social welfare issue but as a diversity issue that warrants unconditional fulfillment of the rights of individuals not unlike the concerns around workplace response to people of color or those who are gay. Increasingly, the word *consumer* has been utilized to describe the person with disability who seeks service. This label conveys not only the individual's rights but also the responsibility of the professional to be sensitive to those rights in a competitive world where the person with disability can go elsewhere to "buy" services if the particular professional offering those services is not meeting the consumer's (customer's) demands and expectations (Tower 1994).

Policy

Historically, disability as a public policy issue fell under the rubric of support for the worthy poor, and the response was focused on income maintenance support through workers' compensation, a "no fault" insurance to those injured at the workplace, through Social Security Disability Insurance (SSDI) for workers whose disability made it impossible for them to continue any "substantial gainful employment," and through Supplemental Security Income for those who, because of disability, never developed a viable connection with a workplace that resulted in Social Security coverage. Additionally, federally supported but state-administered vocational rehabilitation programs offered some training for people with disabilities who might be rendered employable by such training (Bevilacqua 1999).

But disability has received more extensive public policy attention recently. Emboldened by the successful demands of other minorities for independence and the protection of their civil rights, people with disabilities, as the largest single minority (Gliedman & Roth 1980), united to claim protection from discrimination in their interactions with various societal systems. Most relevant to the workplace are several pieces of legislation. The Individuals with Disabilities Education Act (IDEA) assures children assessment, evaluation, due process, and the right to free public education in the least restrictive environment, thereby assisting people with disabilities to be at the same educational starting gate as other future labor market participants. The 1990 Americans with Disabilities Act (ADA) through its Title 1, prohibits discrimination by employers of fifteen or more employees in all aspects of employment (job application, hiring, advancement, discharge, compensation, and other terms and conditions of employment) against a qualified individual with a disability who can perform the essential functions of a particular job when provided with reasonable accommodation that does not represent an undue hardship to the employer. The same legislation bars unions from discriminatory practices in relation to membership rights and union representation. Additional protection stems from the Family and Medical Leave Act of 1993, which provides that a worker in a work organization that has more than fifty employees within a seventy-five-mile radius, who is in need of leave for his or her own or a family member's health condition, may take up to twelve weeks per year without pay but with continuing health benefit coverage and guaranteed rights to return to the same or similar job. Additionally, some states, namely New York, New Jersey, Rhode Island, California, and Hawaii, provide short-term income maintenance (usually up to twenty-six weeks of coverage) for short-term leave when an individual is unable to work because of a disability. Of course, the Social Security Act through its disability benefits insurance offers long-term income support for those former workers who qualify as being unable to earn substantial gainful employment income as a result of disability that has lasted for six months and is expected to last for more than a year or to end in death. Social workers are in a position to help people understand these laws and help integrate legal requirements with any disability policy or income maintenance program at the particular workplace. They also can provide guidance in developing a structural response to the legal requirements and can offer advocacy to assist those individuals whose rights are inadequately supported.

An interesting alternative aspect of the link between disability and the workplace has emerged in the last few years. The public policy of moving large segments of the population—those on welfare, those with mental health conditions as well as other disabilities, those with a history of substance abuse and incarceration—from dependency to work has placed demands at the door of employers to open work opportunities. For employers, being able to respond to the needs of these unfamiliar populations has made the possible contribution of social work clear.

The Mix of Policy, Program Development, and Direct Practice

Given this varied agenda concerning disability at the workplace, the potential for social work action is worth reviewing. Consider for a moment the experience of employees whose onset of disability occurs while working, either because they sustain a disabling injury or illness or have a condition that worsens causing the disability to interfere with continued employment on their present jobs. Or consider others for whom a change in technology occurs that makes their disability more troublesome in performing their existing assignment. In these circumstances, an individual who the day before was meeting the requirements of the job, now may face an inability to do so. Such a person is likely to experience a sense of loss and vulnerability, deterioration of self-image, fear, anger, uncertainty, and other negative psychological responses along with a determination to overcome the problem. In the period of turmoil immediately following the change of situation, the individual continues to see him- or herself as a worker. But if that status is not secure, the person begins to experience anger and isolation. The worker may wonder, will I be rewarded for my prior years of service by some accommodation to my or the workplace's new circumstances?

A process begins to evolve in which the individual seeks to resolve ambiguity. The longer the time that elapses between the occurrence of disability and contact by someone from the workplace who has credibility and the power to negotiate a suitable alternative arrangement, the more likely the individual is to interpret the situation as threatening to his or her status as worker. The eventual outcome of inaction by the employing organization is that a productive worker is turned into an unemployed person with a "disability mentality"—that is, a mindset that reduces employment expectations and seeks, as an alternative, protection for the family's financial situation. A focus on benefits takes the place of the commitment to work. For most employers the development of a disability mentality in an employee is a costly outcome. It means that considerable fiscal resources must be allocated to a reserve fund to protect against future costs of long-term disability, in short, money thrown out. The important issue is that the choice is the employer's to make. The way the employer deals with a newly disabled individual is all-important. A policy that manages disability throughout the system can avoid not only the cost of the reserve account and the loss of a good worker but also the morale downer that spreads through a workforce when a good worker is ignored (Akabas & Gates 1993).

These truths are obvious to social workers, who can use their internal position to provide leadership to the development of a disability management initiative. At the very least, there is a chance for an EAP staffer or a social worker in human resources perhaps administering the organization's diversity effort to deliver direct services by contacting the individual and providing counseling and case management services. But assuming that internally employed social workers will have ties with many different units within the organization and will have built sufficient social capital so that they can gather information and support for their suggestions, or that they actually carry that responsibility as the corporate EEO officer, they are in an ideal position to proceed with policy and program development. The first step in assuming a policy role is to carry out a needs assessment to find out what the system is currently doing about disability and where the gaps are that account for high human and fiscal loss. This will certainly involve human resources, medical, risk management, legal and benefits representatives, and perhaps someone from industrial relations in a mutual exploration of issues and costs generated by disability. In settings with collective bargaining agreements, the union should be included in this needs assessment and in all policy and program action that flows thereafter.

The next step is to captivate those and others within the system identified as having some interest in the issue to join in an initiative to respond programmatically and together to establish a policy and coordinating team for doing so. In this effort, the social worker may be guided by the advice of Brager and Holloway (1978) who note that one is most likely to accomplish organizational change if not seeking credit for it. This initial stage toward establishing disability policy and procedures is similar to what a social worker might do to achieve any organizational change in a system. A Lewinian force field analysis (1951) that calls for the identification of promoting and restraining forces in the field can be a helpful tool in understanding how to influence the system. Ultimately, policy guidelines should include

an assumption that the individual wants to and can be at work, and the employer is interested in sustaining, at work, the individual experiencing disability,

an understanding that the worker with the disability is in a frightening and threatening situation that requires support and that support will be available through the workplace,

a belief that a total system that involves all potential parties will avoid splintered responses and will provide objective, consistent, fair solutions to the variety of presenting problems,

knowledge that flexibility will be essential to creating favorable outcomes and that transitional employment and accommodation are available,

an assurance that everyone communicates so that all options are explored and that all can contribute to the solution, and

a realization that money spent up-front usually provides the least costly answer over the long term.

The implementation stage calls on an even greater array of social work skills to assure an appropriate program development (Mudrick 1991;

Akabas and Gates 1997). The workplace culture must establish a means for finding, early, those who may require attention around disability. Likely sources for such case finding include attendance records, safety and accident reports, filings for extensive health care, workers' compensation, and short-term disability claims, requests for family and medical leave, and sometimes grievance cases under collective bargaining contract provisions. Supervisors need to be trained to identify when individuals already working with a disability seem to be experiencing increased difficulty in job performance or when a planned change in technology might be expected to cause such difficulty for an employee with a disability. These efforts at case finding establish the circumstances under which to provide policies and services for the varying issues that may arise in relation to job, finances, health care, and family when disability occurs. At the same time, procedures need to be developed to establish employment options, to provide accommodation, or to resolve any other job maintenance or return-to-work needs. Throughout, such efforts should respect the right of the employees to make choices based on their own evaluations of the situation and should assure the maximum confidentiality possible when requested by the employee.

Case management services are the bread and butter of social work practice. Providing such services within the functional community of the workplace allows one to marshal resources that can be the envy of any professional trying to serve a consumer without the benefit of such a connection. Here flexibility in response is essential. It does no good to pay someone to stay at home, yet that is the usual corporate policy. Options such as part-time return to work, return to an alternative job for a work-hardening period, family support, and a multitude of other interventions can assure the retention of a valued employee and minimize the cost involved. For example, one of the authors provided disability management consultation to a large steel mill with a 10 percent absence rate due to disability. This required the mill to employ 110 percent of the labor force actually needed for staffing the production process. A culture had evolved to keep out on disability any employee not able to perform 100 percent of the job requirements, a very costly solution. Some employees felt disability was a free ticket to a vacation, but most reported feeling depressed and isolated during their enforced leave. This occurred at a time when the mill was switching over to computerized production, and at the consultant's advice a decision was made to try to change the culture of the workplace to make those workers experiencing disability feel that they were needed even when they had a functional limitation. As a result, all employees absent because of disability, who could manage to sit, were offered an option to receive training on computers and full pay while doing so instead of the proportional payments typical of workers' compensation and disability benefits for staying home. Almost everyone out on disability chose to take advantage of the opportunity. In the end, they were trained ahead of their coworkers. Their training costs were modest, representing only the difference between their rate of workers' compensation and full pay since the mill was self-insured. To train everyone else, employees had to be taken off line at a training cost of full pay for each day of training. Additionally, those with disabilities who were trained were able to provide leadership to their respective departments on return to work rather than finding themselves inconsequential in a workplace that had, in their absence, adopted new systems with which they were unfamiliar.

Once the disability management system is in place, maintenance needs warrant attention. New tasks have been assigned to supervisors and others throughout the system that necessitate training. Design should include someone from the training department and representation from employee/consumers so that the training is imbedded in the system and reflects the real experience of people with disabilities. Furthermore, a management information recording system needs to be established to monitor and evaluate the operation and eventually to establish the cost-benefit record of the initiative. Involving the internal computer gurus can be helpful at this juncture if not earlier. Finally, the collected data can be analyzed as a source of information for designing a prevention system. Social workers are uniquely able to lead such a systemic initiative because the various tasks call on exactly the modalities of intervention underlying the profession's competencies along with the ability to facilitate and negotiate group outcomes (Black 1994; Akabas & Bikson 2001). Although the preceding assumes that social work has an internal position within the work organization, it is possible for the roles described to fall under the purview of a professional working under contract with a particular workplace. In such circumstances, the activities described represent a "product" that the contracting firm can "sell" to the interested employing organization, allowing the social worker to serve as an organizational change consultant (Akabas & Gates 2002).

Opportunities for Making Connections from the Community into the Workplace

Consider the presenting problems in the following case.

MARIE SANTOS, A MOTHER WITH PROBLEMS

Marie Santos is a thirty-five-year-old divorced mother of two children, ages nine and seven. Marie's former husband had been very faithful about meeting his financial obligations since their divorce. The settlement gave her 50 percent of his earnings, up to twenty thousand dollars a year. Marie has managed to scrape along on that since her divorce. She has not worked since a few months before her first child was born. She has never felt comfortable leaving her children with anyone else, particularly since the older daughter suffers from severe asthma. Now, she has little choice since her child care payments are endangered because her former husband had a car accident recently. His injuries are serious and he is not expected to be able to return to his work as an electrician for at least one year. She does not wish to press him for payments because he was so dependable about them when he was employed and now his disability payments will not be sufficient to cover even his expenses. Marie rejects any thought of seeking public assistance.

Marie worked as a receptionist in a law office from the time she graduated high school until her daughter's birth. The pay was good but it never instilled any confidence in her because she feels that the job merely required her to look pretty and greet people pleasantly. She feels her present appearance (she has gained fifty pounds since her first delivery), lack of appropriate clothes, and absence of any real skills or knowledge of new technologies like computers make her undesirable as an employee. She is despairing of ever finding a job that she will enjoy or one that will give her even the minimum income she requires to take care of her family.

Other problems plague Marie as well. Her mother, who was an important backup for her, moved back to Italy to take care of her own aging parents just last year. Marie feels lonely and lost without her. She has few friends and feels she does not have any alternative caretaking possibilities for her daughters. She is only interested in a job that will get her home by the time school closes. The teacher called her recently to ask if everything was all right at home because her younger daughter has become very withdrawn in school and seems to be having trouble reading, a problem that was not identified in the previous year. Marie finds herself crying frequently, overwhelmed, and discouraged.

You are a social worker in a community mental health program and you have just done an intake on Marie who has come seeking service. What are the presenting problems in this case? What else do you need to know?

(continued)

Where might you gain this information? What other community resources, if any, will be needed to meet Marie's needs? Assume that there are many people with problems comparable to those presented by Marie. What kind of program development and policy advocacy would you recommend to provide prevention, deliver services, and offer rehabilitation?

Practitioners in community social service organizations too often pay little or no attention to the work, or potential for work, of their clients. The professional literature provides rare examples of discussion of the significance of work in people's lives or the practice involved in helping secure employment for those who are customarily excluded from participation in the workplace. One of the many results of this isolation is apparent in the fact that fewer than a third of people with a disability are competitively employed, and for people with mental health conditions the record is even more abysmal. Yet studies of people with disabilities repeatedly find that more than two-thirds of those who are unemployed have a strong desire, and the ability, to work (Harris & Associates 1995; White 2000). A likely cause of this unemployment is the separation of the typical community social worker from the world of work. The remedy is to "think work" for every person receiving service. This does not mean that people should be forced to work. But just because they have a disability, neither should they be condemned to dependency and a lifetime at the poverty level that the safety net of government benefits provides to recipients. Nor should they be robbed of the sense of accomplishment and self-efficacy that work provides. People with disabilities should be able to receive appropriate help and support from their service provider if they wish to be employed. Too often this scenario completely escapes the practice of the community-based social worker. A startling example of this gap in professional sensitivity occurred recently.

One of the authors was invited to make a presentation to the social work department of a world-famous rehabilitation hospital on how to introduce a discussion of work into practice with clients. Ten minutes into the presentation, it was clear the audience had not been captured. The presenter stopped and asked for help in understanding the lack of interest. A senior staffer responded, "We are too busy securing benefits to keep our patients eating to spend time thinking about helping them find employment." This realistic but limited vision provided a good starting point for discussion. Were there any patients who had a recent history of work to which they might return? Were there any patients who were not dependent on benefits and had a secure financial position that might remain so even if they returned to work? Were there any patients for whom a lifetime on benefits would be self-destructive?

The perfect case emerged. John was a twenty-five-year-old year old former bank computer technician who had been severely injured in an automobile accident in which both his parents had been killed and his two younger siblings had sustained serious though not life-threatening injuries. John's left leg had been amputated and the other severely compromised. Increasingly depressed, and confined to a wheelchair, his one desire was to gain custody of his younger siblings. The children all agreed on this goal. They were being thwarted by the courts and their maternal grandmother, both of whom pointed to John's present situation as evidence that he could not support a family.

Eventually a significant financial settlement was expected in the death claim so that finances were not a major concern. Furthermore, John's employer had remained in contact with him, and he was receiving full pay under their disability plan, which would continue for two years. Yet no one had explored the possibilities of John's return to work. Discussion identified that the courts were likely to view a return to work as major evidence of John's future ability to sustain his family. Additionally, work could serve as a goal that might help redress John's depression. Excitement was generated around this planning and by the end of the session the director of the hospital, who had been sitting in on the discussion, summarized the general consensus:

- not talking about work carries a message to patients that we do not think they are capable of return to work
- discussion of work does not have to take extensive time, but rather can be ongoing content in helping patients talk about themselves and their benefit eligibility
- in reality, a life dependent on benefits is a life condemned to living in poverty
- return to functional performance is the main intent of a rehabilitation service
- for those patients who were working just prior to hospitalization, return to work should be at the top of the agenda and patients are poorly served when this is ignored
- for all patients, a rehabilitation hospital should be fostering a functional outlook rather than serving to create a disability mentality

John's situation exemplifies the dilemmas faced by social work. As a profession, social work has paid little attention to the outcome of work, believing that, as advocates, their priority is to secure benefits. It can be argued that this has been a disservice to the populations being served. Focusing on securing benefits as the long term goal has reduced clients' options and has nurtured a "benefit mentality" among professionals and consumers. As cutbacks in welfare have occurred, for example, the profession's outcry has been marshaled appropriately against the cuts in benefits. But evidence of a comparable outrage concerning the lack of enforcement of the ADA, of funds for training, and of the development of jobs that would support families has been scanty.

Consider what might have happened to John and his family if, from the first, the social worker had considered return to work as the major goal for him. First, she would have to know the extent of John's interest in returning to work. This discussion with John might provide a positive focus to his counseling sessions and mitigate the depression he experienced by paying attention to the strengths he still has rather than attending to reconciling him to the losses he has suffered. Assuming that the discussion made John feel competent, she could then develop a strategy with him. Contact with his employer and discussion concerning John's readiness and interest in return to work, by John, by his social worker, or by both together, could then result in a joint effort with a workplace representative. A review of the tasks, routines, relationships, and physical environment involved in John's job description and an assessment of his present functional capacity as related to those job requirements would follow. John, his social worker, and probably his supervisor could identify the accommodations that might need to be made in each of the aspects of TRRE (see chap. 6) task, routine, relationship, and environment (Neff 1985) that would foster John's return to work. Planning could establish a process that would revise the work space so that John, in a wheelchair, could function independently. Establishing a graduated work schedule would begin a work-hardening process by which he would gradually increase his hours at work. The employer would gain productivity for wages rather than paying John full earnings as disability benefits to stay in the hospital. Coworkers would feel better about John, seeing him at work rather than having to visit him in the hospital, and better about their employer who has been helpful to John. The social worker has learned a little about dealing with parties at the workplace. She has served John and additionally has built a relationship with the employer that could be parlayed into jobs for other patients at the rehabilitation center or into the bank's philanthropic support for a service-delivery program of the rehabilitation hospital. But most of all, John would have clear evidence to present to the court and his grandmother of his capacity to sustain his family both psychologically and financially. The win-win situation is the outcome of a social worker moving from the community agency back into the workplace.

As our national policy causes benefit recipients to look over their shoulders constantly to assure themselves that they are not exceeding the allowable earnings level or the time allowed for a time-limited benefit status, work is increasingly an important opportunity for community social workers to seek for their clients. The handwriting is on the wall. Clients who depend on benefits for subsistence are under threats that can be expected to escalate. They will be degraded constantly by public pressure to seek employment. This alone might be reason to help them explore the work option. But a more important argument concerns their well-being. All measures of quality of life and evaluations of mental health demonstrate that work makes an important contribution to personal satisfaction, health, and happiness and does not result, as has long been believed, in decompensation for people, even those with serious and persistent mental illness (Bond et al. 2001). It is vital that the profession play catch-up in this regard. Social workers need to believe not only that work is important in people's lives but also that entitlement to a financially and emotionally fulfilling job is an outcome worthy of constant attention from the social work profession. Such an attitude also creates an opportunity for a two-way interaction between social workers in the employing organization and those in the community agency.

Because of its interest in treatment of those with serious and persistent mental health conditions, the profession has staked a place for itself in the mental health arena. As Vourlekis et al. (1998: 567) note, "The rise of social work in public mental health through aftercare of people with serious mental illnesses illustrated the important reality that strengthening a profession takes place by creating turf, not just defending it." Mental health issues are one of the most accessible avenues on which social workers in and out of the workplace can, and increasingly do, meet. And an alliance between in-house and community social workers is clearly vital if the employment of people with serious and persistent mental illness is to be expanded. Research has verified that regardless of diagnosis or symptoms, people with a serious mental health condition can work provided that the symptoms are stable and they can establish a block of time each day during which they can work (Akabas & Gates 2000). Research also has shown that such people require accommodation and ongoing support to be able to sustain work (Bond 1998).

The role of social workers in the workplace is as agents of change. They need to serve as negotiator/facilitator, educator/trainer, and counselor/ advocate. Each role is a well-traveled road for the professional. Not unlike the work of providing leadership to establishing a systemic response to disability in the role of an internal social worker, similar tasks have to be completed to succeed as a change agent in bridging systems between the community and the workplace. First, the internal social worker must negotiate an opportunity for the parties to meet and facilitate their communication. Reducing the stigma that employers may attribute to a mental health condition and the fear of disclosure that consumers hold and that providers customarily support can help establish the conditions necessary for communication among the parties. Thereafter, the provider needs education in workplace concerns and what is meant by a "qualified" employee and training in understanding the needs, expectations, and language of the workplace. The work organization needs education about the skills, knowledge, and potential contribution of qualified people with mental health conditions who are well matched with the requirements of the job. Eventually, supervisors and coworkers need training on the provisions of relevant laws, for example, the ADA and FMLA, and how to establish and accept any "reasonable" accommodation that may be indicated. The final components of the change agent's role are to provide counseling to all parties, to serve as advocate for the process of identifying and implementing accommodation for the individual, and to maintain the bridge that allows the provider to continue ongoing support to sustain the employee with the mental health condition as the job or the employee's circumstances change.

A search for mutual interests suggests that both employers and providers can benefit, each in their separate ways, by achieving employment for people with mental health conditions. Employers, faced with a responsibility to achieve diversity in the labor force and a need for workers who are reliable and can get the job done, are well served by employing qualified workers with disabilities, including those with mental health conditions. The interests of service providers are furthered when they can gain access to jobs, thereby allowing them to respond to consumers' needs and interests in employment. The question this poses is how can the systems communicate with each other so that employment (their mutual interest) can be the outcome. The matchmakers can be the social workers contractually connected to or at the workplace. They can offer introductions to the workplace to providers, reassurance to the human resource representative concerning the competence of people with mental health conditions that will mitigate the stigma attributed to mental health conditions, and protection to the employer from charges of discrimination under the Americans with Disabilities Act. In partnership with the community agency representative, they can organize an educational intervention for the workplace and an ongoing support system for the employed person with the mental health condition.

A project conducted by the Workplace Center of Columbia University School of Social Work, concerned with the workplace consequences of serious and persistent mental illness identified the need for understanding and acceptance of the "special" treatment represented by an accommodation. The center offered an innovative strategy for solidifying employment relationships (Gates, Akabas, & Oran-Sabia 1998). Based on earlier research findings that identified accommodation as a social process rather than a technical effort as it is usually treated (Gates 2000), the center staff tested a psycho-education intervention that involves the coworkers, the supervisors, and the workplace representatives who can sanction accommodation in an effort to develop social support for it. After an individual secured employment, but before any resentment arose as to the impact of accommodation on the work assignments or consideration required from coworkers, the coworker group was called together with the new employee and the community social worker (of course with the informed consent of the individual with the mental health condition). The psycho-education session has several components, including:

a general discussion of the nature of mental health conditions and their symptoms
a review of the provisions of the ADA
an exchange on the generic nature of accommodation to normalize the accommodation process
an exercise in identifying appropriate accommodation
an explanation of the particular individual's need for accommodation

The process is a powerful intervention that attacks the myths about people with mental health conditions. It also reduces fear and isolation and provides understanding about the accommodation process, which reduces the possibility of resentment and jealousy that arise because the accommodation is often viewed as undeserved and unfair and is misunderstood as "special" treatment. The outcome usually is social support from coworkers and supervisors who comprise the natural system at the workplace. That support, in turn, provides the necessary and sufficient conditions for sustained successful employment of the individual with a mental health condition.

* * *

This chapter uses disability as the metaphor for describing the rich opportunity for social workers in the workplace to provide leadership around issues that are their typical terrain, to serve as the point of access in helping individual clients who need assistance, and to act as a connecting link in a bridge designed to establish a more purposeful relationship between the community professional and the workplace. It is possible to substitute many other aspects of social work practice as equally relevant examples of issues that lead to similar opportunities. The reader has only to consider the field of family and children's services or the arena of contemporary urban problems such as AIDS, incarceration, and substance abuse or the issues facing the increasingly large cohort of aging individuals, to name just a few. Following the example offered in relation to disability, the social worker can help the work organization identify similar ways in which the workplace can respond, in its own interest, to develop systems within the work organization and to establish relationships with community agencies to deal with one of these themes. For example, contemporary urban problems present themselves in every work organization. What does the organization need to do to understand the problem, to identify its impact on the organization, to identify the options available for dealing with the problem both internally and by creating connections to the community of social agencies? How can the social worker become a key actor in developing the response?

The turf represented by these social welfare–related issues often sits in an organizational vacuum waiting for some group to claim it as territory. The profession of social work has an affinity for this domain. It waits only for the practitioner to be assertive and effective in dealing with the possibilities. This means that social workers have to go outside the proverbial box to seize the opportunity, to think and act as generalists, using the full array of knowledge and skills to which they have access. It offers the challenge to be not only do-gooders but good doers. Can we afford to ignore this opportunity?

Study Questions

1. "Disability" has various definitions. Is there a definition that makes the most sense for a workplace trying to develop a consistent response to the issue? If yes, which is it? If not, how would you handle the need for a definition in offering guidance to a workplace?

2. Public policy concerning people with disabilities places many responsibilities on the world of work. If you were a consultant to a work organization (union or employer) what advice would you offer concerning the implica-

tions of laws for organizational action? What roles are available for social workers to assume in these systems?

3. The authors argue that employment for people with mental health conditions represents a mutual interest arena for coordinated effort by the workplace and the community. What is the division of labor you would suggest for each entity? What is necessary to prepare a social worker for each role?

4. How would you apply the systemic approach described in this chapter to achieving an improved workplace response to family/work tensions or to improved career opportunities for people of color?

5. Psycho-education is an intervention that originally attempted to achieve effective involvement of family members in the treatment of people with schizophrenia. The authors suggest its use to create understanding within a work group. In what way could a work group be viewed as similar to a family? What do you think about applying a family-derived intervention to a work group to influence its behavior?

CHAPTER 8

Social Workers as Workers, Social Agencies as Employers

We have described many connections between social work and the world of work, reviewing both historic activities and potential opportunities. In this chapter we focus on social work itself as work and on social agencies as employers. This offers a chance to consider the immediate impact and interconnections of the ideas, concepts, and structures of social work in the workplace on the profession of social work and its service delivery arrangements. We begin with a description of the social work labor force and then apply the elements of evidence-based best human resource practice in other sectors to the social service sector to suggest a prescription for social agency management of its social work labor force.

Most modern managers would agree that people are the most important ingredient of a successful enterprise. It has even been suggested that many corporate takeovers are motivated by the need to gain access to the skilled labor force of the object of the merger. Theorists have given significant support to the understanding of employees' contributions. Ouchi (1981) based his management recommendations in *Theory Z* on his realization that the successful organization is one that raises the interests of employees to the top of its agenda. Peters and Waterman (1982), in *In Search of Excellence*, identified that excellent organizations, defined by such variables as the most profitable firms and those with the largest or fastest-growing market share, inevitably were those that paid the most effective attention to the needs of their employees. Research points in the same direction. For example, Habeck and colleagues (1991) found that organizations with the lowest cost of workers' compensation following injury, when controlled for industry, are those firms that consistently pay attention to employees' needs.

More recently, practitioners have begun to identify how to achieve the employee commitment that seems to have a cause-and-effect relationship with organizational success. Kim and Mauborgne (1997) have put forth a concept of procedural justice, a process based on first engaging workers in open discussion of organizational issues, then explaining a decision, even when it is not in line with workers' recommendations, and finally, making expectations based on the decision clear, as the key to achieving that level of voluntary cooperation that leads to individual commitment and its accompanying exceptional organizational performance. These and similar pronouncements may not receive universal accord, but despite debates and uncertainties, there is a pervasive theme in the literature supporting a philosophy that recognizes workers as key stakeholders whose dedication is essential to organizational success. As a result, the role of human resource management has expanded geometrically in most work settings as each organization seeks to gain competitive advantage through the performance of its employees.

If paying attention to employees is vital for organizations in general, how much more so must it be for social agencies? In social agencies the largest contributor among the four L factors of production—land (office facility, paid by rent), labor (staff, paid by wages and benefits), lumber, (supplies like paper, pencils, and discs), and loan (capital investment like duplicating machines, computers, and postage meters)—is labor. In the production function of social service providers, labor is not only the paramount factor, with the other three factors contributing relatively little, but also the major portion of other factors. For example, staff input is expected to cause the client or community change that is the product of social agency action. But the capital investment made by staff in their own education and the capital investment made by the agency in training and development of staff constitute most of the capital (value) of the agency. "Between 1929 and 1982, education prior to work accounted for 26 percent of the growth in productive capacity of the United States, and learning on the job contributed an additional 55 percent" (Gummer 1995: 98). Yet historically, social agencies seem to be so involved with the needs of clients and demands for accountability, whether publicly or privately funded, that they tend to "get on with the work" while forgetting or even ignoring the importance of their employees in the process.

This chapter hypothesizes that agencies do so at their peril. Exploitation of staff, however unintentional, cannot achieve the outcomes everyone agrees are the goal of service. Social workers are workers, too, and like all workers, they perform best when motivated and devoted to their jobs. Meeting the needs of the various other constituencies of the social agency (i.e., consumer/clients, funders, community residents) is impossible without the effective contribution of the staff. As in all work organizations, social agencies that provide an environment conducive to workforce commitment are able to achieve more effective outcomes, have happier customers (consumers/clients), and contain unit costs more successfully (thereby achieving fiscal accountability) than those that lack such an outlook (Molloy & Kurzman 1993). Whether as administrators looking for means of increasing agency funding or as individual professionals seeking more satisfying employment options, we are all well served by attention to the work environment, the work culture, and the work rewards. Reisman (1986: 390), observing that the humanistic approach and concern for employees are pervasive in successful businesses, poses the relevant question, "if such a management approach works so well in organizations 'not motivated by altruism,' should not such an approach work even better in social agencies?"

Who Is the Social Work Labor Force?

Identifying social workers is more difficult than defining many other occupational groupings because there are a variety of sources from which the members of the category can be culled, and data inconsistencies exist between one data set and another (Barth 2003). For the National Association of Social Workers (NASW), the eligibility requirement is that someone has a Council on Social Work Education–accredited degree in social work at the bachelor's or master's levels (doctoral degrees are included in membership eligibility but are accredited by other educational authorities) and chooses to join the association (Gibelman & Schervish 1997). For the U.S. Department of Labor's Bureau of Labor Statistics, social workers are defined by the jobs they hold, and the title can include those without formal training who perform the tasks social workers customarily do or have been doing the job for years and have been grandfathered into the profession despite a newer job-related requirement that individuals in the title hold a university-level degree in the field. Under this definition, and based on reports of the current population survey and the total employment by occupation and industry, approximately 604,000 social workers were employed in the United States in 1998 (U.S. Department of Labor 2000), of whom 150,000 are members of the NASW.

Although these workers make up less than 1 percent of the total labor force, they are distributed throughout the United States in a variety of industries and work settings. Seventy-one percent have graduated from one of the 430 accredited BSW programs (342,000) or 160 accredited master's programs (235,000). Others have a BA without social work–specific training. In greater proportion than most workers, they belong to unions (23.2 percent). Actually, because one does not have to be a member of a union to be employed under a union contract, 25.4 percent of all social workers are employed under union contracts. They are most likely to be members of the American Federation of Government Employees; the Teamsters; the American Federation of State, County, and Municipal Employees; the Communication Workers of America; or the Service Employees International Union but could be in almost any union, including the United Auto Workers (if they live in Michigan) (personal communication, Pamela Wilson AFL-CIO June 2000). Unions play an important role in establishing conditions of employment. For social workers, the bargaining relationship is often directed at assuring that clients receive adequate levels of service in addition to the usual concerns about wages, hours of employment, and benefits. Historically, social service workers have depended on their unions to give voice to the members' concerns about their clients. For example, a union protest in the Brockton office of the Massachusetts Department of Social Services used balloons to demonstrate that workers were being asked to carry caseloads far in excess of the already heavy 18 families per employee provided in the collective bargaining agreement as a level at which adequate services could be provided. According to a story in the *Boston Globe* (Smith 1997), workers demonstrated against their excessive caseloads by blowing balloons that showed that, on average, they were carrying 26 families, comprised of 40 parents, 64 children, and 146 "collateral contacts." Not surprisingly, no worker could hold that many balloons. Some balloons popped, many just blew away and attested clearly to what actually was happening to clients.

Unions can be an important intermediary in the provision of social services in the community as well as a channel for worker participation in agency decision making. They have been a repository of rank-and-file interest in social action and reform, as well as directed at protection of social work employment conditions (Scanlon 1999). Social work unionists can join with agency management in making the public case for higher priority status and better funding for the provision of social services. The NASW Code of Ethics recommends that social work managers respect and accept the right of their employees to organize and bargain collectively for hours, wages, and working conditions, especially because "[in] the public policy arena, the union and NASW share many political objectives" (Tambor 1995: 2423). There is evidence, however, that agencies fight unionization as zealously as the most autocratic of employers (Peters & Masaoka 2000). This unfortunate response is in direct conflict not only with the profession's values of empowerment, participation, and self-determination but also with the best practice findings of research concerning sophisticated management practices.

By personal characteristics social workers are more likely to be women (71.5 percent) than men, white (72.3 percent) than people of color, and younger (62.3 percent, forty-four or under). Only a small proportion are self-employed full time (1.6 percent), while 41.1 percent work for private employers and the rest for government on the federal, state, and local levels. The Bureau of Labor Statistics lists twelve areas of social work practice: clinical, child welfare and family, child or adult protection, mental health, health care, schools, criminal justice, occupational, gerontology, social work administration, social work planning, and policy making. Gibelman and Schervish (1997) add five more: supervision, management, research, community organization, and education and training (cited in Barth 2003). A large proportion of all social workers are employed in the health services (26.4 percent) and education (5.28 percent), while most of the rest are in general social services such as welfare, mental health, child welfare, housing, and corrections. This situation is constantly evolving. For example, Cohen (2003: 36) noted: "For some time clinical social workers have performed the largest proportion of psychotherapeutic work done in the United states. Clinical social workers provide as much as 65 percent of all psychotherapy and mental health services." Those employed in world of work settings, for either employers or unions, are small in number but have had a significant impact on policies and practices in work settings. For example, more than half of all the professionals providing employee assistance services are social workers, with psychologists, nurses, vocational counselors, and psychiatrists making up the remaining service deliverers. The social work concept of person-in-environment probably makes the best fit of any professional model among the mental health care providers in EAP practice.

Earnings for social workers are highest in the federal government, where the median annual income is $45,300; with the exception of education and hospitals, the lowest median in the range, $30,800, is in state government (U.S. Department of Labor 2000). Clearly, social workers are not selecting their work because of its potential for high earnings. This is yet another issue that supports the significance of treating social workers in line with the best of human resource practices, since the extrinsic rewards of their work (income) cannot assure their continuity in the profession. Furthermore, for the general well-being of society, it is important that social workers achieve job satisfaction since they will be needed more than ever in the future (Ewalt 1991). Employment of social workers is projected to increase much faster than the average for all occupations through 2008.

Creating a Supportive Work Environment

The need to create a supportive work environment is great in agencies delivering social service, not just because of the importance of gaining commitment from the labor force as the single, prime factor of production necessary to achieve outcome goals but also because it is vital to the credibility of the potential contribution of the work of social work in the workplace. The recommendations and actions of social workers in other work settings are validated, in part, by the way in which social work managers operate social agencies (Akabas 1990). If, on social work turf, we model the environment, structures, and behavior of what is considered effective human resource practice, we gain credibility. Alternatively, if agencies managed by social workers are not viable in relation to providing an acceptable work environment within their own houses, how can the profession's potential contribution be taken seriously in other work settings?

The situation facing a social work director of a community mental health center is instructive.

CASE EXAMPLE

A community mental health center in the Midwest has been in operation for seven years. Of the total staff (forty professionals and fourteen support personnel) 70 percent have been there since the center opened. Turnover has been very limited, most of the additional 30 percent representing staff expansion. Little expansion has occurred during the last three years. Because of their long tenure and the practice of annual raises based on percent of salary without regard to merit, staff were receiving relatively high salaries. Contributing further to high morale was the initial missionary quality of founding a new service in an untouched area. But recently, some of this esprit de corps has fallen off. Funding from the federal and state governments has been reduced, and there is pressure to take on more Medicaid and Medicare patients. Staff members are complaining about the lack of new program initiatives and the increasingly heavy treatment load, particularly of severely ill people. With no expansion, there has been little room for promotion or change of work assignment. A general apathy has set in among some of the workers. Others are engaging in private practice and seem to reserve their energy and commitment for those activities rather than for their work at the center.

(continued)

The director, a social worker, recognized the importance of a new initiative. She wanted to find a new client constituency of less severely ill people and to generate new sources of funds for the center She explored entering a managed care network that would offer services to workplaces and to employed people who would have their costs paid for by insurance, covered by their employers or unions. She knew that other centers had moved in this direction with success. The move, however, raised many difficulties. Any new initiative would require an investment in various resources. For example, the center was not computerized and would need to become so to serve a managed care constituency. Redecorating so the space would be attractive to corporate clients would be necessary. Funds also would be needed for a marketing and a computer specialist and to cover the cost of materials, training, and other developmental expenses.

Because salaries were high and inflation low, the director considered eliminating raises for the next year. She knew such an action would be unpopular and realized, wisely, that she would have to involve the staff in the initiative decision. She called together the staff, identified their apathy and discontent, and presented her vision for a solution. She asked them to elect a task force to consider her proposal and to identify any potential problems with the idea. The task force was also asked to identify staff professionals who might be candidates for marketing and computer jobs, to make recommendations as to criteria for selecting treatment staff who should be reassigned to administer the program, design the training needed for the entire center staff to help them understand the business sector, treat this new group of clients appropriately, invest in this new program, and attain the computer skills necessary for this kind of work. She indicated that she was thinking of using the funds previously allocated to salary raises to finance the effort. She also asked that they move in a timely manner since she would like to have a plan in place within the quarter.

When the staff met without the director, fear and grumbling were evident and the focus was on the idea of eliminating wage increases. They decided to ask for the appointment of an impartial consultant to facilitate the change process, to which the director agreed, and one of the authors was invited to take that role. The consultant realized that the director and staff had many mutual interests that could be served by the director's vision but that staff members had concerns and ideas, and they wanted to be heard. The consultant met with each staffer individually and held regular feedback sessions for the whole staff as themes and ideas began to emerge. Once their original worries were expressed, many began to seek out the consultant to offer suggestions. They were concerned that a change of clients might mean a change of work hours, and those with family responsibilities, private practices, or both were unwilling to consider different work schedules. They were irritated that redecoration could be placed ahead of their salary increases. Some felt unwilling to treat what they considered "the worried well" and felt that the center's mission should be to continue to serve those most in need of care. But they all admired the director for wanting to revitalize their workplace and continued to be committed to their jobs. There were candidates for reassignment, and as they created individual inventories of their skills and interests, several came forth with hobbies in computer technology that could serve as a base for a skilled force to computerize the center. Three staff members had actually studied marketing in college and felt that they would enjoy the challenge of developing a plan for the center's initiative. Several themes emerged.

About half saw no need for change and wanted their positions and assignments to remain untouched. (They would require attention to bring them on board.)

A few were exceedingly enthusiastic and were ready, indeed eager, to take on totally new assignments. They made suggestions about redecorating and expressed a willingness to contribute furnishings and time to the process; they also had ideas about training and recommendations for every aspect of the planning process. (They would accept any request willingly, including forgoing salary increases.)

The rest were prepared to accept training, were willing to give the new initiative a chance, but had a more wait-and-see attitude. (They could be won over with relatively little effort so long as they did not lose their annual increment.)

Apprised of the situation, the director opted to give staff a cost of living increase (they had been accustomed to more), with a promise to try for a larger increase in the coming year if her plan generated the expected revenue stream. She proposed a task force made up of half her selected appointees and half volunteers to help her institute the change and to interview and select among their colleagues to fill the new staff positions, and she indicated that increments above cost of living in the future would be based on merit measured by contribution to the work of the center, with each staff member being able to make his or her own case to her in an annual review. A year later the consultant came in to evaluate the situation and found that the director's vision and flexibility had been well rewarded. There was a new energy among the staff and a very successful initiative involving the world of work. Two staff members had left the center, but five

(*continued*)

new staffers were on board because of increased demand for the center's services. The involvement of staff in decision making had paid off in real productivity and a renewed culture of commitment.

A supportive work environment is essential to the realization of social work values such as participatory management, teamwork, consensus building, and respect for collective bargaining among staff. It is also in keeping with the profession's underlying commitment to empowerment. There can be no distinction between the rights of clients and those of employees on the issue of achieving enfranchisement. Finally, a supportive work environment is essential as a strategy to mitigate the burnout that occurs among employees as a result of the stressful nature of human service delivery (Zanz 1998). Let us review each of these concerns in turn.

* * *

Consider the nature of the social work environment and its relation to social work values. Like other professions, social workers are socialized to a set of values and ethics that guide their practice (Weinbach 1998). Social work values are based largely on altruism, client self-determination, and meeting the needs of the most needy, or as Patti (1982) suggests, social workers are led by norms that invest in advocacy of subdominant values. They are faced with maintaining these values in a hostile task environment where the general public is unfriendly toward their services, in part, as has become all too apparent in this era of "from welfare to work," because the public sees the service recipients as different from—and costly to—themselves (Akabas 2000). Additionally, social work practitioners experience difficulty in defining their goals and, therefore, in measuring outcomes. Does the profession seek to reach those most difficult to serve and, therefore, consider success to be the enrolment of a few but very needy clients? Or do social workers seek to serve the greatest number that allocated resources can reach, regardless of level of need (Lewis 1975)? This tension often results in public uncertainty about what they are being asked to support. Too often the outcome is meager funding and inappropriate demands for accountability in a quest for quantity at the cost of quality. Ultimately, the work environment of the social agency is at risk of losing its connection to social work values and is not supportive in the ways that research has found are essential to individuals' well-being and organizational commitment.

Social workers' work, itself, is extremely stressful (Acker 1999). Social agencies live in a task environment where their assigned job is to do society's "dirty work." The general public is unfriendly and unwilling to pay for services they never expect to use themselves. Funding is uncertain and the pressure is for efficiency over quality. The profession has allowed the business mentality to dictate measures of efficiency and effectiveness. But the analogy between business and social agencies is fraught with inaccuracies. Business seeks to hold its customers, while social workers' desire most to lose them through their own growth and development. Business seeks to gain the most interested and willing customers, while social agencies expend large amounts of effort (and funds) on attracting the least advantaged and, therefore, most difficult and reluctant consumers. Competition among social agencies brings inefficiency whereas in business it provides the framework for efficiency. In this hostile environment, social workers must be good doers as well as do-gooders.

Additionally, in the general conditions of the social agency and even the private practice workplace social workers often face resistant clients, have limited authority that is not equal to their responsibility, or have to deal with excessive paperwork and routinization of procedures because of bureaucratic regulations that demean their professional skills and knowledge. Working conditions are frequently dangerous, with angry clients who may place blame inappropriately on the counselor who, by regulation, is forced to reject a request for service that the client considers reasonable (Shields & Kiser 2003; Newhill 1995). Individually, social workers report such personal issues as underutilization of their skills, role conflict, excessive workload, role ambiguity, depersonalization, and uncertainty. The profession as a whole experiences low salaries, low status of its work in the eyes of the community, and limited advancement opportunities in organizations that have minimal hierarchical arrangements.

All these factors compound the level of stress experienced by workers, leading to a syndrome identified as *burnout* (Sze & Ivker 1986; McNeely 1988; Rauktis & Koeske 1994). Oktay (1992: 432), quoting Johnson and Stone, defines burnout as "a state of exhaustion resulting from involvement with people in emotionally demanding situations." According to the literature, burnout, as experienced by human service workers, has as its outcome reduced commitment, inability to concentrate, loss of creativity in problem solving, and general malaise concerning one's work. Individuals often try to ameliorate burnout by changing employers or opting out of the social work profession. This is particularly so for those who experience inflexibility in job assignment and poor relationships with immediate supervisors (Samantrai 1992). To be known as a profession that loses its own members because of unsatisfactory working conditions jeopardizes practitioners' credibility in all settings. Powell (1994: 234), in a study of alienation and burnout among social workers, suggests that burnout is not an individual's problem but reflects the workplace milieu: "The data suggest that lack of power over the conditions of one's social work practice and a sense of isolation may be strongly linked to burnout and that burnout rises in conjunction with powerlessness."

Powell links the issues of empowerment and burnout. His article offers a systems approach as a potential guide for palliative intervention, that is, a reworking of the conditions under which work is done in any given setting. Let the issue be clear. Social work is a satisfying, meaningful career option and there is significant evidence that workers value their choice of profession in relation to its purpose and outcome (Butler 1990). But they wish to do the work for which they have been prepared. Too often they find this impossible given the excessive bureaucratic structure of service delivery and the intense pressure to achieve quantitative outcomes, particularly in this era of managed care (Finkle 1998). What then must the agency administrator do to foster the productivity that is demanded of all managers today? Interestingly, they must do the same thing that all effective and successful managers must do regardless of industry or site, namely, pay attention to their employees and their needs (Giffords & Dina 2003). But for social work managers, this may be clearer than for most managers since if they create an environment in keeping with social work values, the result will be a culture of participation, teamwork, individual authority in decision making, and respect for diversity, that is, a culture that regards meeting employees' needs as the key to organizational success.

Even though what a social worker manager needs to do should come naturally, imbedded as it is in the profession's culture, this is more easily said than done. Similar solution sets pervade the recommendations found throughout the research reports on workforce well-being. So too, the formula for motivation and job satisfaction is universal, and it is well described throughout the literature and, therefore, is accessible to agency and facility managers. Yet it is a rare organization, profit making or not-for-profit, that succeeds with this agenda. In short, social workers are carriers of initiatives that can lead to improved workplace responsiveness for all members of the community, but they have not been able to capture it in their own work settings. It is time that the profession's work environment caught up with best practices elsewhere (Akabas 1990;

Akabas and Gates 1990). What follows are some guidelines for undertaking that journey.

Prescription for Gaining Staff Commitment and Organizational Effectiveness

Achieving a productive work environment within an organization starts with establishing a personnel or human resource process that is respectful of the knowledge, skill, and values extant in both the recruitment pool and among the employees eventually selected. That work environment should be supported by a commitment to diversity of personnel that is connected to the way work is done. It hinges on a quality of leadership that prioritizes staff needs in its vision of the organizational mission and advocates on their behalf, knowing that otherwise the work of social work can lead to vicarious trauma that requires remedial attention. It is fortified by supportive supervision, open communication, and fairness in compensation, assignment of work, and choice of agency procedures as qualities inherent in the work culture. It is nurtured further by providing mentoring, development, training, and promotional opportunities that ensure a multicultural, continuous-learning environment. And it is insured when staff, themselves, take responsibility for achieving such circumstance by joining together, whether in a union or by other means, to advocate for their own self-determination. Finally, it thrives in a safe environment where security is a matter of conscious agency effort and where there exists a process of staff self-monitoring and accountability that assures that anyone with impaired behavior, of whatever type and for whatever reason, is helped to find assistance toward recovery, whether it be from substance abuse or from some other cause. Lest we be accused of holding social agencies to a higher standard than the one required of all other work organizations, it is worthwhile to remember that the outcome of such standards is not just individual job satisfaction but also superior organizational performance, a goal that can be considered essential to the survival of all organizations, not just human service agencies.

Human Resource Process

As Drucker (1990) has noted, organizations work best when they operate from an identified strategic plan. A planning function that assesses the personnel needs of the organization begins the human resource process. It continues through the recruitment and selection phase and includes orientation, training and development, ongoing appraisal, promotion, and compensation. It ends in separation (whether by dismissal, resignation, or retirement). Each time a staff member is added or replaced represents an opportunity for an agency to rethink its mission and service product since it is the knowledge, skill, and experience of the staff that determine the activities in which the agency can engage. If the hospital social service department wishes to initiate an in-house employee assistance program, it will seek new social work employees with experience and interest in that activity. If a mental health clinic recognizes increasing demand for career counseling, it will be well served by looking for a social worker with vocational assessment experience. If the school wishes to increase the assistance it offers students in their transition to work, it might search for an employee who has had social work practice experience in the corporate sector.

Achieving Diversity

The important issue in planning and evaluation for staffing, both for existing programs and for new initiatives, is to incorporate the broadest possible search as well as nondiscriminatory hiring practices. This is equally applicable to the possible promotional and lateral moves that any position offers for present staff as it is to generating a pool of interested outside candidates for any position. Such actions are essential to fulfill existing legal requirements (e.g., the requirements of Title 7 of the Civil Rights Act of 1964, the Americans with Disabilities Act, the Age Discrimination in Employment Act), and as Gibelman (1996) advises, they are in keeping with the NASW Code of Ethics, which requires that colleagues be treated with respect. She asks, "how do the values that embody this Code influence the personnel recruitment and hiring process in human service organizations?" (59). In raising this question she is calling on the profession to employ the greatest possible care in doing, in practice, what it espouses in theory. And it all starts with the recruitment and hiring process.

In practical terms, practicing what we preach requires devotion to diversity as a guiding principle in recruitment and selection. Gummer (1995) has described three stages in the fulfillment of an organizational diversity plan. He points out that most organizations are at the discrimination-fairness stage in which the players recognize that America is a diverse society and that discrimination in selection based on personal characteristics such as color, gender, and the like is wrong and, therefore, should not be used as hiring criteria. In this stage, fair recruitment seeks to achieve diversity. Nonetheless, once hired, everyone is expected to adhere to the dominant culture regardless of differences. Gummer asserts that organizations gain little in this stage beyond an image that makes them look, to the outside, like they are an open system. If the organization progresses to stage two, it reaches the access-legitimacy paradigm under which it identifies the mix in the world at large and recruits and selects a diverse staff and utilizes them to match and care for those who exemplify the differences. For example, they hire a Spanish-speaking Latina social worker and then, regardless of language needs, they assign all clients with Latino names to that worker. This niche approach, too, misses the opportunity posed by diversity in that it merely fragments the service rather than improving the quality of service overall. It may, in fact, result in hostility among ethnic groups who compete for limited staff resources. To achieve real benefit from diversity, an organization must reach Gummer's learning-effectiveness stage, under which diversity is valued for what each person can teach other people thus achieving true organizational effectiveness. In such a milieu, all staffers can work effectively with the Latina client because they have all shared knowledge and evaluated each other's practice to reflect the similarities and differences among ethnic populations, and they are available as consultants when an issue requires specific expertise. Then, all staffers will be sensitive to the needs of Latino clients, and only those clients who do not speak any language but Spanish will need a Spanish-speaking (though not necessarily Latino) therapist—because of language needs not because they are Latino.

Structural changes within the agency may be needed to promote inclusion, to adapt clinical interventions for use with varying populations, and to be responsive to the great variety in the kinds of needs both different staff and consumers may present (Seck et al. 1993). Research findings (Gant 1996) indicate that true cultures of diversity are universal, and they value people for what they bring in relation to their differences. Such cultures "reduce dependence on a sole staff member to be the spokesperson for a particular ethnic community" (Fong & Gibbs 1995: 19). They are marked by a high level of comfort among staff, who develop a sense of social identity from participating in the agency, and by an openness to supervisory support regardless of the personal characteristics of the supervisor (Hopkins 1997).

Such a formula for staffing raises a related issue with which social agencies often struggle, namely, what are the roles and potential contributions of peers who are believed to make up for their lack of professional training by real life experience? Mental health agencies are faced with considering the desirability of including consumers in recovery as staff members and of defining their role and responsibility. Substance abuse treatment services deal with the same question, made more intense by the belief of some, especially those dedicated to an Alcoholics Anonymous model of care, that the most effective (and perhaps only) treatment should come from those who have experienced and overcome the problem. Programs offering an array of services for other presenting problems, from those treating victims of domestic violence or other sexual assaults to those organizing community groups of tenants or welfare mothers, face the dilemma of how to utilize the knowledge and skills of their clients in a direct service capacity as well as on advisory boards. Disappointments with paraprofessional staffing (Kurzman 1970a) during the sixties and seventies should not deter agencies from exploring this dimension of diversity. Rather, it should suggest that careful and specific planning is essential to successfully incorporate the values and value of peers in developing and implementing services. It should also reflect a recognition that there are boundaries to the contributions peers can make. Clarity concerning boundaries can enhance both peer and professional contributions to services.

Agency Leadership

Integrating diversity and other human resource initiatives at a level that will promote organizational effectiveness and innovation depends on agency design, the agency culture, and the vision of agency managers and leaders (Carnochan & Austin 2002). Their activities should be directed at establishing an ongoing learning environment, which includes objectives that provide knowledge and information about variations among cultures, help staff identify how they feel about different cultures, and train for skills in how to interact with clients and coworkers who are of other cultures. The importance of leadership cannot be overstated. The dynamics of an organizational change process depends on vision and certainty of the leader (Shin and McClomb 1998). Reminding their readers that all people resist change, Kets de Vries and Balazs (1999: 658) suggest that it is up to leaders to identify organizational shortcomings, manage employee resistance to change, present viable alternatives, provide the staff with a sense of organizational pride and hope, and articulate a vision. They conclude, "leaders need to communicate values by setting an example with clarity and consistency . . . those who drive the process have to 'walk the talk.'" Support for their position comes from research reported by Goleman (2000) who identifies six styles of leadership: coercive, authoritative, affiliative, democratic, pacesetting, and coaching. Although he reports that good leaders use a mix, he indicates that to spark the best performance in most situations leaders need to use four styles: authoritative (i.e., mobilize people through a vision), affiliative (i.e., give employees a sense of community and emotional bonds), democratic (i.e., provide opportunity for participation), and coaching (i.e., mentor for growth and development). He, too, stresses vision, clarity, egalitarian spirit, and good communications as the keys to organizational change. For social work managers, such advice should be like "preaching to the choir." It should be a matter of doing what comes naturally. Yet as Hopkins and Hyde (2002) point out, too often leaders feel under attack and tend to retreat to micro responses at an intraagency solution level rather than opening themselves to the staff empowerment, community collaborative linkages, and experimentation that mark a learning organization. Such micro-response behavior destroys the great potential of social work leadership in administration and makes the social agency no better in its management than a typical, traditional, process-focused business operation.

Supervisory Support

An environment that allows staff to make beneficial use of supervisory support has been found to buffer and mediate stress at the workplace (Rauktis and Koeske 1994). Clearly, it is a valuable ingredient for effective social agency management. In fact, in any list of qualities that are the key to agency effectiveness, perhaps none is more important than supervisory support. House (1981) has identified four types of support needed in the workplace: informational (knowing what you need to know to do your job), instrumental (receiving help doing your job when you need it), appraisal (feedback that tells you how you are doing), and emotional (someone caring when you are having a bad day or an unusually good one). Some research suggests that what workers want most from their supervisors is help in doing a good job, which would stress the informational and instrumental aspect of supervision. Other researchers (Butler 1990: 116) have indicated the importance of appraisal and emotional support: "Social workers . . . do not have many grateful clients, nor does the outside world often express appreciation, [therefore] . . . [they have a] need for hearing regularly from management that their work is important and appreciated." Yet some find that even the full array of support may not be enough when the conditions of work and the workload demands are excessive (Karabanow 1999; Rauktis & Koeske 1994).

The work of social service personnel is difficult both because of the conditions surrounding work and the very nature of the work, itself. Much is expected of the social worker in relation to meeting the needs of the most oppressed, the most poverty stricken, the most demoralized, and the most traumatized members of our society. Working with such populations and with their presenting problems requires more support than even the most effective supervisors can offer. Much has been written recently about vicarious traumatization (McCann & Pearlman 1990). This issue has received greater attention since 9/11 because of the trauma debriefing needed by surviving coworkers and the impact on the social workers who did the debriefings. Attending to the needs of others experiencing trauma requires, first, a realization that serving the traumatized can be cumulative and leaves the server debilitated in a way that exceeds, on an intrapsychic level, what we usually think of as burnout. As one observer has noted, "There is a cost to caring" (Figley 1995). Even when work conditions are exemplary, therefore, the nature of some of the work in social work places empathetic professionals at risk because they may view the experience of clients' traumas as so painful as to cause a transforming negative reaction in themselves as helpers. This indirect or vicarious traumatization when the social worker absorbs the trauma of the client has sometimes been found to make the professional feel helpless and confused. When such reactions occur, they are disruptive of the social worker's own ability to be responsive to the needs of the client. Such developments require attention from the environment that encourages respite and self-care for the professional.

An aspect of taking care of one's self revolves around concerns with personal safety. According to Newhill (1995), after police, social workers run the highest risk of work-related violence. The personal disappointment of clients (e.g., parents whose children have been removed from the home or abusers who believe the social worker is implicated in the separation resulting from the court delivered order of protection), as well as the actual living conditions and circumstances of many clients, place the social worker in dangerous circumstances that agencies too often neglect to recognize. Professionals may contribute to their own danger by feeling that they can handle problematic behavior and the dangers of neighborhoods in which they find themselves on home visiting assignments. Such basic cautions as placing panic buttons in interviewing rooms, having guards available at sites, being accompanied on home visits, and receiving in-service training on how to deal with threatening situations (other than feeling that they are a sign of personal inadequacy) can protect social workers from needless danger and its aftermath.

Vicarious and real trauma are part of a continuum of problems that therapists themselves may bring to the practice situation. For example, adult children of alcoholics have difficulty serving clients who are experiencing substance abuse disorders (Fewell, King, & Weinstein 1993). There are numerous other examples where therapists engage in behavior that according to the NASW Code of Ethics is incompetent, unprofessional, exploitive, or otherwise unethical and is in the end harmful to their clients or colleagues (Reamer 1992a; Strom-Gottfried 1999). In such situations, it is absolutely essential, and usually possible, for coworkers and supervisors to identify that the individual social worker is impaired and to utilize appropriate professional monitoring to hold the individual accountable.

It is also possible that some supervisors in social agencies have difficulty meeting the demands of the supervisory role. Though supervision calls on many skills that are "expected" among trained social workers, the reality is that a social work degree does not guarantee supervisory ability. Supervisors, in social work as elsewhere, reach supervisory status for a host of reasons. Some do so because they have done a superior job as line workers, while others are merely rewarded for their seniority or because they are skilled in completing written civil service exams. Regardless of the reasons for appointment, the supervisory skills are not a replica of those required for competent line performance be it as direct service counselors or program developers or research analysts. Agencies, facing high demand for services and a shortage of funds, may opt for adding another worker rather than investing in training and development for existing staff. So supervisors rarely receive the kind of training needed to perform the managerial tasks of assuring productivity while meeting human needs as effectively as possible.

Mentoring programs offer a means to a relatively low-cost staff development effort when training funds are sparse. They have a serendipitous by-product of offering recognition and reward to the experienced and knowledgeable senior staffers. New supervisors can be assigned to or invited to select an agency manager who can provide advice and encouragement as the supervisor develops a style and action plan that will lead to job satisfaction and productivity among subordinates. Mentoring has another advantage over training. Training is usually focused on conveying specific skills, while mentoring attends to personal development on a broader scale that may improve self-efficacy. This, in turn, leads to more effective supervisory action in the short run and the potential for developing candidates for succession to leadership over the longer run (Pearlmutter 1998). Both are vital to the successful organization.

Team Building and Empowerment

Another decisive element in creating a workplace culture that drives productivity is the perception of participation, that is, that workers sense that they have a voice in the decision-making process. Typically, human beings who feel valued are committed and creative in relation to their work and are likely to function at a level of high productivity. For social work managers, what needs to be done should come naturally since it is a perfect fit with the profession's commitment to empowerment. It is hard to make a case for empowering clients while denying empowerment to employees. Encouraging participation and team effort can have a positive impact only when it is real. Workers must believe that their opinions count. If, for example, a team is brought together to examine the image the surrounding community has of the mental health clinic and recommend changes that will bring in more full-pay customers/clients, then management must be committed to acting on the recommendations that result or have a very good reason why they do not. Research carried out by Kim and Mauborgne (1997: 65–66) has led them to conclude that although economic issues are important to workers, the real key to motivation and productivity is fair process: "Outcomes matter but no more than the fairness of the process that produces them. . . . Fair process profoundly influences attitudes and behaviors critical to high performance. It builds trust and unlocks ideas. With it, managers can achieve even the most painful and difficult goals while gaining the voluntary cooperation of the employees affected. Without fair process, even outcomes that employees might favor can be difficult to achieve."

They recommend that managers involve individuals in decisions that affect them, make sure that everyone understands the reasons for the final decision (even when their own ideas are not accepted), and state the new rules precisely so that expectations are clear. They conclude that "every company can tap into the voluntary cooperation of its people by building trust through fair processes" (75). These suggestions are confirmed by Ramsdell (1994: 69) who identifies six categories of benefit when staff are involved in decision making: data flow to inform organizational leaders' decision-making, access to expertise and creativity is increased, staff motivation and commitment blossoms, productivity and service quality swell, morale and job satisfaction flourish, and burnout and turnover decline. Yet she finds on empirical study a relatively low level of staff participation. Observing the discrepancy between recognizing the value of staff participation and the limited realization of participation in practice, Ramsdell concludes that there is a "need for new and improved mechanisms for staff participation in organizational decision-making in order to address the continuing critical need for human service organizations to develop and study more effective and efficient management practices." Regular staff meetings, appointment of task forces to solve agency problems, team interviewing of job candidates, opportunities to attend and present at professional conferences, and placement of information on staff and agency accomplishments in the local press are some of the means available to achieve participation in fact as well as in promise.

An interesting example of staff participation was reported by Fischel-Wolovick and colleagues in 1988. Noting that the changing labor force at the time (more working mothers in particular) made it important to find innovative approaches to traditional nine to five scheduling, Mount Sinai Hospital in New York City convened an Alternative Work Schedule Committee of social workers. The impetus was requests from staff who were finding it increasingly difficult to meet the sometimes opposing demands of work and personal and family needs. To be considered were all the alternative work schedule (AWS) possibilities, not just flex-time but job sharing, compressed work week, and other possibilities. Cost was a key concern as was the social workers' worry that their request for schedule changes might be misinterpreted by the rest of the hospital staff as a lack of commitment to their responsibilities. The committee, which agreed that AWS would be desirable on services where it was structurally feasible, overcame opposition, even within its own department, and instituted an experiment with the approval of senior management. Measured by the number of cases opened monthly and the number of direct services provided, productivity of the department improved. Requested feedback has been uniformly positive and the authors conclude that "AWS . . . provides managers with a way of retaining valuable staff and solidifying the mutually held commitment to excellence in professional practice" (102).

An obvious means of staff participation occurs when workers are organized into a union. Participation becomes formalized as can be seen in the following vignette.

CASE EXAMPLE

Exceptional Children's Resource Center runs several day programs for three hundred cognitively impaired and emotionally troubled children under the age of sixteen, of whom, at any point in time, thirty youngsters of all ages are accommodated in respite care around the clock, seven days a week. The respite care center is always full. A union represents the line professionals

(*continued*)

and all clerical, maintenance, and transportation personnel in the agency. Their contract had expired. They agreed to a one-month extension but indicated that they would strike at the end of that period. Although negotiations continued, they were halfhearted until the day before the end of the month when it was generally accepted that the union would go out on strike.

In preparation for a possible strike, the agency emptied the respite care center. It knew it could close down the day programs, but at least half the children were with the center for the entire day while their parents worked, and if services to those children were interrupted their parents would be unable to work. In addition, the client population required consistency in program. There was serious concern that considerable progress would be lost if services were interrupted.

Ordinarily supervisors might be used to keep the program open, but almost all the supervisors had been promoted from the ranks and they indicated that they would not cross a picket line because they were sympathetic to the issues the workers were bringing, and further, they would have a difficult time supervising them after the strike if they did the work of the striking employees during a strike. They also indicated that if a strike took place and there was an attempt to keep the program open, they would inform parents, with whom they had intimate relationships, that their children were at risk because the staffing would be inadequate.

The agency was in a tight budget situation. It wanted to avoid a strike that would result in further loss of income. About half the children served were paid for by their parents on a sliding fee scale. As costs had risen, the slide had been downward—that is, in 1990, with a sliding schedule, fees collected covered 80 percent of the actual costs for these children. Now, based on family income, less than 50 percent of these fees were collected. For the other half of the children, government funds covered fees. Here, too, the negotiated fee covered total cost per child in 1990, but was down to 90 percent now. With an endowment income and an annual fund drive, the agency had been able to make up the shortfall from parental and government payments until last year when a $100,000 deficit occurred. A bank loan on the building was secured to cover that cost and provide some cushion into the next period while the administration attempted to negotiate a higher contract fee and the development director attempted to increase the contribution base. Management claimed to have allocated all its remaining loan to cover increased labor contract costs to which it had already agreed, particularly increased health insurance costs and an already agreed upon 3 percent annual salary increment for the next three years. They insisted that there was no further money about which to bargain and suggested that the union was trying to close the agency down. They wondered aloud whether the workers really cared about the children for whose care they were responsible and suggested that concerned workers would not be putting their desires ahead of the children's needs for an ongoing program.

The union pointed to a 35 percent annual turnover rate as evidence that salary and working conditions were inadequate. They wanted several additional benefits including a prescription and dental plan (which all members in the local except for those working for the center already had) and an increase in vacation time. The present schedule gave workers two weeks after the first year and a third week after five years. The union insisted that, in this difficult work environment, employees needed more leisure time and wanted two additional days for each year of service past the first year until workers reached a month of vacation annually. (They claimed this as standard in their other contracts.) The union also wanted a fixed ratio of staff to clients of one to three during the daytime hours including Saturday and Sunday for respite care, and one to six for afternoon and evening shifts for respite care. They claimed this as a quality-of-care issue—workers were not able to devote adequate time to each child and that for these children learning is contingent on extensive one to one work. Worse yet, they believed that often they were so short staffed that the children were in danger. (Management and labor agreed such staffing would require a 20 percent increase in staff for which, according to management, no funds were available.)

Even though the parties reached a relative impasse, the impending deadline represented an opportunity to consider creative solutions. It was in everyone's interest to avoid a strike. A last-minute mediation brought forth a suggestion from the director that the parties use the concepts established by the Camp David accord to try to move forward (Fisher, Ury, & Patton 1991). That concept required that the parties put the past discussion and its ill will behind and, with a fresh view of each other, identify their mutual interests and then brainstorm new solutions no matter how outlandish. Everyone cared about the children and their growth and development. Both labor and management knew they needed more money and more staff, and they admitted that more personnel would be helpful in improving services and outcomes. Having identified their mutual interests and their needs, they began brainstorming, which led to many ideas:

(*continued*)

- hire more staff
- recruit volunteers
- cut down on the cost of turnover and absenteeism by increasing vacation time
- become a training site for special education teachers and social work students
- close the respite care center and reallocate staff to a Saturday program
- use the political power of the union to lobby for higher payments for care
- improve the performance of the development director
- reduce hierarchy by having supervisors work alongside, rather than in observation of, staff
- increase training of parents to gain greater continuity of care from center to home (which could reduce work demands)
- reassign staff so that there are more personnel at peak times and lighter coverage early in the day when everyone is fresh
- add part time workers for peak time, limiting the cost of additional staffing
- reduce costly turnover by meeting industry standards for working conditions
- contact "alumni" families for contributions
- form an association of comparable agencies to lobby the legislature for an increase in payment schedules
- develop ties with community businesses to increase contributors
- solicit care-improvement ideas from staff and reward innovative ideas

The brainstorming process brought the parties together. As they looked at their ideas they realized that they needed each other. Management recognized the value of better communication systems and a less adversarial relationship. The union recognized management's budget dilemma. It had considerable political clout but had never used it to promote higher fee schedules for client populations. It suggested joining with management to make a presentation to the state legislature. Management acknowledged that its workforce was entitled to conditions equal to others in similar work and agreed to work toward benchmarking its wages and benefits to industry standards. A strike threat was called off in response to management's establishing a schedule over a three-year contract period for meeting the union demands.

They agreed to have each side pick the idea that most appealed to it plus the next three most-appealing ideas and to prioritize their action on that basis. Management agreed to take a chance on spending their loan money up front rather than holding it to meet the next three years' raises, while the union agreed to join in lobbying the legislature and other organizations for support. An ongoing joint task force was established to oversee the implementation of the agreement.

Developing a contract between the agency and the representatives of its workforce is a process of partnership. It requires the review of wages, hours, and conditions of employment that bear on all aspects of the employment relationship including management style, benefits (vacation and sick leave, health care, and pension coverage), promotion and seniority rights, workload and quality of supervision, discipline and grievance procedures, and other structural provisions surrounding work. The negotiating committee representing the employees gains credibility to the extent that it solicits information from the membership and then pursues their identified interests so that all workers gain a sense of participation. There is an old saying that "management gets the union it deserves." A supercharged emotional environment sometimes accompanies an organizing drive, and agencies have been known to fight fiercely against unionization campaigns (Peters & Masaoka 2000) though the NASW Code of Ethics specifically recognizes the right of workers to unionize and bargain collectively. Under such circumstances, the agency is likely to encourage adversarial relations with the union and its membership, which can be reflected in difficulty getting the work done. But where the agency is respectful of the union's team as the spokesperson for its employees and bargains in good faith, as the law requires, management can empower its employees and develop the union into a committed partner in meeting even excessive client needs and in approaching public and even private funding sources.

Summary

Staff participation, whether through a union or without one in place, is the perfect complement to the efforts of an organization dedicated to a learning effectiveness model of diversity prescribed by Gummer (1995). Taken together, staff participation and organizational dedication to growth through learning provide the basis for an environment that respects social workers as workers and creates organizational effectiveness for social agencies as employers. Several additional initiatives can be identified that reduce stress and burnout and induce desired organizational outcomes. They include training and development, teamwork, communication and feedback, fair compensation and promotional policies, and structural developments (also known as process reengineering) that minimize bureaucratic regimens. These are all interrelated initiatives and require expression in policy and in modeling by executive leadership.

Operating an organization with flexibility as its guiding principle presents challenges to the managers, but the rewards make it worth the effort. One of the authors employs four mothers of young children. Their hours, which reflect a policy of negotiable work schedules and responsiveness to the need for achieving a work/family balance, include one working a three-day compressed week, another telecommuting one day a week, and two sharing a job. Our biggest problem has been to assure some hours each week of overlapping time to strategize future plans. Although together the time they work is equal to only three full-time equivalents, they represent an incredibly creative, experienced, talented, and committed staff that could not be duplicated by any three women willing to work a typical nine to five day on site, to say nothing of the additional hours of coverage represented by their unique schedules. Another example of a policy that supports flexibility is the disability management program that allows valuable workers experiencing disability to sustain employment on terms that accommodate their health conditions (see chap. 7). Another way to nod in the direction of flexibility is to offer a cafeteria-style benefits package that covers a basic set of benefits and then offers options that can meet the varying needs of gay employees, single workers, members of two-earner families, and older workers. An array of possibilities that allows one employee to opt for partner health care and another to take money instead of health care, that provides educational benefits for one and increased pension contributions for another confirms a managerial commitment to diversity and caring.

For many agencies, what may be required is a cultural upheaval that has to start at the top with the leadership. Whatever the agency mission, a reward/punishment model that applies pressure for productivity clearly cannot accomplish the productivity goal that is being sought. Pressure to "get out the work" may not be achieved merely by the fact that social workers are satisfied that their work is meaningful and challenging. According to Herzberg (1987), these are hygiene factors and do not serve as motivators in a social service delivery environment that has been identified as having the potential to cause burnout, vicarious traumatization, and alienation (Powell 1994; Himle et al. 1989). A balance is necessary (Banerjee 1995). Social work values can replace command-and-control methods of achieving productivity with a model guided by expectations for staff involvement and participation and encouragement of consumer decision making that measures productivity by qualitative as well as quantitative outcomes. All organizations, not just social agencies, when focused on social work values gain productivity through pride of belonging and perceptions of fairness.

Agency structure needs to be geared to fulfilling the initiatives enumerated above, in part based on what Banerjee (1995) calls, "a healthy disrespect for the impossible." The result is the establishment of a state of mind that provides constant, dedicated, enthusiastic effort throughout the system to find better ways so that workers can work smarter, not harder. It leads to job satisfaction, use of skills, responsibility equal to authority, autonomy characterized by decision-making power at the lowest possible hierarchical level, self-motivation, equality among the various groups, and feedback that creates a constant-learning environment where continuous quality improvement rules the day. Such a culture reaffirms the importance of the work and the work group, is noncompetitive, and assures, through training, development, and mentoring, that all employees have the skill, knowledge, and interest necessary to do their jobs appropriately.

In the struggle between social work values and fiscal needs based on public accountability, the profession must take on the challenge of helping society set priorities that recognize that equity is as important a goal as efficiency and that services can make the best contribution if there is not only no embarrassment connected with the need for assistance but also no exploitation of staff in the provision of service. Management must build a culture that recognizes the need for a holistic effort rather than stand-alone accomplishments. In such a culture, supervisors are supportive, performance evaluations emphasize growth and development, and staff play a significant self-motivated role. The success of the provision of human services is at stake. We cannot settle for less.

Study Questions

1. This chapter contains a prescription for human resource policy in a social agency. What are the elements described? How well does the agency with which you are connected fulfill the chapter's recommendations? What needs to change and how could you support an argument for such change?
2. The authors note that the U.S. Bureau of Labor Statistics defines the social work labor force to include those without any academic training who carry out the tasks customarily deemed to be social work activities. What impact do you think this has on the power and influence of social work as a profession?

3. What role does leadership play in promoting the flexibility essential for organizational survival? What behaviors have you observed in agency leadership that promote flexibility effectively and what behaviors would you consider a restraint on flexibility?

4. The nature of social work has been identified as sometimes "dangerous to the health of the professional." What are some of the situations that can have such impact and what policies and procedures ameliorate those situations?

5. Throughout the book there are indications of the potential contributions of union membership to worker well-being. What do you think about social workers joining unions? What are the arguments supporting membership as being desirable? Do you see any drawbacks to joining a union, and if so, what are they?

CHAPTER 9

The Future

Issues, Trends, and Potential

Why be a social worker involved in the world of work? The previous chapters have given a glimpse of the difficulties in the world of work. Much of this book has decried the situation that currently exists in the world of work as a condition of the half-empty glass. Trends like globalization, interest in short-term profits, loss of unskilled jobs, decline in proportional membership in labor unions, reduction in longstanding fringe benefits, increasing insecurity of full-time employment, and the growing concentration of wealth combine to have a negative impact on the nature of labor market participation. But that is only one component of the story. The previous chapters have also provided a view of many positive trends such as increasing diversity of the labor force, the close connection between corporate well-being and care for workers, efforts at creating programs to achieve a work/family balance, and programs designed to increase job opportunities for people with disabilities, and have suggested some of the means by which the world of work can strategize to meet and overcome many current challenges. Is the glass half empty or half full? The mission of social work involves recognizing and facing adversity and then organizing one's self to deal optimistically and creatively with the existing adversity in the interest of achieving individual, family, organizational, and community well-being by promoting responses that foster human rights and social justice.

Some old metaphors are much used because they convey the essence of a situation better than anything that has been imagined since their invention. This is certainly the case with the old saw of the glass half empty or half full. The challenge of social work in the workplace is its half-full status. It has been the authors' major contention throughout that the opportunities for making a difference in the lives of people and the circumstances facing organizations and communities are many and varied through targeting the American workplace and promoting the significance of work in people's lives. Though equal opportunity has yet to be achieved in America, it is the American workplace that probably offers greater protection of fairness than any other labor market in the world. Though capitalism tends to value the bottom line more than the people whose labor contributes to it, it is the American workplace that is probably the site of the greatest economic opportunity available in the world, accounting for the continuing immigration stream to America. Though hierarchically organized, it is the American workplace that promotes immigration and accommodates the greatest diversity of participants of any workplace in the world. Though all are not treated equally in America, it is in the American workplace that employers are restrained by law and court actions from engaging in reckless behavior against workers. Though participants work longer hours in America than in any other place in the industrialized world, it is in the American workplace where employees are universally protected by a minimum wage and maximum hour law. Though not all is as social workers might wish it to be, it is in the American workplace that legal and political processes at all levels can be used to move toward improved conditions for all. Toward this end, people's work roles and conditions of employment, the world of work and the general economic context of our lives warrant equal attention from social work as the profession, historically, has given to love and to the individual, the family, and the community.

This chapter explains the authors' conceptualization of the half-full glass in the context of the goodness of fit between social work and the world of work in its multiple dimensions. The future opportunities for social workers and the social work profession are cited to help those who wish to move their own careers or their agencies' policies and practices in a direction that incorporates a world of work perspective. This builds on the current ideology and accompanying trends that perceive economic growth and global competition as the potential panacea for achieving improved well-being. Although we may decry the loss of the kind of community spirit that framed the progressive laws and actions of the New Deal, we recognize that both major political parties, reflecting the change in prevailing public opinion, have supported the dismantling of federal responsibility for the provision of entitlements for the American people. Dismantling of federal responsibility has altered the rules of the game. Now, reaching the social work goals of general well-being and social justice involves increased attention to the workplace and increased significance on the importance of having a job. It behooves social workers to develop their knowledge of the world of work, to acquire skills to practice in this world, and to hone their capacity to identify and advocate for job opportunities and entitlements for their clients, for financial support for their agencies, and for benevolent legislative regulation for their communities in and from this world of work.

Human Resource Management: A Land of Social Work Opportunity

The labor force has become increasingly diverse, suggesting that workers present new needs to the workplace. As well, a new kind of worker has emerged in the twenty-first century, one who is hired for brains, not brawn, and who expects a balanced lifestyle that includes leisure as well as work and the opportunity to balance the many overlapping work and family roles. These expectations become important as more and more employing organizations compete on the quality of their labor force, with the most successful enterprise likely to be the one that includes the most satisfied, creative, and therefore, we argue, the most productive workers. As a result, the human resource function has been elevated in importance within the strategic plan of many employing organizations.

Thinking about the future of social work and the workplace, an obvious locus from which to pursue organizationally relevant objectives is one within the human resource management arena.

Whether in a social agency or a profit-making corporation, the issues involved in assuring a motivated, productive, and creative workforce fall naturally within the purview of social work. The explanation for this is an evidence-based understanding that feelings are a significant factor in the way we think, behave, and make decisions. Being aware of our own feelings and the feelings of those with whom we interact and being able to manage these emotions to facilitate interpersonal relations, problem solving, and functional performance have been identified as important keys to organizational success (George 2000). Helping an organization release the emotional intelligence of its management can provide an organization with the competitive edge that each seeks.

A recent innovation that is well suited to this goal, and to social work skills, is executive coaching or life coaching. The two may be differentiated largely by their target. Executive coaching is focused on the highest-level executives in an organization and directed at their ability to stay focused and to lead by a shared vision rather than the less effective means of leadership by position. Life coaching, meanwhile, seeks to help the recipients gain general well-being and the capacity to improve their performance, job satisfaction, and thereby, organizational performance. Life coaches are helpful at a time of career transition since they focus on present situations, offer objective advice, and serve as a partner in helping motivate the service consumer to be confident, establish goals and develop action plans that can be achievable through specific steps. The approach allies a strengths perspective with an activist role as the counselor/coach. As Kochman (2003) has suggested, "Coaches help people create a future, not get over a past." Coaching has been likened to the model of the sports coach or personal trainer, but the skill it assumes as its goal is not athletic prowess but psychodynamic understanding and competence based on conscious use of self. Coaching is seen as a means to return to the employer the investment it makes in its leaders.

Effective coaches have been observed to personify maturity and objectivity and to use professional counseling skills, understanding of the importance of culture in human behavior, knowledge of systems dynamics, good communication skills, and the ability to be honest and ask hard questions. Surely this sounds like the skill list of an experienced clinician. And being a coach places the social worker in a position to exert influence at the highest organizational level. Organizations that use coaching are characterized by a commitment to lifelong learning, a quality that has been identified as key to effective diversity integration in a workplace. This dedication to being a learning organization is significant in that it not only characterizes units likely to be interested in coaching but also can be used as a marker of organizations where social workers will find a wide array of demand for their services under the human resource function, particularly those related to diversity management efforts, work/family initiatives, and their related training functions. By their content, these issues are core to the knowledge base of social work.

Diversity management, for example, involves recruiting from new resources, many of which are likely to be grassroots organizations in poor, immigrant, and minority communities or community facilities that serve people moving from welfare to work or those with physical disabilities, ex-offenders, individuals with serious and persistent mental health or substance abuse problems, or both, and others disadvantaged in their ability to compete in the labor market. Social workers, with their knowledge of community resources, their ability to carry out needs assessments to determine what these newly introduced populations may require to succeed in the workplace, and their capacity to deliver support services to these individuals and training for their coworkers and supervisors, offer the ideal staff for meeting the needs of a human resources unit charged with bringing integrated diversity to reality within an organization.

A similar skill set is needed to promote the achievement of a work/family responsive initiative. The variety of family units today places significant demands on an organization seeking to meet the full range of employee needs and expectations. Policies and procedures adopted to fulfill the wants of a traditional family with two parents, only one of whom is a worker, and two children, may not be responsive to the single middle-aged women caring for a pair of fragile, elderly parents, the gay couple who have adopted three special needs children, or the young marrieds with the employed wife supporting a husband who is a medical student. A sensitive needs assessment will be appropriate to assure the universality of the program; community resources will have to be inventoried to create appropriate partnerships between the employer and the community; consultation and training will be required to help the organizational culture become accepting of workers who access the benefits created; and counseling may be essential to help workers plan long-term strategies to meet changing family needs. It would be hard to envision any professional other than a social worker who could answer such a job description.

Nor is the opportunity for social workers to meet staffing needs of a workplace's human resource department limited to the issues described above. The general day-to-day work of the typical human resources department reflects the fact that although workers are hired, human beings answer the call. Two employees have difficulty working together and one requests a transfer; a charge of sexual harassment is lodged against someone who is regarded as the heir apparent to the chief financial officer; several minority employees complain that they are unfairly passed over for promotion; a long-term supervisor, just two years before being eligible for retirement, shows signs of cognitive impairment that is affecting the unit's work; an anonymous letter arrives suggesting that petty cash is being stolen and expense accounts padded through a conspiracy between a clerk in the accounting department and a product manager. Each of these delicate situations requires sensitive, careful investigation and advice concerning the company's response. The control-and-command response typical of management of an earlier period is no longer allowable in the more litigious and competitive environment in which the world of work operates today. This places abundant opportunity to make a meaningful contribution in the path of the occupational social worker who walks the human resource route to professional practice.

A Parallel Fertile Ground: Union Employment

Affiliation with a trade union, too, offers countless options to the interested occupational social worker. An important question for the future of social work, both within the world of work and in general, is, "what will be the profession's relationship to the trade union movement?" The question warrants attention in at least three arenas: unions as a partner in assuring society's social welfare agenda, unions as purveyors of social services, and unions as representative of the employees of social agencies. The early history of the profession suggests that even before 1948, when C. Wright Mills identified labor leaders as "the new men of power" in his book by the same title, social workers understood the importance of unions and their political clout. We realized the essential protection from the power of corporate America represented by the countervailing force of unions. The union commitment to strive to increase labor's share of the wealth, to achieve worker empowerment through membership participation, to struggle for social and workplace justice is consonant with the profession's goals. Unions are the largest single organization in the United States promoting a progressive, albeit self-serving, agenda in the political arena. All these mutual interests between social work and trade unions suggest that an alliance between them would seem to constitute a natural phenomena. In New York City the local chapter of the National Association of Social Workers (NASW) has, in fact, made a pact with Local 1199 of the Health and Human Service Employees Union (SEIU) to promote a plan for improved health coverage for all New Yorkers, a plan that would, parenthetically, increase employment in the sector covered by the union. In return, the local effectively lent support to NASW's successful effort to gain licensure in New York, a move that improves the availability and accessibility of insured mental health care for everyone in the state while offering the profession status in the managed care arena.

Such reciprocal support can be available throughout the country to social workers interested in political action directed at helping low-income, disadvantaged workers. The lobbying power of unions can be enlisted to promote goals as diverse as support for better local transit, essential in assisting the poor to reach employment opportunities, to parity in mental health care coverage, needed to assure treatment for adolescent children of working-class families who too often have had to surrender their children experiencing serious emotional disturbance to foster arrangements to gain access to adequate care. This natural affinity between the goals of the labor movement and the goals of the profession can be promoted by occupational social workers who are sensitive to and empathize with the interests and needs of trade unions and speak the language of the world of work.

It has often been said that unions organize discontent and sit on it in preparation for the struggle to come. Unions campaign to moderate management prerogatives and gain greater control for workers over how work is done and to ensure due process at the workplace, as well as to achieve the right of input into issues dealing with quality of the final product and with efficiency and effectiveness of the production of goods and services. The extent to which unions can succeed in any effort depends on membership loyalty. Needs assessments that identify the interests of union members can be vital to inspire the required support from union leadership. Loyalty can also be fostered by the delivery of training and the management of benefits and services, all activities that utilize the skills and knowledge of social workers. Furthermore, labor organizing—mobilizing a group for action and building a community of interest and support—are familiar techniques among social workers involved in community organizing. Employment in union settings can marry the staffing needs of unions with the practice inclinations of the individual professional. Such consonance offers the social worker protection from the burnout that often plagues practitioners.

Yet, in the world of social welfare there is ambiguity concerning the feasibility and extent of an alliance between social work and unions. The directors of social agencies, like managers anywhere, may fear that unionization of the labor force will result in a loss of agency flexibility and reduce management prerogative and worker accountability. Board members of social agencies sometimes view employees as a cost item, to be paid at the minimum wage feasible for maintaining their employment. They may see unionization as creating costs that endanger the life of the organization (see the case of the Exceptional Children's Resource Center in chap. 8). Practitioners themselves often question whether a union can represent their concerns while effectively protecting their "professional" responsibilities. It is the occupational social worker, armed with awareness of the mutual interests and competent in advocacy and negotiation, who can provide leadership within the profession to guide the parties to fruitful relationships that overcome these suspicions. Such an outcome would fulfill the mandate in the NASW Code of Ethics, which supports the right of practitioners to organize and bargain collectively, as the law requires, over wages, hours, and working conditions.

EAPs Today

Sometimes within, but always related to, the work of the human resource department or the union administration, employee and member assistance programs continue to be the principal employers of occupational social workers. Members of the social work profession usually are preferred when staffing employee assistance programs because the diverse expertise and comprehensive service model typical of social work are viewed as more responsive to and a better fit with the vested interest of labor and management for the stable and productive workforce on which they *both* depend (Tanner 1991). Not just a counseling or job jeopardy program responding to problems on a tertiary basis, most EAPs today have embraced a comprehensive service paradigm, long advocated by the authors of this text (Kurzman & Akabas 1993). Eschewing the old-fashioned "core technology" model (Roman & Blum 1988), with its primary focus on alcoholism and substance abuse, the comprehensive service program design of social work subscribes to a proactive program conceptualization that responds to the human service needs of workers and to the corresponding needs of work organizations. Services include not only assessment and intervention but also education, prevention, case management, and managed behavioral health care functions (see chaps. 4 and 6). This is exciting terrain for a professional social worker schooled in generalist practice, systems theory, the ecological, life model, and an empowerment perspective.

The majority of the workforce today has an EAP available to it. Many internal (in-house) programs continue, and their advantages are spelled out elsewhere in this volume. The predilection of most employers today, however, is toward the external (contractual) program design. Explanations for this trend include program flexibility, suitability for small businesses, comprehensiveness, perception of greater confidentiality, and consistency with current corporate trends and practices. The contractual model is in sync with the way companies do business today, where services, production, and even labor frequently are contracted out to firms that provide flexible and focused support roles, permitting employers to focus on their core responsibilities and functions.

In either an internal or external EAP setting, occupational social workers have occasion to interface with public and private benefit programs, interpret (and establish) protocols for compliance with work-centered statutes, secure public entitlements for current, displaced, and retired workers, and identify the natural helping networks in the community that can best serve their clients. Responding to the diverse and rapidly changing composition of the workforce, the disparate status of current employees, the several loci of work units (here and abroad), EAP staff, with their comfort with interorganizational and interdisciplinary collaboration and their competence in multicultural practice, can serve as a vital arm of today's human resource functions. Understanding (and often assuming) managed care administration, EAP practitioners are able to bring the profession's systems sophistication into play when working with insurance carriers, health maintenance organizations, government agencies, and preferred providers. To fulfill these potential roles, social workers need to be conversant with the new technology of communication, data storage, and information retrieval and to use this technology not only in the performance of the duties suggested above but also in the monitoring of their own practice to substantiate the value added that EAPs bring to the sponsoring organization. Such action is intimately related to the future connection between the profession and the world of work.

Managed Care

Managed care has reshaped the private practice experience of professionals by removing the locus of control from the professional-client dyad to the hands of a third party who is the payer. Many social workers have complained that this changed relationship results in limited choice and restricted access to care that is outside the best interests of the client. But others point out that the seller of service, namely the mental health professional, may not be the best source for decision making to assure that people get the care they need and do not receive care that they do not need. Supporters of this argument point out that the United States spends half again what most industrialized countries spend on health care yet does not achieve better results when measured by public health criteria such as longevity, infant mortality, or universal availability of care. This issue should be of concern to social workers interested in the workplace because employers are the major source of health care dollars for most covered Americans and have been the most vocal supporters of managed care initiatives. It is also of interest to occupational social workers because managed care has the potential to offer increased employment opportunities to the same social workers who complain about it. Private practitioners might find managed care less problematic if they concentrated more extensively on the work outcomes of their patients.

The Social Service Sector as a Workplace

Within the social service sector, itself, there are issues that warrant attention and provide opportunities for social workers knowledgeable concerning the world of work. The government's monthly survey of the U.S.

labor market, the Current Population Survey (CPS), noted in 1999 that almost six hundred thousand people with at least a baccalaureate degree self-identified as social workers (Barth 2003). While NASW would only consider individuals with a bachelor's, master's, or doctoral degree in social work to be members of the profession (which would represent approximately half of the CPS survey number), this still means there are around three hundred thousand professional social workers in all, about half of whom choose to belong to NASW. It is important for us to look at this population in a book on work, workers, and work organizations because social workers, too, are workers, performing an often arduous (yet rewarding) work function under the auspices of public, proprietary, and nonprofit organizations. While it is a broadly accepted axiom that social work in part is a calling, much like the ministry, social workers have intrinsic and extrinsic needs similar to all other members of the American workforce. Pride, respect, and self-esteem are examples of intrinsic rewards while tangible, or extrinsic, rewards include a reasonable salary, family-friendly benefits, and appropriate working conditions.

All social workers rightly expect to be treated with equity as well as equality and to be properly compensated (in cash and in kind) for their participation and contribution. Government data, however, show that social workers are found to earn about 11 percent less than people working in all other occupations. Additionally, from 1992 to 1998 the wages of MSWs grew only 1 percent annually, while the cost-of-living in the United States was increasing from 2 to 4 percent per annum (Barth 2003). Registered nurses, holding only a baccalaureate (four-year) or even an associate (two-year) undergraduate degree were being paid more than MSWs, both upon entry and ten years later in their professional careers. It is not surprising, therefore, to find that burnout is a major issue raised in the social work literature. Defined as a "term to describe workers who feel apathy or anger as a result of on-the-job stress and frustration" (Barker 2003: 57), burnout would appear to be widely prevalent in social agency settings. For social workers, who often feel that they have more responsibility than authority and greater work demand than reward, the burnout issue is reported to be broader than a question of adequate compensation (Gillespie 1987). Working generally with the poor and disenfranchised who have chronic conditions and marginal social prestige, members of the profession have a status that, too often, is reflective of the clients they serve.

Social workers are responding to this dilemma in three ways. First, the organized profession, led by NASW, has been aggressively seeking legal recognition for its members. For example, thirty years ago (1974), only thirteen states provided for the legal regulation of social work practice. By

1994 all fifty states did. Similarly, as a result of concerted advocacy on both a state and federal level, qualified social workers currently enjoy vendor privileges in thirty-five states, whereas such status did not exist in a single state in 1974. As a result, clinical social workers today are nationally recognized as autonomous providers of mental health care. In fact, they have become the professional provider of choice in the mental health system, as they are in EAPs (Cohen 2003). This achievement has led to the second response. An increasing number of social workers are engaging in private practice—not as their primary position but as a supplement to agency-based practice. As independent practitioners, such social workers have more autonomy, additional financial compensation, and enhanced status and recognition as professional providers in their community. Third, social workers have joined labor unions at almost twice the percentage for workers as a whole (Tambor 1995). More than half of all social workers are employed in the highly organized public sector (federal, state, or local government), which is the one sector of the world of work where unions remain strong. With the strength of collective representation, factors that promote equity and that mitigate against burnout are present. Unions fight not only for good wages and benefits but also for job security and favorable working conditions—including reasonable workloads. These advantages give social workers greater control over their work and an increased sense of status and respect, and serve as an effective antidote to the sometimes oppressive demands of both their clients and their employers.

Employment Policy and Implications for Practice

Changes in public and corporate policy during the last few decades have opened new roles for social work practice in the employment arena. Shifts in public welfare policies and provisions have moved great numbers of public assistance recipients, of necessity, into the world of work. Remarkable advances in psychotropic medications mean that a significant cohort of people not thought to be candidates for traditional workforce participation now hold gainful employment. Companies have moved the sites of production and service—not just from the North to the South, but to Mexico, India, Eastern Europe, and the Pacific Rim causing disruption to the labor force at home. In each case, the connection between policy and practice is clearly evident, opening new options for professional social workers who are attracted and intrigued by the opportunities for stimulating practice in and with work settings.

We have witnessed a major change in public assistance over the past few decades. Starting with the federal Work Incentive Program (WIN) in 1967, continuing under the Family Support Act of 1988, and intensifying as a result of provisions of the omnibus welfare reform laws of 1996, most welfare mothers today are expected to work. Current statutes impose a time limit on the receipt of welfare, cut benefits for immigrant workers, and impose a stringent work requirement on all recipients (see chaps. 3 and 4). Regardless of the social work profession's general opinion about the equity of these more coercive mandates, the outcome has been a new emphasis on the need to move welfare mothers from welfare to work. Despite our predilection toward less restrictive regulations, these requirements do provide us with an excellent opportunity to serve poor, disenfranchised women (often of color), who represent an exemplar of our own commitment and our raison d'être as a profession. In particular, group work and community organization expertise should prove useful to individuals and organizations helping public assistance recipients identify their individual and group strengths, pursue education and skills training opportunities, and advocate for community resources, government entitlements, and due process. Caution is needed in this area. Although the "work first" strategy has reduced welfare rolls significantly, it has not increased self-sufficiency because women in general experience discrimination that limits their earnings, and most of the welfare-to-work population are unskilled women with significant child care problems, further limiting their earnings and turning them into a "vast new service proletariat" (Lens 2002) that requires a whole new dimension of advocacy from occupational social workers.

A dramatic change also has occurred over the last decade in the treatment of people with serious and persistent mental health conditions (see chap. 7). Such people have been included both as part of the general social policy movement that encourages employment for everyone and through a specific public policy commitment to a recovery model under which care is goal oriented, with the preferred outcome being employment (Lukens 2003). Clients with diagnoses of major depression, bipolar disorder, and schizophrenia are no longer confined to institutional settings for residence, SSI and SSDI for income, or sheltered workshops for employment. New laws, psychotropic medications, and evidence-based practices (such as supported housing, family psycho-education, and a strengths-based clinical perspective) have established the necessary conditions to move many people with chronic and persistent mental health conditions out of the world of dependency. Equally relevant with regard to opportunities for social workers has been the emergence of nonpsychiatric practitioners as the dominant treatment personnel for assisting this population (Cohen 2003). Joining with the advocacy of and support from the National Alliance for the Mentally Ill, consumer organizations, and clients' families, social workers are providing leadership as such formerly dependent clients move into the mainstream of American life—the workplace. Experiencing greater opportunity, reduced stigma, and increased acceptance, people with severe and persistent mental health conditions are being maintained in competitive work settings, while social workers, from both community agencies and EAPs, offer the essential coaching, advocacy, supportive counseling, advice about accommodation, and case management that are the hallmarks of evidence-based supported employment practices.

The theoretical orientation of the social work profession to a person-in-environment and strengths perspective and the world of work knowledge that an occupational social worker brings to practice provide ideal circumstances for helping normalize the lives of people with mental health conditions. Recognition of this potential accounts for the required staffing, for example, of assertive community treatment (ACT) teams. These teams are mandated, in addition to a nurse, a case manager, and a peer, to include counselors who are knowledgeable about vocational planning and employment support. ACT teams represent cutting-edge alternatives to hospitalization for people with serious and persistent mental health conditions. The teams are expected to achieve normative community living for the target population. The definition of normative, not unexpectedly, includes appropriate work. This movement has the potential to end a long history during which people with mental health conditions have been denied their human rights including the opportunity to secure competitive employment. But to accomplish the mandated goal of employment, teams clearly require the participation of a professional knowledgeable in bridging the social welfare and work arenas, the natural work space of occupational social workers.

In a similar vein, globalization, merger-mania, technological change, and downsizing have generated seismic changes in the lives of many workers and their families. One career, largely with just one or two employers, rarely is the reality for today's workforce participants. Instead, six to eight jobs in the context of three or four separate careers is the more likely scenario—often involving very difficult employment transitions. Outplacement, retraining and upgrading, career coaching, and linkage to resources and entitlements become critical functions at the new junctures of job displacement. Who better to assume these functions and perform these roles than a generalist social worker who can provide individual (and family) counseling, form and lead both support and activity-focused groups, identify and access community resources, and advocate with government, labor, civic, and employment organizations for resources and policy commitments (see chap. 6)?

In all these examples, we can see the link between policy and practice. In order to ensure a fair distribution of jobs to disadvantaged populations in light of the frequently biased and unequal marketplace of employment, occupational social workers are becoming an individual and collective force on behalf of dislocated workers, welfare-to-work mothers, and people with chronic mental health conditions. New laws, medical advances, evolving mores and values, and environmental changes all have created practice opportunities for social workers who are sensitive to the meaning of work, and the centrality of praxis—the practical application of skills and knowledge to changing customs and convention—and have brought about favorable conditions for achieving "distributive justice" (Rawls 1971) via the workplace.

Community Relations and Philanthropy

Changes in public policies and more particularly in corporate and union policies are also reflected in corporate philanthropy and union fundraising efforts. Labor and management have a long history of involvement with and commitment to the communities in which they are located and to which they provide their manpower, products, and services. While the nature of their participation has changed over time, both trade unions and employers generally have viewed such relationships as being ideal means of combining their own self-interest with creating a public image of "doing good." Particularly in the banking, insurance, and utilities industries, corporations frequently have been directly involved in health, education, and welfare issues in the geographic and functional communities with which their staff and customers interact. As Akabas (1995a: 1781) has noted "Philip Morris's dedication to American cultural enterprises, Mutual of New York's philanthropic mission in relation to acquired immune deficiency syndrome [AIDS] services, McDonald's financing of entertainment for sick children, and the AFL-CIO's ongoing sponsorship of scouting are select examples of a massive commitment by the auspices of the world of work to fulfill their social responsibilities."

A significant amount of funding for nonprofit social agencies comes from such earmarked corporate giving and through corporate foundations. The *National Directory of Corporate Giving* (Foundation Center

2003) lists twenty-three hundred corporate foundations and thirteen hundred direct corporate giving programs. Their philanthropic contributions often are supplemented by family foundations, endowed by the fortunes or estates of successful entrepreneurs and focusing primarily on human service agencies and initiatives. The Ford Foundation and the Gates Foundation are two of the more dramatic examples of this use of personal wealth. The trustees and boards of foundations that link the interests of philanthropy and the world of work have welcomed social workers as managers who can evaluate proposals, advise on appropriate missions to support, and monitor grant expenditures.

Labor unions also have been active in the community services arena. Starting with Samuel Gompers, the AFL's leader at the turn of the twentieth century, the trade union movement has shown an interest in promoting social services and social justice—"bread and roses." As Molloy and Kurzman (1993) have observed, social work's commitment to advocacy for clients and for progressive social change has made it a natural ally of labor in pursuit of the goals of social justice. Unions look to social workers to cultivate an advocacy capacity for their members within the social service system—a system to which they pay taxes as wage earners and to which they make generous United Way contributions through voluntary deductions from their paychecks. For occupational social workers, the natural question is, what are the inherent alliances of mutual interest that can be formed here, using the social work profession's community organization, program development, research, and planning expertise? There are many examples. Often sharing a common ideology with unions and advocating for the needs and rights of the working class and the working poor, social workers, social agencies, and schools of social work have mounted successful community social service and social action initiatives with the United Auto Workers, Service Employees International Union, United Needle Industrial and Textile Employees, and the American Federation of State, County, and Municipal Employees, to name but a few. Ultimately, both management and labor recognize that fulfilling their social obligations is "good business" because it is good for marketing and community relations, creates loyalty to the leadership, and to the products and services they together provide. As a result, occupational social work opportunities exist in the domains of charitable allocations, community services, urban affairs, affirmative action, social responsibility, and community relations, and from the union side, in the areas of retiree services, dependent care advocacy, community service programming, United Way partnerships, and political action.

* * *

We have argued that the economy and economic issues predetermine much of what happens to people. This provides a rationale for social work to be invested in the workplace where the economic issues are at the base of most decision making. Another theme throughout has been the significance of work in people's lives. This alone would provide adequate reason for social work to be involved in work. But the significance of work goes beyond individual impact. Trends in the labor market such as utilizing contingency workers, multiple job holders, and individuals accepting part-time work because the full-time work they seek is not available, all augur for increasing problems stemming from the workplace. The aging of baby boomers, the reduction of fringe benefits, and the decreasing proportion of workers represented by unions represent additional threats to the well-being of the workforce and, indeed, to our way of life. Every indication is that the middle class is threatened with extinction—that is, workers who use skills and knowledge that have made them the most productive labor force in the world look like they may have priced themselves out of the competitive market in the swift trend toward globalization. Work and family/community are intertwined in policy and practice and have reciprocal impact. The social work profession's long-time dedication to individuals, families, and communities cannot be realized without looking at the impact of work on those units and their well-being. Additionally, occupational social work reflects the national focus on production, economy, and the partnership of key sectors, yet another reason for its significance to the future of the social work profession. Instead of remaining outside, critical of the conservative policies that propose to reduce taxes and increase self-sufficiency regardless of the cost to disadvantaged populations, it befits social work to strive from inside to help create alternatives to shrinking dollars and public commitment by developing new coalitions with more powerful entities. Occupational social work provides such a vantage and the chance to make a difference. It is an opportunity for the profession that should not be missed.

REFERENCES

Abramovitz, M. (1995). Aid to families with dependent children. In R. L. Edwards et al. (Eds.), *Encyclopedia of social work* (19th ed.) (1:183–94). Washington, D.C.: NASW Press.

———. (1996). *Regulating the lives of women.* (Rev. ed.). Boston: South End Press.

———. (1997). Temporary assistance to needy families. In R. L. Edwards et al. (Eds.), *Encyclopedia of social work* (19th ed. supplement) (311–33). Washington, D.C.: NASW Press.

———. (1998). Social work and social reform: An arena of struggle. *Social Work* 43(6), 512–26.

Abramson, A., and Salamon, L. (1986). *The non-profit sector and the new federal budget.* Washington, D.C.: Urban Institute.

Achtenberg, R. (Ed.). (1985). *Sexual orientation and the law.* New York: Clark Boardman Ltd.

Acker, G. (1999). The impact of clients' mental illness on workers' job satisfaction and burnout. *Health and Social Work* 24(2), 112–19.

AFL-CIO. (1997). *America@work Magazine* 2(8).

———. (1998). *America@work Magazine* 3(4).

———. (1999). *America@work Magazine* 4(5).

———. (2003). *America@work Magazine* 8(7).

———. (n.d.). The union difference: Trends in union membership. Retrieved February 10, 2004, from http://www.aflcio.org/aboutunions/joinunions/whyjoin/uniondifference/uniondiff11.cfm.

Akabas, S. H. (1970). Labor force characteristics, mental illness and earnings in the men's clothing industry. *Dissertation abstracts international* 31(11), 5609-A. Ph.D. diss., New York University.

———. (1977). Labor: Social policy and human services. In J. B. Turner et al. (Eds.), *Encyclopedia of social work* (17th ed.) (1:738–44). Washington, D.C.: NASW.

——. (1983). Industrial social work: Influencing the system at the workplace. In M. Dinerman (Ed.), *Social work in a turbulent world* (pp. 131–41). Silver Spring, Md.: NASW.

——. (1984a). Expanded view for worksite counseling. *Business and Health,*1, 24–28.

——. (1984b). Workers are parents too. *Child Welfare* 63(5), 387–98.

——. (1990). Reconciling the demands of work with the needs of families. *Families in Society* 71(6), 366–71.

——. (1995a). Occupational social work. In R. L. Edwards et al. (Eds.) *Encyclopedia of social work* (19th ed.) (2:1779–86). Washington, D.C.: NASW Press.

——. (1995b). Supervisors: The linchpin in effective employment for people with disabilities. *Journal of the California Alliance for the Mentally Ill* 6(4),17–18.

——. (2000). Practice in the world of work: Promise unrealized. In P. Meares and C. Gervin (Eds.), *The handbook of social work direct practice* (pp. 499–517). Thousand Oaks, Calif.: Sage.

Akabas, S, H,, and Bikson, L. (2001). Work and job jeopardy. In A. Gitterman (Ed.), *Social work practice with vulnerable and resilient populations* (2nd ed.) (pp. 841–60). New York: Columbia University Press.

Akabas, S. H., and Farrell, B. G. (1993). Prevention: An organizing concept for workplace services. In P. A. Kurzman and S. H. Akabas (Eds.), *Work and well-being: The occupational social work advantage* (pp. 86–101). Washington, D.C.: NASW Press.

Akabas, S. H., and Gates, L. (1990). Workforce diversity. In J. Klein and J. Miller (Eds.), *The American edge* (pp. 113–35). New York: McGraw-Hill.

—— (1993). Managing disability in the workplace: A role for social workers. In P. A. Kurzman and S. H. Akabas (Eds.), *Work and well-being: The occupational social work advantage* (pp. 239–55). Washington, D.C.: NASW Press.

——. (1997). *Planning for disability management: An approach to controlling costs while caring for employees.* Scottsdale, Ariz.: American Compensation Association.

——. (2000). A social work role: Promoting employment equity for people with serious and persistent mental illness. *Administration in Social Work* 23(3/4), 163–84.

——. (2002). *The role of employee assistance programs in supporting workers with mental health conditions.* New York: Center for Social Policy and Practice in the Workplace, Columbia University.

——. (In review). Work opportunities for rewarding carriers: A model to guide practice with mental health consumers.

Akabas, S. H., Gates, L. B., and Galvin, D. E. (1992). *Disability management.* New York: AMACOM.

Akabas, S. H., and Krauskopf, M.S. (1986). A buyer's market for EAPs. *Business and Health*, 3, 30–35.

Akabas, S. H., and Kurzman, P. A. (1982a). The industrial social welfare specialist: What's so special? In S. H. Akabas and P. A. Kurzman (Eds.), *Work, workers, and work organizations: A view from social work* (pp. 197–235). Englewood Cliffs, N.J.: Prentice Hall.

———. (Eds.). (1982b). *Work, workers, and work organizations: A view from social work.* Englewood Cliffs, N.J.: Prentice-Hall.

Akabas, S. H., Kurzman, P. A., and Kolben, N. S. (1979). *Labor and industrial settings: Sites for social work practice.* New York: Columbia University, Hunter College and CSWE.

Alderfer, C. P. (1987). An intergroup perspective on group dynamics. In J. Lorsch (Ed.), *Handbook on organizational behavior* (pp. 190–222). Englewood Cliffs, N.J.: Prentice-Hall.

Allen, T., Freeman, D., Russell, J., Reizenstein, J., and Rentz, J. (2001). Survivor reactions to organizational downsizing: Does time ease the pain? *Journal of Occupational and Organizational Psychology* 74 (June), 145–64.

Allen, Z. (1996). The 1996 election. *Public Employee Press* 37(20, November 29), 8–9.

Anthony, W. (2003). Studying evidence-based processes, not practices. *Psychiatric Services* 54 (1), 7.

Antoniades, R., and Bellinger, S. (1983). Organized worksites: A help or hindrance in the delivery of social work services in and to the workplace. In R. J. Thomlison (Ed.), *Perspectives on industrial social work practice* (pp. 29–38). Ottawa: Family Service Canada.

APA (American Psychiatric Association). (1994). *Diagnostic and statistical manual of mental disorders.* (4th ed.). Washington, D.C.: Author.

Aronowitz, S. (1994). *The jobless future.* Minneapolis: University of Minnesota Press.

Asch, A., and Abelson, P. (1993). Serving workers through managed mental health care: The social work role. In P. A. Kurzman and S. H. Akabas (Eds.), *Work and well-being: The occupational social work advantage* (pp. 123–37). Washington, D.C.: NASW Press.

Asch, A., and Mudrick, N. R. (1995). Disability. In R. L. Edwards et al. (Eds.), *Encyclopedia of social work* (19th ed.) (1:752–61). Washington, D.C.: NASW Press.

Austrian, S. (1998). Clinical social work in the 21st century: Behavioral managed care is here to stay! In R. Dorfman (Ed.), *Paradigms of clinical social work* (2:315–36). New York: Brunner/Mazel, Publishers.

Axinn, J., and Stern, M. J. (2001). *Social welfare: A history of the American response to need.* (5th ed.). Boston: Allyn and Bacon.

Bacon, D. (2000). Immigrant workers ask labor: Which side are you on? *Working USA* 3(5), 7–18.

Bailey, D. (1995). Management: Diverse workplaces. In R. L. Edwards et al. (Eds.), *Encyclopedia of social work* (19th ed.) (2:1659–63). Washington, D.C.: NASW Press.

Bakalinsky, R. (1980). People vs. Profits: Social work in industry. *Social Work,* 25(6), 471–475.

Bane, M. J., and Ellwood, D. T. (1994). *Welfare realities: From rhetoric to reform.* Cambridge, Mass.: Harvard University Press.

Banerjee, M. (1995). Desired service outcomes: Toward attaining an elusive goal. *Administration in Social Work* 19(1), 33–53.

Bargal, D., and Katan, Y. (1998). Social work in the world of work: The Israeli case. In F. Lowenberg (Ed.), *The challenges of a changing society* (pp. 257–78). Jerusalem: Magnes Press.

Bargal, D., and Schmid, H. (1992). Organizational change and development in human service organizations: A prefatory essay. *Administration in Social Work* 16(3/4), 5.

Barker, K. (2003). Contingent work in the United States. In R. A. English (Ed.), *Encyclopedia of social work* (19th ed.) (2003 supplement, pp. 9–20). Washington, D.C.: NASW Press.

Barker, K., and Christensen, K. (1998). Controversy and challenges raised by contingent work arrangements. In K. Barker and K. Christensen (Eds.), *Contingent work: American employment relations in transition* (pp. 1–18). Ithaca, N.Y.: ILR Press.

Barker, R. L. (1999). *Milestones in the development of social work and social welfare.* Washington, D.C.: NASW Press.

———. (2003). *The social work dictionary* (5th ed.). Washington, D.C.: NASW Press.

Barnes, P. (1991). Managed mental health care: A balancing act. *Administration and Policy in Mental Health* 19(1), 51–55.

Barth, M. C. (2003). Social work labor market: A first look. *Social Work* 48(1), 9–19.

Batavick, L. (1997). Community-based family support and youth development: Two movements, one philosophy. *Child Welfare* 76(5), 639–63.

Beggs, J. (1995). The institutional environment: Implications for race and gender inequality in the U.S. labor market. *American Sociological Review* 60(4), 612–25.

Bell, D. (1992). *Faces at the bottom of the well: The permanence of racism.* New York: Basic Books.

Beller, D. J., and Lawrence, H. H. (1992). Trends in private pension plan coverage. In J. A. Turner and D. J. Beller (Eds.), *Trends in pensions* (pp.35–57). Washington, D.C.: United States Department of Labor.

Bernstein, J. (1999). Reformulating welfare reform. *Hunter College School of Social Work Update* 3–4 (Spring), 6.

Bernstein, N. (1996). Giant companies entering race to run state welfare program. *New York Times,* September 15, pp. A1, A26.

Bevilacqua, J. (1999). The state vocational rehabilitation agency. *Journal of Disability Policy Studies* 10(1), 90–98.

Bevilacqua, J. J., and Darnauer, P. F. (1977). Military social work. In J. B. Turner et al. (Eds.). *Encyclopedia of social work* (17th ed.) (2:927–31). Washington, D.C.: NASW.

Bielby, W. (2000). Minimizing workplace gender and racial bias. *Contemporary Sociology, 29*(1), 120–29.

Bielski, V. (1996). The way we work: Our magnificent obsession. *Family Therapy Newsletter 20*, 25–35.

Bishop, J. E. (1979). Age of anxiety: Stress of American life is increasingly blamed for emotional turmoil. *New York Times,* April 2, pp. 1, D14.

Black, R. (1994). Diversity and populations at risk: People with disabilities. In F. Reamer (Ed.), *The Foundation of Social Work Knowledge* (pp. 393–416). New York: Columbia University Press.

Blair, B. (1987). Internal and external models. In J. Spicer (Ed.), *The EAP solution* (pp. 12–17). Center City, Minn.: Hazelden Foundation.

Blank, R. (1994). Outlook of the U.S. labor market and prospects for low-wage entry jobs (unpublished working paper). Evanston, Ill.: Northwestern University, Center for Urban Affairs.

Bloom, M. (1995). Primary prevention overview. In R. L. Edwards et al. (Eds.), *Encyclopedia of social work* (19th ed.) (3:1895–905). Washington, D.C.: NASW Press.

Bluestone, B., and Rose, S. (1997). Overworked and underemployed. *American Prospect* (March–April), 58–69. [No volume provided].

Blum, T., Martin, J., and Roman, P. (1992). A research note on EAP prevalence, components, and utilization. *Journal of Employee Assistance Research* 1(1), 209–29.

Blum, T., and Roman, P. (1987). Internal vs. external EAPs. In *EAPs: Benefits, problems and prospects* (Ch. 13). Washington, D.C.: Bureau of National Affairs. [no pagination].

Bok, D. (1996). *The state of the nation: Government and the quest for a better society.* Cambridge, Mass.: Harvard University Press.

Bok, D. C., and Dunlop, J. T. (1970). *Labor and the American community.* New York: Simon and Schuster.

Bombyk, M. (1995). Progressive social work. In R. L. Edwards et al. (Eds.), *Encyclopedia of social work* (19th ed.) (3:1933–42). Washington, D.C.: NASW Press.

Bond, G. (1998). Principles of the individual placement and support model: Empirical support. *Psychiatric Rehabilitation Journal* 22(1), 11–23.

Bond, G., Becker, D., Drake, R., Rapp, C., Meisler, N., Lehman, A., Bell, M, and Blyler, C. (2001). Implementing supported employment as an evidence-based practice. *Psychiatric Services, 52*(3), 313–22.

Bourdieu, P. (1965). *Travail et travailleurs en Algérie.* Paris: Editions Mouton.

Brager, G., and Holloway, S. (1978). *Changing human service organizations: Politics and practice.* New York: Free Press.

Brandes, S. D. (1976). *American welfare capitalism, 1880–1940.* Chicago: University of Chicago Press.

Bravo, E. (1999). Letter to the editor. *New York Times*, May 23, sec. 4, p. 14.

Brayfield, A. (1995). Juggling jobs and kids: The impact of employment schedules on fathers' caring for children. *Journal of Marriage and the Family* 57(2), 321–32.

Brenner, M. H. (1973). *Mental illness and the economy.* Cambridge, Mass.: Harvard University Press.

Briar, K. H., and Vinet, M. (1985). Ethical questions concerning an EAP: Who is the client? In S. H. Klarreich, J. L. Francek and E. C. Moore (Eds.), *The human resources management handbook* (pp. 342–59). New York: Praeger.

Brick, M. (2001). New increases in worker output. *New York Times*, February 8, p. C16.

Brilliant, E. L., and Rice, K. A. (1988). Influencing corporate philanthropy. In G. M. Gould and M. L. Smith (Eds.), *Social work in the workplace: Practice and principles* (pp. 299-313). New York: Springer.

Brocato, J., and Wagner, E. (2003) Harm reduction: A social work practice model and social justice agenda. *Health and Social Work* 28(2), 117–25.

Browne, A., Salomon, A., and Bassuk, S. (1999). The impact of recent partner violence on poor women's capacity to maintain work. *Violence Against Women*, 5(4), 393–426.

Bruhnsen, K. (1999). Brief interventions and moderation approaches for preventing alcohol problems. In J. Oher (Ed.), *The employee assistance handbook* (pp. 221–46). New York: John Wiley and Sons.

Buhler, P. (2003). Managing in the new millennium. *SuperVision* 64(10), 20-22.

Burghardt, S., and Fabricant, M. (1987). *Working under the safety net.* Beverly Hills, Calif.: Sage.

Butler, B. (1990). Job satisfaction: Management's continuing challenge. *Social Work* 35(2, March), 112–17.

Carnochan, S., and Austin, M. (2002). Implementing welfare reform and building organizational change. *Administration in Social Work* 26(1), 61–77.

Carnoy, M. (1999). The family, flexible work and social cohesion at risk. *International Labour Review* 138(4), 411–29.

Carson, R. (1962). *Silent spring.* Boston: Houghton-Mifflin.

Casner-Lotto, J. (2000). Holding a job, having a life—the next level in work redesign. *Employment Relations Today* (Summer), 29–41.

Cassidy, J. (1999). A new study shows America's fat cats getting fatter. *New Yorker*, September 13, 32.

Chestang, L. W. (1982). Work, personal change, and human development. In S. H. Akabas and P. A. Kurzman (Eds.), *Work, workers, and work organizations: A view from social work* (pp. 61–89). Englewood Cliffs, N.J.: Prentice-Hall.

Clark, E. J. (2003). The future of social work practice. In R. A. English (Ed.), *Encyclopedia of social work* (2003 supplement, pp. 61–70). Washington, D.C.: NASW Press.

Clark, S. (2000). Work/family border theory: A new theory of work/family balance. *Human Relations* 53(4), 747–65.

Clemetson, L. (2003). More Americans in poverty in 2002, Census study finds. *New York Times*, September 27, p. A10.

Cohen, J. A. (2003). Managed care and the evolving role of the clinical social worker in mental health. *Social Work* 48(1), 34–43.

Conway, H., and Svenson, J. (1998). Occupational injury and illness rates, 1992–96: Why they fell. *Monthly Labor Review* 121(11, November), 36–58.

Coulton, C. J. (1996). Poverty, work and community: A research agenda for an era of diminishing federal responsibility. *Social Work* 41(5), 509–19.

Counseling and consultation at Polaroid. (1978). *Practice Digest* 1, 6–7.

Csiernik, R. (1998). An integrated model of occupational assistance. *Social Worker* 66(3), 37–47.

———. (1999). Internal versus external employee assistance programs: What the Canadian data adds to the debate. *Employee Assistance Quarterly* 15(2), 1–12.

Cunningham, G. (1994). *Effective EAPs.* Thousand Oaks, Calif.: Sage.

CSWE (Council on Social Work Education). (2001). *Educational policy and accreditation standards.* Alexandria, Va.: Author.

———. (2002). *Handbook of accreditation standards and procedures.* (5th ed.). Alexandria, Va.: Author.

Davidson, B., and Herlihy, P. (1999). The EAP and the work-family connection. In J. Oher (Ed.), *The Employee Assistance Handbook* (pp. 405–19). New York: John Wiley and Sons.

Denning, P. (2000). *Practicing harm reduction psychotherapy: An alternative approach to addictions.* New York: Guilford.

DeParle, J. (1998). What welfare-to-work really means. *New York Times Magazine*, December 20, pp. 50–64.

Dickinson, N. S. (1995). Federal social legislation from 1961 to 1994. In R. L. Edwards et al. (Eds.), *Encyclopedia of social work* (19th ed.) (2:1005–13). Washington, D.C.: NASW Press.

———. (1997). Federal social legislation from 1994 to 1997. In R. L. Edwards et al. (Eds.), *Encyclopedia of social work* (19th ed. supplement) (pp. 125–31). Washington, D.C.: NASW Press.

DiNatale, M., and Boraas, S. (2002). The labor force experience of women from Generation X. *Monthly Labor Review* 125, 3–15.

District Council 37, AFSCME. (1998). *Public Employee Press* (October 2), p. 4.

Donovan, R. (1984). The dollars and "sense" of human services at the workplace: A review of cost-effectiveness research. *Social Work Papers* 18, 65–73.

———. (1987). Home care work: A legacy of slavery in U.S. health care. *Affilia* 2(3), 33–44.

———. (1989a). We care for the most important people in your life: Home care workers in New York City. *Women's Studies Quarterly* 17(1and 2), 56–65.

——. (1989b). Work stress and job satisfaction: A study of home care workers in New York City. *Home Care Services Quarterly* 10(1 and 2), 93–114.

Donovan, R., Kurzman, P. A., and Rotman, C. (1993). Improving the lives of home care workers: A partnership of social work and labor. *Social Work* 38(5), 579–85.

Dowd, M. (1983). Many women in poll value jobs as much as family life. *New York Times*, December 4, pp. 1, 66.

Downsizing of America. (1996). *New York Times*, March 3, pp. 27–28.

Drucker, P. (1990) *Managing the non-profit organization: Practices and principles.* New York: Harper Collins.

Dunn, E. F. (1998). Historical review of U.S. policy on diversity. In A. Daly (Ed.), *Workplace diversity: Issues and perspectives* (pp.70–87). Washington, D.C.: NASW Press.

Dusenbury, L. (1999). Workplace drug abuse prevention initiatives: A review. *Journal of Primary Prevention* 20(2), 145–56.

Edwards, R. L., Cooke, P. W., and Reid, P. (1996) Social work management in an era of diminishing federal responsibility. *Social Work* 41(5), 468–79.

Ehrenreich, B. (2000). *Nickel and dimed: On (not) making it in America.* New York: Owl Books.

Eichner, A. (1973). The search for output measures. *Social Policy* 9(2), 48–53.

Ellin, A. (2002). Stock options? Try union dues. *New York Times*, September 15, p. 3.9

Ellison, R. (1952). *Invisible man.* New York: Random House.

Ending welfare. (Editorial.) (1998). *New York Times,* July 27, p. A22.

Ewalt, P. (1991). Trends affecting recruitment and retention of social work staff in human services agencies. *Social Work* 36(3), 214–17.

Fabricant, M., and Burghardt, S. (1992). *The welfare state crisis and the transformation of social service work.* Armonk, New York: M. E. Sharpe.

Feather, N. T. (1990). *The psychological impact of unemployment.* New York: Springer-Verlag.

Feinstein, B. B., and Brown, E. G. (1982). *The new partnership: Human services, business and industry.* Cambridge, Mass.: Schenkman.

Fewell, C. H., King, B. L., and Weinstein, D. L. (1993). Alcohol and other drug abuse among social work colleagues and their families: Impact on practice, *Social Work* 38(5, September), 565–70.

Figley, C. (1995). Compassion fatigue as secondary traumatic stress disorder: An overview. In C. Figley (Ed.), *Compassion fatigue: Coping with secondary traumatic stress disorder in those who treat the traumatized.* Levittown, Pa.: Brunner/Mazel.

Filipowicz, C. A. (1979). The troubled employee: Whose responsibility? *The Personnel Administrator,* 24(6), 17–22, 33.

Fine, M., Akabas, S., and Bellinger, S. (1982). Cultures of drinking: A workplace perspective. *Social Work* 27(5), 436–40.

Fine, M., and Asch, A. (1988). Disability beyond stigma: Social interaction, discrimination, and activism. *Journal of Social Issues* 44(1), 3–21.

Finkle, A. (1998). Mental health in the managed care era: An opportunity for EAPs. *Employee Assistance Quarterly* 13(3), 33–45.

Fischel-Wolovick, L., Cotter, C., Masser, I., Kelman-Bravo, E., Jaffe, S., Rosenberg, G. and Wittenberg, B. (1988). Alternative work scheduling for professional social workers. *Administration in Social Work* 12(4), 93–102.

Fisher, J. (1980). *The response of social work to the Depression.* Cambridge, Mass.: Schenkman.

Fisher, R., Ury, W., and Patton, B. (1991). *Getting to yes: Negotiating agreement without giving in.* (2nd ed.) New York: Penguin Books.

Fleisher, D., and Kaplan, B. H. (1988). Employee assistance/Counseling typologies. In G. M. Gould and M. L. Smith (Eds.), *Social work in the workplace: Practice and principles* (pp. 31–44). New York: Springer.

Folbre, N. (1995). *The new field guide to the U.S. economy.* New York: New Press.

Fong, L. and Gibbs, J. (1995). Facilitating services to multi-cultural communities in a dominant culture setting: An organizational perspective. *Administration in Social Work* 19(2), 1–24.

Foote, A. (Ed.). (1978). *Cost effectiveness of occupational EAPs.* Ann Arbor, Mich.: Institute of Labor and Industrial Relations of the University of Michigan.

Foster, B., and Schore, L. (1990). Job loss and the occupational social worker. In S. L. A. Straussner (Ed.), *Occupational social work today* (pp. 77–97). New York: Haworth Press.

Foundation Center, The. (2003). *The national directory of corporate giving* (9th ed.). New York: Author.

Fredriksen, K., and Scharlach, A. (1999). Employee family care responsibilities. *Family Relations* 48(2), 189–96.

Freedman, R., Litchfield, L., and Warfield, M. (1995). Balancing work and family: Perspectives of parents of children with developmental disabilities. *Families in Society* 76(8), 507–14.

Freeman, R. (1996). Toward an apartheid economy. *Harvard Business Review* 74(September–October), 114–21.

Freud, S. (1930). *Civilization and its discontents.* London: Hogarth Press.

Freudenheim, M. (1993). The price of worker health care. *New York Times,* March 2, pp. D1, D20.

———. (1994).Companies assess psychotherapy by the numbers. *New York Times,* April 12, pp. A1, D2.

Friedlander, D., and Burtless, G. (1995). *Five years after: The long-term effects of welfare-to-work programs.* New York: Russell-Sage.

Friedman, G. A., and Havinghurst, R. J. (1954). *The meaning of work and retirement*. Chicago: University of Chicago Press.

Frumkin, P., and Andre-Clark, A. (1999). The rise of the corporate social worker. *Social Science and Public Policy* 36(6), 46–52.

Gabriel, P. (Ed.) (2000). *Mental health in the workplace: Situation analysis United States*. Geneva, Switzerland: ILO.

Gamble, D. N., and Weil, M. O. (1995). Citizen participation. In R. L. Edwards et al. (Eds.), *Encyclopedia of social work* (19th ed.) (1:483–94). Washington, D.C.: NASW Press.

Gant, L. (1996). Are culturally sophisticated agencies better workplaces for social work staff and administrators? *Social Work* 41(2), 163–71.

Garraty, J. A. (1986). *Employment in history*. New York: Harper and Row.

Gates, L. (2000). Workplace accommodation as a social process. *Journal of Occupational Rehabilitation* 10(1), 85–98.

Gates, L., Akabas, S., and Oran-Sabia, V. (1998). Relationship accommodations involving the work group: Improving work prognosis for persons with mental health conditions. *Psychiatric Rehabilitation Journal* 21(3), 264–72.

Gates, L., Taler. Y., and Akabas, S. (1989) Optimizing return to work among newly disabled workers: A new approach to cost containment. *Benefits Quarterly* 5(2), 19–27.

Gebhardt, D., and Crump, C. (1990). Employee fitness and wellness programs in the workplace. *American Psychologist* 45(2), 262–72.

George, J. (2000). Emotions and leadership: The role of emotional intelligence. *Human Relations* 53(8), 1027–55.

Germain, C. B. (1973). An ecological perspective in casework practice. *Social Casework* 54(6), 323–30.

Germain, C. B., and Gitterman, A. (1995). Ecological perspective. In R. L. Edwards et al. (Eds.), *Encyclopedia of social work* (19th ed.) (1:816–24). Washington, D.C.: NASW Press.

——. (1996). *The life model of social work practice* (2nd ed.). New York: Columbia University Press.

Gibelman, M. (1996). Managerial manners—notably lacking in personnel recruiting. *Administration in Social Work* 20(1), 59–72.

Gibelman, M., and Schervish, P. (1997). *Who we are: A second look*. (2nd ed.) Washington, D.C.: NASW Press.

Giffords, E., and Dina, R. (2003). Changing organizational cultures: The challenge in forging successful mergers. *Administration in Social Work* 27(1), 69–81.

Gilberto, L. (1997). Downsized expectations: Older women coping with job loss. Doctor of social welfare diss., City University of New York.

Gillespie, D. (Ed.). (1987). *Burnout among social workers*. New York: Haworth Press.

Gilson, S., and DePoy, E. (2002). Theoretical approaches to disability content in social work education. *Journal of Social Work Education* 38(1),153–65.

Giovannoni, J. M. (1995). Childhood. In R. L. Edwards et al. (Eds.), *Encyclopedia of social work* (19th ed.) (1:433–41). Washington, D.C.: NASW Press.

Gitterman, A. (Ed.). (2001). *Handbook of social work practice with vulnerable and resilient populations.* (2nd ed.). New York: Columbia University Press.

Giuliani, R. (1998). Why we will end welfare by 2000. *New York Post,* July 21. p. 27

Giuliano, G. (1998). Information technology, work patterns, and intra-metropolitan location. *Urban Studies* 35(7), 1077–95.

Gladstone, J., and Reynolds, T. (1997). Single session group work intervention in response to employee stress during workforce transition. *Social Work with Groups,* 20(1), 33–49.

Glass, J., and Estes, S. (1997). The family responsive workplace. *Annual Review of Sociology* 23, 289–313.

Gliedman, J., and Roth W. (1980). *The unexpected minority.* New York: Harcourt Brace Jovanovich.

Gold, I. (1996). Unions held on to contract gains in 1995. *AFL-CIO News,* 41(6, March 25), 5.

Goldstein, E. G. (1995). Psychosocial approach. In R. L. Edwards et al. (Eds.), *Encyclopedia of social work* (19th ed.) (2:1948–54). Washington, D.C.: NASW Press.

Goleman, D. (2000). Leadership that gets results. *Harvard Business Review* 78(2), 78–90.

Googins, B. K. (1991). *Work-family conflicts: Private lives, public responses.* Westport, Conn.: Auburn House (Greenwood Publishers).

Googins, B., and Burden, D. (1987). Vulnerability of working parents: Balancing work and home roles. *Social Work* 32(4), 295–300.

Googins, B. and Davidson, B. (1993). The organization as client: Broadening the concept of employee assistance programs. *Social Work* 38(4), 477–84.

Googins, B., and Godfrey, J. (1987). *Occupational social work.* Englewood Cliffs, N.J.: Prentice-Hall.

Gould, G. M., and Smith, M. L. (Eds.) (1988). *Social work in the workplace: Practice and principles.* New York: Springer.

Gowdy, E., Carlson, L., and Rapp, C. (2003). Practices differentiating high-performance from low-performance supported employment programs. *Psychiatric Rehabilitation Journal* 26(3), 232–39.

Gray, M., and Barrow, F. (1993). Ethnic, cultural and racial diversity in the workplace. In P. A. Kurzman and S. H. Akabas (Eds.), *Work and well-being: The occupational social work advantage* (pp. 138–52). Washington, D.C.: NASW Press.

Greenhouse, S. (1996a). Strikes at 50-year low. *New York Times,* January 29, p. A12.

———. (1996b). Labor leaders say union is rejoining AFL-CIO. *New York Times,* February 18, p. 39.

———. (1997). Item in tax bill poses threat to the job benefit. *New York Times,* July 20, p. 18.

———. (1998a). Equal work, less equal perks. *New York Times,* June 30, pp. D1, D6.

———. (1998b). Labor unrest masks peaceful trend. *New York Times,* July 12, sec. 4, p. 4.

———. (1998c). Unions growing bolder, no longer shun strikes. *New York Times,* September 7, p. A12.

———. (1999a). Labor revitalized with new recruiting. *New York Times,* October 9, p. A14.

———. (1999b). Unions need not apply. *New York Times,* July 26, pp. C1, C19.

———. (2000). Growth in unions' membership in 1999 was best in two decades. *New York Times,* January 20, p. A10.

———. (2001a). Americans' international lead in hours working grew in '90s. *New York Times,* September 1, p. A6.

———. (2001b). Child care, perk of tomorrow? *New York Times,* May 13, sec. 4, p. 14.

Grinstein, A. (1960). *The index of psychoanalytic writings.* (Vols. 1–5). New York: Free Press.

Gueron, J. M., and Pauly, E. (1991). *From welfare to work.* New York: Russell Sage.

Gullason, E. (2000). The dynamics of the U.S. occupational structure during the 1990s. *Journal of Labor Research* 21(2), 363–75.

Gummer, B. (1995). American managers discover secret weapon—their employees! Developing human capacities in organizations. *Administration in Social Work* 19(1), 93–110.

———. (1998). Current perspectives on diversity in the workforce: How diverse is diverse? *Administration in Social Work* 22(1), 83–100.

Guralnik, J., Yanagishita, M., and Schneider, E. (1988). Projecting the older population of the United States: Lessons from the past and prospects for the future. *Milbank Quarterly* 66(2), 283–308.

Gutierrez, L., Kruzich, J., Jones. T., and Coronado, N. (2000). Identifying goals and outcome measures for diversity training: A multi-dimensional framework for decision-makers. *Administration in Social Work* 24(3), 53–70.

Habeck, R., Leahy, M., Fong, C., and Welch, E. (1991). Employer factors related to workers' compensation claim and disability management. *Rehabilitation Counseling Bulletin* 34(3), 210–26.

Hacker, A. (1992). *Two nations: Black and white, separate and unequal.* New York: Scribners.

Hagen, J. L. (1995). JOBS Program. In R. L. Edwards et al. (Eds.), *Encyclopedia of social work* (19th ed.) (2:1546–52). Washington, D.C.: NASW Press.

———. (2003). Temporary assistance for needy families. In R. A. English (Ed.), *Encyclopedia of social work* (19th ed.) (2003 supplement, pp. 163–76). Washington, D.C.: NASW Press.

Hamilton, G. (1940). *Theory and practice of social casework.* New York: Columbia University Press.

Hanson, M. (1993). Serving the substance abuser in the workplace. In P. A. Kurzman and S. H. Akabas (Eds.), *Work and well-being: The occupational social work advantage* (pp. 218–38). Washington, D.C.: NASW Press.

Hardesty, R. (1995). *AFL-CIO News,* 40(16, July 31), 1.

Harlow, K. C. (1987). A comparison of internal and external EAPs. *New England Journal of Human Services* 7(2), 16–21.

Harris, J. (1993). Military social work as occupational practice. In P. A. Kurzman and S. H. Akabas (Eds.), *Work and well-being: The occupational social work advantage* (pp. 276–90). Washington, D.C.: NASW Press.

Harris L., and Associates. (1995). *The NOD and Harris survey on employment of people with disabilities.* New York: Author.

Hartman, A. (1978). Diagrammatic assessment of family relationships. *Social Casework 59,* 465–76.

Hartman, A., and Feinauer, D. (1994). Human resources for the next decade. *Administration and Policy in Mental Health* 22(1), 27–37.

Hartwell, T. D., Steele, P., French, M. T., Potter, F. J., Rodman, N. F., and Zarkin, G. A. (1996). Aiding troubled employees: The prevalence, cost, and characteristics of EAPs in the U.S. *American Journal of Public Health* 1(1), 209–29.

Hasenfeld, Y. (2000). Social services and welfare-to-work: Prospects for the social work profession. *Administration in Social Work* 23(4), 185–99.

Health care benefits. (2003). *Monthly Labor Review* 126(10), 2.

Heffner, R. D. (Ed.). (1956). *Alexis de Tocqueville's democracy in America.* New York: Mentor Books.

Heintz, J., and Folbre, N. (2000). *The ultimate field guide to the U.S. economy.* New York: New Press.

Herbert, B. (1996). In America: Supply side seducer. *New York Times,* August 12, p. A15.

——. (2000). The crime fighter. *New York Times,* July 20, p. A25.

Herzberg, F. (1987). One more time: How do you motivate employees? *Harvard Business Review* 65(5, September–October), 109–21.

Herzberg, F., Mausner, B., and Snyderman, B. B. (1959). *The Motivation to work* (2nd ed.). New York: Wiley.

Hiatt, J., and Jackson, L. (1997). Union survival strategies for the twenty-first century. *Journal of Labor Research* 18(4), 487–501.

Himle, D., Jayaratne, S., and Thyness, P. (1989). The buffering effects of four types of supervisory support on work stress. *Administration in Social Work* 13(1), 19–34.

Hochschild, A. R. (1997). *The time bind when work becomes home and home becomes work.* New York: Metropolitan Books.

Hockenberry, J. (1995). *Moving violations: A memoir.* New York: Hyperion.

Hoefer, R., and Colby, I. C. (1997). Social welfare expenditures: Private. In R. L. Edwards et al. (Eds.), *Encyclopedia of social work* (19th ed. supplement) (pp. 274–81). Washington, D.C.: NASW Press.

Hoffmann, J., and Larison, C. (1999). Drug use, workplace accidents and employee turnover. *Journal of Drug Issues* 29(2), 341–64.

Hollis, F. (1964). *Casework: A psychosocial therapy.* New York: Random House.

Hollis, F., and Woods, M. E. (1990). *Casework: A psychosocial therapy* (4th ed.). New York: McGraw-Hill.

Holmes, S. A. (1990). House passes measure on family leave. *New York Times,* May 11, p. B6.

Holusha, J. (1990). Unions are expanding their role to survive in the '90s. *New York Times,* August 19, p. F12.

Hooper-Briar, K. and Seck, E. T. (1995). Jobs and Earnings. In R. L. Edwards et al. (Eds.), *Encyclopedia of social work* (19th ed). (2:1539–45.) Washington, D.C.: NASW Press.

Hopkins, H. L. (1934). Social planning for the future. *Social Service Review* 8(3, September), 383–89.

——. (1935a). Relief through work demanded by Hopkins. *New York Times,* March 10, p. E5.

——. (1935b). They'd rather work. *Collier's* (November 16), 7.

Hopkins, K. (1997). Supervisor intervention with troubled workers: A social identity perspective. *Human Relations* 50(10), 1215–38.

Hopkins K., and Hyde, C. (2002). The human service managerial dilemma: New expectations, chronic challenges and old solutions. *Administration in Social Work* 26(3), 1–15.

House, J. (1981). *Work stress and social support.* Reading, Mass.: Addison-Wesley.

Hudson, K. (1999). No shortage of nonstandard jobs (briefing paper). Washington, D.C.: Economic Policy Institute. Available at http://www.epinet.org/briefingpapers/hudson/hudson.pdf.

Hunter, M. (1971). House clears poverty bill despite Nixon veto threat. *New York Times,* December 8, pp. 1, 51.

——. (1999). Work, work, work, work! *Modern Maturity* 42(3), 35–41.

Iversen, R. R. (1998). Occupational social work for the 21st century. *Social Work* 43(6, November), 551–66.

Jahoda, M. (1988). Economic recession and mental health: Some conceptual issues. *Journal of Social Issues* 44, 13–23.

Jansson, B. S. (2001). *The sixteen-trillion-dollar mistake: How the U.S. bungled its national priorities from the New Deal to the present.* New York: Columbia University Press.

Jansson, B. S., and Smith, S. (1996). Articulating a new nationalism in American social policy. *Social Work* 41(5), 441–51.

John Paul II. (1981). *On human work: Encyclical laborem exercens.* Washington, D.C.: U.S. Catholic Conference Publications.

Johnson, P., and Indvik, J. (1999). The organizational benefits of assisting domestically abused employees. *Public Personnel Management* 28(3), 365–74.

Johnston, D. C. (1997). On payday, union jobs stack up very well. *New York Times*, August 31, sec. 3, pp. 1, 9.

———. (1999). Study contradicts foes of estate tax. *New York Times*, July 25, sec. 1, p. 18.

Johnston, W. B., and Packer, A. E. (1987). *Workforce 2000: Work and workers for the 21st century.* Indianapolis: Hudson Institute.

Jonsen, A. R., and Hellegers, A. E. (1976). Conceptual foundations for an ethics of medical care. In R. M. Veatch and R. Branson (Eds.), *Ethics and Health Policy.* Cambridge, Mass.: Ballinger.

Josephson, M. (1952). *Sidney Hillman: Statesman of American labor.* Garden City, N.Y.: Doubleday.

Judy, R. W., and D'Amico, C. (1997). *Workforce 2000: Work and workers in the 21st century.* Indianapolis: Hudson Institute.

Kahn, A. J. (1973). *Social policy and social services* (chap.3). New York: Random House.

Kahne, H. (1994). Part-time work: A reassessment for a changing economy. *Social Service Review* 68(3, September), 417–36.

Kameras, D. (1997a). When CEOs take the money and run. *America@work*, 2(1), 12.

———. (1997b). Follow the leader? *America@work*, 2(4), 19.

Kamerman, S. B., and Kahn, A. J. (1987). *The responsive workplace: Employers and a changing labor force.* New York: Columbia University Press.

———. (1995). *Starting right.* New York: Oxford University Press,

Kanter, R. M. (1977). *Work and family in the United States.* New York: Russell Sage.

Karabanow, J. (1999). When caring is not enough: Emotional labor and youth shelter workers. *Social Service Review* 73(3), 340–57.

Karger, H. J. (1989). The common and conflicting goals of labor and social work. *Administration in Social Work* 13(1), 1–18.

———. (Ed.). (1988). *Social workers and labor unions.* Westport, Conn.: Greenwood Press.

Karger, H. J., and Stoesz, D. (2002). *American social welfare policy* (4th ed.). Boston: Allyn and Bacon.

Karls, J. M., and Wandrei, K. E. (1994). *The P.I.E. manual.* Washington, D.C.: NASW Press.

———. (1995). Person in environment. In R. L. Edwards et al. (Eds.), *Encyclopedia of social work* (19th ed.) (3:1818–27). Washington, D.C.: NASW Press.

Karuntzos, G., Dunlap, L., Zarkin, G., and French, M. (1998). Designing an employee assistance program (EAP) intervention for women and minorities: Lessons from the Rockford EAP study. *Employee Assistance Quarterly* 14(1), 49–67.

Kates, N., Greiff, B. S., and Hagen, D. Q. (1990). *The psychological impact of job loss.* Washington, D.C.: American Psychiatric Association.

Kaufman, R., and Guerra, I. (2002). A perspective adjustment to add value to external clients, including society. *Human Resource Development Quarterly* 13(1), 109–15.

Kennedy, D. M. (1999). *Freedom from fear.* New York: Oxford University Press.

Kerns, W. L. (1995). Role of the private sector in financing social welfare programs. *Social Security Bulletin* 58 (1), 66–73.

——. (1997). Private social welfare expenditure, 1972–94. *Social Security Bulletin* 60(1), 54–60.

Kets de Vries, M., and Balazs, K. (1999). Transforming the mind-set of the organization: A clinical perspective. *Administration and Society* 30(6), 640–75.

Kilborn, P. T. (1999). Denver's Hispanic residents point to ills of the uninsured. *New York Times,* April 9, pp. A1, A16.

Kim, W., and Mauborgne, R. (1997). Fair process: Managing in the knowledge economy. *Harvard Business Review* 75(4), 65–75.

Kivel, B. D., and Wells, J. W. (1998). Working it out: What managers should know about gay men, lesbians, and bisexual people and their employment issues. In A. Daly (Ed.), *Workplace diversity: Issues and perspectives* (pp. 103–15). Washington, D.C.: NASW Press.

Kobasa, S. C., Maddi, S. R., and Kahn, S. (1982). Hardiness and health: A prospective study. *Journal of Personality and Social Psychology* 42, 168–77.

Kobasa, S. C., and Purccetti, M. C. (1983). Personality and social resources in stress resistance. *Journal of Personality and Social Psychology* 45, 839–50.

Kochman, M. (2003). Coach or couch, choose your therapy. *New York Times,* July 13, p. 14NJ.1.

Kossek, E., Huber-Yoder, M., Castellino, D., and Lerner, J. (1997). The working poor: Locked out of career and the organizational mainstream? *Academy of Management Executive* 11(1), 76–92.

Kossoudji, S., and Cobb-Clark, D. (1996). Finding good opportunities within unauthorized markets: U.S. occupational mobility for male Latino workers. *International Migration Review* 30(4), 901–24.

Krueger, A. (2000). Fewer workplace injuries and illnesses are adding to economic strength. *New York Times,* September 14, p. C2.

Krugman, P. (1999). Labor pains. *New York Times,* May 23, sec. 6, p. 24–25.

Kurzman, P. A. (1970a). The new career movement and social change. *Social Casework* 51(1), 22–27.

——. (1970b). Poor relief in medieval England: The forgotten chapter in the history of social welfare. *Child Welfare* 49(9), 495–501.

——. (1974). *Harry Hopkins and the New Deal.* Fair Lawn, N.J.: R. E. Burdick.

REFERENCES **253**

—. (1977). Rules and regulations in large-scale organizations: A theoretical approach to the problem. *Administration in Social Work* 1(4), 421–31.

—. (1983). Ethical issues in industrial social work practice. *Social Casework* 64, 105–11.

—. (1987). Industrial/occupational social work. In A. Minahan et al. (Eds.), *Encyclopedia of social work* (18th ed.) (1:899–910). Silver Spring, Md.: NASW Press.

—. (1988a). The ethical base for social work in the workplace. In G. M. Gould and M. L. Smith (Eds.), *Social work in the workplace: Practice and principles* (pp. 16–27). New York: Springer.

—. (1988b). Work and family: Some major dilemmas. In C. S. Chilman et al. (Eds.), *Employment and economic problems: Families in trouble* (pp. 67–83). Newbury Park, Calif.: Sage.

—. (1992). EAP staffing: Past, present, and future. *Employee Assistance Quarterly* 8(2), 79–88.

—. (1993). Employee assistance programs: Toward a comprehensive service model. In P. A. Kurzman and S. H. Akabas (Eds.), *Work and well-being: The occupational social work advantage* (pp. 26–45). Washington, D.C.: NASW Press.

—. (1998). Workplace ethics: Issues for human service professionals. In *Encyclopedia of Applied Ethics* (4:555–60). San Diego, Calif.: Academic Press.

—. (2000). Bakalinsky's conundrum: Should social workers practice in the world of work? *Administration in Social Work* 23(3/4), 157–61.

Kurzman, P. A., and Akabas, S. H. (1981). Industrial social work as an arena for practice. *Social Work* 26, 52–60.

—. (Eds.). (1993). *Work and well-being: The occupational social work advantage.* Washington, D.C.: NASW Press.

Lambert, S. (1993). Workplace policies as social policy. *Social Service Review* 67(2), 237–60.

—. (1999). Lower-wage workers and the new realities of work and family. *Annals of the American Academy of Political and Social Science* 562, 174–90.

Landon, P. S. (1995). Generalist and advanced generalist practice. In R. L. Edwards et al. (Eds.), *Encyclopedia of social work* (19th ed.) (2:1101–8). Washington, D.C.: NASW Press.

Landy, D. (1960). Problems of persons seeking help in our culture. In *Social Work Forum—1960* (pp. 127–45). New York: Columbia University Press.

Langdon, D. S., McMenamin, T. M., and Krolik, T. J. (2002). U.S. labor market in 2001: Economy enters a recession. *Monthly Labor Review* 125(2), 3–33.

Langman-Dorwart, N., Wahl, R., Singer, C., and Dorwart, R. (1992). Managed mental health: From cost containment to quality assurance. *Administration and Policy in Mental Health* 19(5), 345–52.

Lantos, B. (1943). Work and the instincts. *International Journal of Psychoanalysis* 24, 114–19.

LaPlante, M. (1991). The demographics of disability. *Milbank Quarterly* 69 (supplements 1/2), 55–77.

Lawson, B. Z. (1987). Work-related post-traumatic stress reactions. *Health and Social Work* 12(4), 250–58.

Leana, C. R., and Feldman, D. C. (1992). *Coping with job loss.* New York: Lexington Books.

Leashore, B. R. (1995). African-Americans: Overview. In R. L. Edwards et al. (Eds.), *Encyclopedia of social work* (19th ed.) (1:101–15). Washington, D.C.: NASW Press.

Lechner, V. (1993). Racial group responses to work and parent care. *Families in Society,* 74(2), 93–103.

Lechner, V., and Sasaki, M. (1995). Japan and the United States struggle with who will care for our aging parents when caregivers are employed. *Journal of Gerontological Social Work* 24(1/2), 97–114.

Leiter, M., and Wahlen, J. (1996). The role of employee assistance counselors in addressing organizational problems. *Employee Assistance Quarterly* 12(1), 15–28.

Lens, V. (2002). TANF: What went wrong and what to do next. *Social Work* 47(3), 279–90.

Leonhardt, D. (2000). Executive pay drops off the political radar. *New York Times,* April 16, sec. IV, p. 5.

——. (2003). Gap between pay of men and women smallest on record. *New York Times,* February 17, p. A1.

Lerner, M. (1980). Stress at the work place: The approach of the institute for labor and mental health. *Catalyst* 8, 75–82.

Levin, D. P. (1993). Back to school for Honda workers. *New York Times,* March 29, pp. D1, D3.

Levinson, A. (2003). Tentative ties: When the worker and the workplace come and go (Unpublished policy paper). New York: Hunter College School of Social Work.

Lewin, K. (1951). *Field theory in social science: Selected theoretical papers.* Chicago: University of Chicago Press.

Lewis, A. (1996). The fraying of hope. *New York Times,* March 8, p. A31.

Lewis, H. (1975). Management in the nonprofit social service agency *Child Welfare* 54(9), 615–23.

——. (1985). The whistle blower and the whistle-blowing profession. *Child and Adolescent Social Work Journal* 2(1), 3–12.

Liebow, E. (1967). *Tally's corner: A study of Negro street corner men.* Boston: Little, Brown.

Lifton, R. J. (1980). *The broken connection.* New York: Simon and Schuster.

Lipset, S. M. (1985). *Consensus and conflict: Essays in political sociology.* New Brunswick, N.J.: Transaction Books.

Lukens, E. (2003). Treatment for people with severe and persistent mental illness. In R. A. English (Ed.), *Encyclopedia of social work* (19th ed.) (2003 supplement, pp. 176–86). Washington, D.C.: NASW Press.

Lynd, R., and Lynd, H. (1929). *A study of modern American culture.* New York: Harcourt, Brace and World.

Mackelprang, R., and Salsgiver, R. (1996). People with disabilities and social work: Historical and contemporary issues. *Social Work* 41(1), 7–14.

Madonia, J. F. (1983). The trauma of unemployment and its consequences. *Social Casework* 64, 482–88.

Madrick, J. (1995). *The end of American affluence.* New York: Simon and Schuster.

Maiden, R. P. (2001). The evolution and practice of occupational social work in the U.S. *Employee Assistance Quarterly* 17(2), 119–61.

Maloof, B., Governale, N., and Berman, D. (1997). The salvation of the EAP. *Behavioral Health Management* 17(4), 34–38.

Manton, K., Singer, B., and Suzman, R. (1993). The scientific and policy needs for improved health forecasting models for elderly populations. In K. Manton, B. Singer, and R. Suzman (Eds.), *Forecasting the health of elderly populations* (pp. 3–35). New York: Springer-Verlag.

Marlatt, G. A., and Witkiewitz, K. (2002). Human resource approaches to alcohol use: Health promotion, prevention, and treatment. *Addictive Behavior* 27, 867–86.

Marrone, J., Hoff, D., and Gold, M. (1999). Organizational change for community employment. *Journal of Rehabilitation* 65(2), 10–19.

Martin, L. (2000). Budgeting for outcomes in state agencies. *Administration in Social Work* 24(3), 71–88.

Marx, J. (1996). Strategic philanthropy: An opportunity for partnership between corporations and health/human service agencies. *Administration in Social Work* 20(3), 57–73.

Marx, K. (1967). *Capital: A critique of political economy.* New York: International Publishers.

Masi, D.A. (1982). *Social work in industry.* Lexington, Mass.: Lexington Books.

Maslow, A. (1954). *Motivation and personality.* New York: Harper.

Maurer, H. (1981). *Not working.* New York: New American Library.

Mayo-Quiñones, Y. (1998). Latinos in the work force. In A. Daly (Ed.), *Workplace diversity: Issues and perspectives* (pp. 45–55). Washington, D.C.: NASW Press.

McCann, I., and Pearlman, L. (1990). Vicarious traumatization: A framework for understanding the psychological effects of working with victims. *Journal of Traumatic Stress* 3(1), 131–49.

McCroskey, J., and Scharlach, A. (1993). Family and work: Trends and prospects for dependent care. In P. A. Kurzman and S. H. Akabas (Eds.), *Work and well-being: The occupational social work advantage* (pp. 153–69). Washington, D.C.: NASW Press.

McGowan, B. G. (1984). *Trends in employee counseling programs*. New York: Pergamon.

——. (1995). Advocacy. In R. L. Edwards et al. (Eds.), *Encyclopedia of social work* (19th ed.) (1:89–95). Washington, D.C.: NASW Press.

McNeely, R. (1988). Five morale-enhancing innovations for human service settings. *Social Casework* (April), 204–13.

Medjuck, S., Keefe, J., and Fancey, P. (1998). Available but not accessible: An examination of the use of workplace policies for caregivers of elderly kin. *Journal of Family Issues* 19(3), 274–99.

Meeting human service needs in the workplace: A role for social work. (1980). New York: Columbia University, Hunter College and Council on Social Work Education.

Menninger, K. (1942). Work as sublimation. *Bulletin of the Menninger Clinic* 6, 170–82.

Merrifield, A. (1999). Class formation, capital accumulation, and the downsizing of America. *Monthly Review* 51(5), pp. 32–44.

Merton, R. K. (1968). *Social theory and social structure*. (Rev. ed.). New York: Free Press.

Meyer, C. H. (1976). *Social work practice: The changing landscape* (2nd ed.). New York: Free Press.

——. (1987). Direct practice in social work. In A. Minahan et al. (Eds.), *Encyclopedia of social work* (18th ed.) (1:409–22). Silver Spring, Md.: NASW Press.

——. (1995). Assessment. In R. L. Edwards et al. (Eds.), *Encyclopedia of social work* (19th ed.) (1:260–70). Washington, D.C.: NASW Press.

Milford Conference. (1929). *Generic and specific: A report*. Classics Series, 1974 Reprint. Washington, D.C.: NASW Press.

Miller, L. (1977). A counseling program in industry: Polaroid. *Social Thought* 3(1):42.

Mills, C. W. (1948). *The new men of power: America's labor leaders*. New York: Harcourt Brace.

Mishel, L., and Bernstein, J. (1994). *The state of working America, 1994–1995*. New York: M. E. Sharpe.

Mishel, L. R., Bernstein, J., and Schmidt, J. (1999). *The state of working America, 1998–1999*. Ithaca, N.Y.: ILR Press of Cornell University.

Mishel, L. R., Bernstein, J., and Boushey, H. (2003). *The state of working America, 2002–2003*. Ithaca, N.Y.: ILR Press of Cornell University.

Molloy, D., and Burmeister, L. (1989). Social workers in union-based programs. *Employee Assistance Quarterly* 5(1), 37–51.

Molloy, D. J., and Kurzman, P. A. (1993). Practice with unions: Collaborating toward an empowerment model. In P. A. Kurzman and S. H. Akabas (Eds.), *Work and well-being: The occupational social work advantage* (pp. 46–60). Washington, D.C.: NASW Press.

Mor Barak, M. (2000a). The inclusive workplace: An ecosystems approach to diversity management. *Social Work* 45(4), 339–53.

——. (2000b). Repositioning occupational social work in the new millennium. *Administration in Social Work* 23(4), 201–10.

——. (2004). *Managing diversity: Toward a worldwide inclusive workplace.* Thousand Oaks, Calif.: Sage.

Mor Barak, M., and Tynan, M. (1993). Older workers and the workplace: A new challenge for occupational social work. *Social Work* 38(1), 45–55.

Morgan, G. (1997). *Images of organizations.* (2nd ed.) Thousand Oaks, Calif.: Sage.

Motor voter: National voter registration act. (N.d.). Retrieved March 24, 2004, from http://motorvoter.com/.

Mudrick, N. (1991). An underdeveloped role for occupational social work: Facilitating the employment of people with disabilities. *Social Work* 36(6), 490–95.

Murray, R. E. (1998). *The lexicon of labor.* New York: New Press.

Mutchler, J., Burr, J., Pienta, A., and Massagli, M. (1997). Pathways to labor force exit. *Journal of Gerontology: Social Sciences* 52B(1), S4-S12.

Nasar, S. (1999). Where joblessness is a way of making a living. *New York Times,* May 9, sec. 4, p. 5.

NASW (National Association of Social Workers). (1991). *Standards for social work personnel practices.* Washington, D.C.: NASW Press.

——. (1999). Code of ethics. Washington, D.C.: NASW Press.

——. (2000). Alcohol, tobacco, and other substances. In *Social Work Speaks: National Association of Social Work policy statements, 2000–2003,* 5th edition (pp. 19–26). Washington, D.C.: NASW Press.

Neff, W. S. (1985). *Work and human behavior* (3rd ed.). New York: Aldine.

Neidt, C., Riuters, G., Wise, D., and Schoenberger, E. (1999). The effects of the living wage in Baltimore. Working Paper 119. Washington, D.C.: Economic Policy Institute.

New day for labor, A. (Editorial). (1999). *Nation* (September 20), p. 7.

Newhill, C. (1995). Client violence toward social workers: A practice and policy concern for the 1990s. *Social Work* 40(5), 631–36.

Norris, F. (1995). You're fired: But your stock is way up. *New York Times,* September 3, sec. 4, p. 3.

Oktay, J. (1992). Burnout in hospital social workers who work with AIDS patients. *Social Work* 37(5), 432–39.

Orbach, N. (2001). EAPs as a risk management tool. *Behavioral Health Management* 21(4), 44–47.

Osterman, P. (2000). Work reorganization in an era of restructuring: Trends in diffusion and effects on employee welfare. *Industrial and Labor Relations Review* 53(2), 179–96.

Ouchi, W. (1981). *Theory Z: How American business can meet the Japanese challenge*. Reading, Mass.: Addison-Wesley Publishing.

Ozawa, M. N. (1982). Work and social policy. In S. H. Akabas and P. A. Kurzman (Eds.), *Work, workers, and work organizations: A view from social work* (pp. 32–60). Englewood Cliffs, N.J.: Prentice-Hall.

——. (1985). Economics of occupational social work. *Social Work* 30(5), 442–44.

Page, J. A., and O'Brien, M. W. (1973). *Bitter wages*. New York: Grossman.

Parsons, T. (1951). *The social system*. Glencoe, Ill.: Free Press.

Passell, P. (1998). Rich nation, poor nation. *New York Times*, August 13, p. D2.

Patti, R. (1982). Applying business management strategies in social agencies: Prospects and limitations. In S. H. Akabas and P. A. Kurzman (Eds.), *Work, workers, and work organizations: A view from social work* (pp. 147–75). Englewood Cliffs, N.J.: Prentice-Hall.

Pear, R. (1998). Americans lacking health insurance put at 16 percent. *New York Times*, September 26, p. A1.

——. (1999a). White House releases new figures on welfare. *New York Times*, August 1, p.16.

——. (1999b), Clinton hears success stories of ex-welfare recipients. *New York Times*, August 4, p. A12.

——. (2003). Big increase seen in people lacking health insurance. *New York Times*, September 30, p. A1.

Pearlmutter, S. (1998). Self-efficacy and organizational leadership. *Administration in Social Work* 22(3), 23–38.

Perlis, L. (1977). The human contract in the organized workplace. *Social Thought* 3(1), 29–35.

Perlman, H. H. (1968). *Persona: Social role and responsibility*. Chicago: University of Chicago Press.

Peters, H. (1999). A value-driven approach to the operations of a South African EAP vendor. *Employee Assistance Quarterly* 14(1), 83–117.

Peters, J., and Masaoka, J. (2000). A house divided: How nonprofits experience union drives. *Nonprofit Management and Leadership* 10(3), 305–17.

Peters, T., and Waterman, Jr., R. (1982). *In search of excellence: Lessons from America's best-run companies*, New York: Harper and Row.

Piore, M. (1977). The dual labor market. In D. M. Gordon (Ed.) (2nd ed.), *Problems in political economy* (pp. 90–94). Lexington, Mass.: D. C. Heath.

Polivka, A. E. (1996). Contingent and alternative work arrangements defined. *Monthly Labor Review* 119(October), 3–9.

Popple, P. R. (1981). Social work practice in business and industry, 1875–1930. *Social Service Review* 55, 257–69.

Porter, M. (1999). Philanthropy's new agenda: Creating value. *Harvard Business Review* November–December, 121–32.

Poverny, L. M., and Finch, W. A. (1985). Job discrimination against gay and lesbian workers. *Social Work Papers* 19, 35–45.

———. (1988). Integrating work-related issues on gay and lesbian employees into occupational social work practice. *Employee Assistance Quarterly* 4(2), 15–29.

Powell, W. (1994). The relationship between feelings of alienation and burnout in social work. *Families in Society* 75(4, April), 229–35.

Ramsdell, P. (1994). Staff participation in organizational decision-making: An empirical study. *Administration in Social Work* 18(4), 51–71.

Rauktis, M., and Koeske, G. (1994). Maintaining social worker morale: When supportive supervision is not enough. *Administration in Social Work* 18(1), 39–60.

Rawls, J. (1971). *A theory of justice.* Cambridge, Mass.: Harvard University Press.

Reamer, F. G. (1992a). The impaired social worker. *Social Work* 37(2), 165–70.

———. (1992b). Should social workers blow the whistle on incompetent colleagues? In E. Gambrill and R. Pruger (Eds.), *Controversial issues in social work* (pp. 66–78). Boston: Allyn and Bacon.

———. (1998). *Ethical standards in social work: A critical review of the NASW Code of Ethics.* Washington, D.C.: NASW Press.

———. (2001). *Tangled relationships: Managing boundary issues in the human services.* New York: Columbia University Press.

———. (2002). Blowing the whistle: Should you or shouldn't you? *Social Work Today* 2(15), 8–9.

Reich, C. A. (1966). The new property. *Public Interest* 3, 57–89.

Reich, R. B (1998). *Locked in the cabinet.* New York: Vintage Books.

———. (2000). *The future of success.* New York: Alfred A. Knopf.

———. (2002). *I'll be short: Essentials for a decent working society.* Boston: Beacon Press.

———. (2004). *Reason: Why liberals will win the battle for America.* New York: Alfred A. Knopf.

Reid, P. N. (1995). Social welfare history. In R. L. Edwards et al. (Eds.), *Encyclopedia of social work* (19th ed.) (3:2206–75). Washington, D.C.: NASW Press.

Reisch, M, and Gorin, S. (2001). The nature of work and the future of the social work profession. *Social Work* 46 (1), 9–19.

Reisman, B. (1986). Management theory and agency management: A new compatibility. *Social Casework* (September) 387–93.

Reynolds, B. C. (1975). *Social work and social living: Explorations in philosophy and practice.* Washington, D.C.: NASW Press. (Reprint of 1951 edition).

Richmond, M. L. (1917). *Social diagnosis.* New York: Russell Sage.

Richmond, R., Kehoe, L., Heather, N., and Wodak, A. (2000). Evaluation of a workplace brief intervention for excessive alcohol consumption: The workscreen project. *Preventive Medicine* 30, 51–63.

Ridgeway, P., and Rapp, S. (1999). Active ingredients in achieving competitive employment for people with psychiatric disabilities: A research synthesis.

In L. L. Mancuso and J. D. Kottler (Eds.), *A technical assistance kit on employment for people with psychiatric disabilities* (pp. 1–27). Alexandria, Va.: National Association of State Mental Health Program Directors.

Riger, S., and Krieglstein, M. (2000). The impact of welfare reform on men's violence against women. *American Journal of Community Psychology* 28(5), 631–47.

Roark, J. L., et al. (1998). *The American promise: A history of the United States.* Boston: Bedford Books.

Roberts-DeGennaro, M., Laranzola, G., and Phillips, W. (1986). A human needs assessment of a trade union: The need for a union-managed EAP. *Employee Assistance Quarterly* 1(4), 29–42.

Rocha, C. J. (1997). Working poor. In R. L. Edwards (Ed.), *Encyclopedia of social work, 1997 (*19th ed. supplement) (pp. 331–42). Washington, D.C.: NASW Press.

Roman, P., and Blum, T. (1988). The core technology of EAPs: A reaffirmation. *Almacan* 18(8), 17–22.

Root, L. S. (1993a). Employee benefits: The role of social insurance and social services. In P. A. Kurzman and S. H. Akabas (Eds.), *Work and well-being: The occupational social work advantage* (pp. 102–22). Washington, D.C.: NASW Press.

———. (1993b). Unemployment and underemployment. In P. A. Kurzman and S. H. Akabas (Eds.), *Work and well-being: The occupational social work advantage* (pp. 332–49). Washington, D.C.: NASW Press.

———. (2000). Education and training in the workplace: Social work interventions in the private sector. *Administration in Social Work* 23(4), 13–28.

Rosenbaum, D. E. (1984). Recession is seen harming health. *New York Times* (June 28), p. A20.

Rosenman, S. I. (Ed.) (1950). *The public papers and addresses of Franklin Delano Roosevelt.* New York: Random House.

Rosenthal, D., and Olsheski, J. (1999). Disability management and rehabilitation counseling: Present and future opportunities. *Journal of Rehabilitation* 65(1), 31–38.

Rosenthal, J. (1971). Excerpts from Nixon's veto message. *New York Times* (December 10), pp. 1, 20.

Rostow, W. W. (1960). *The stages of economic growth.* Cambridge, England: Cambridge University Press.

Rubery, J., and Grimshaw, D. (2001). ICTs and employment: The problem of job quality. *International Labour Review* 140, 165–92.

Ryan, W. (1976). *Blaming the victim.* (Rev. ed.) New York: Vintage Books.

Saleebey, D. (2003). Strengths-Based Practice. In R. A. English (Ed.), *Encyclopedia of social work* (19th ed.) (2003 supplement, pp. 150–62). Washington, D.C.: NASW Press.

Samantrai, K. (1992). Factors in the decision to leave: Retaining social workers with MSWs in public child welfare. *Social Work* 37(5), 454–58.

Sandler, M., and Gray, M. (1999). *Winning at work.* Palo Alto, Calif.: Davies Black.

Scanlon, E. (1999). Labor and the intellectuals: Where is social work? *Social Work* 44(6), 590–93

Schlesinger, A. M. (1956). *The crisis of the old order.* Boston: Houghton-Mifflin.

Schore, L., and Atkin, J. (1993). Stress in the workplace: A response from union member assistance programs. In P. A. Kurzman and S. H. Akabas (Eds.) *Work and well-being: The occupational social work advantage* (pp. 316–31). Washington, D.C.: NASW Press.

Schorr, A. L. (Ed.). (1977). *Jubilee for our times: A practical program for income equality.* New York: Columbia University Press.

Schwartz, W. (1969). Private troubles and public issues: One social work job or two? *Social Welfare Forum, 1969* (pp. 22–43). New York: Columbia University Press.

Scott, C. J., and Arnold, E. W. (2003). Deauthorization and decertification. *Working USA* 7(3), 6–20.

Seck, E. T., Finch, W. A., Mor Barak, M. E., and Poverny, L. M. (1993). Managing a diverse workforce. *Administration in Social Work* 17(2), 67–79.

Secret, M., Sprang, G., and Bradford, J. (1998). Parenting in the workplace. *Journal of Family Issues* 19(10, November), 795–815.

See, L. A. (1998). Diversity in the workplace: Issues concerning Africans and Asians. In A. Daly (Ed.), *Workplace diversity: Issues and perspectives* (pp. 354–72). Washington, D.C.: NASW Press.

Sellers, J. (1999). Bridging disabilities and work. *Policy and Practice of Public Human Services* 57(2), 18–25.

Shapiro, J. (1993). *No pity: People with disabilities forging a new civil rights movement.* New York: Times Books.

Sheafor, B. W., and Landon, P. S. (1987). Generalist perspective. In A. Minahan et al. (Eds.), *Encyclopedia of social work* (18th ed.) (1:660–69). Silver Spring, Md.: NASW Press.

Sherraden, M. W. (1985). Chronic unemployment: A social work perspective. *Social Work* 30(5), 403–8.

Shields, G., and Kiser, J. (2003). Violence and aggression directed toward human service workers: An exploratory study. *Families in Society* 84(1), 13–20.

Shin, J., and McClomb, G. (1998). Top executive leadership and organizational innovation: An empirical investigation of nonprofit human service organizations. *Administration in Social Work* 22(3), 1–21.

Shostak, A. B. (1982). Work meanings through Western history: From Athens to Detroit and beyond. In S. H. Akabas and P. A. Kurzman (Eds.), *Work, workers, and work organizations: A view from social work* (pp. 5–31). Englewood Cliffs, N.J.: Prentice-Hall.

Sills, D. L. (1957). *The volunteers.* Glencoe, Ill.: Free Press.

Singer, T. L. (1995). Sexual harassment. In R. L. Edwards et al. (Eds.), *Encyclopedia of social work* (19th ed.) (3:2148–56). Washington, D.C.: NASW Press.

Skeels, J. W. (1965). Social welfare programs of labor and industry. In H. L. Lurie (Ed.), *Encyclopedia of social work* (15th ed.) (1:735–40.) New York: NASW.

Smith, D. (1987). The limits of positivism in social work research. *British Journal of Social Work* 17, 401–16.

Smith, H. (1995). *Rethinking America.* New York: Random House.

Smith, M. L. (1988). Social work in the workplace. In G. M. Gould and M. L. Smith (Eds.), *Social work in the workplace: Practice and principles* (pp. 3–15). New York: Springer.

Smith, P. (1997). Caseload overload. *Boston Globe,* June 27, p. B1.

Social Security Bulletin. Annual Statistical Supplement. (2002). Retrieved March 11, 2004, from http://www.ssa.gov/policy/docs/statcomps/supplement/2002/3e.pdf.

Social Security Region VII Fact Sheet (2004). "2004 Social Security Changes." Available at http://www.ssa.gov/kc/fact_sheet_01print.htm.

Solzhenitsyn, A. I. (1963). *One day in the life of Ivan Denisovich.* New York: Praeger.

Spaler-Roth, R., and Deitch, C. (1999). "I don't feel right sized; I feel out-of-work sized": Gender, race, ethnicity, and the unequal costs of displacement. *Work and Occupations* 26(4), 446–82.

Spitzer, K., and Favorini, A. (1993). The emergence of external EAPs. In P. A. Kurzman and S. H. Akabas (Eds.), *Work and well-being: The occupational social work advantage* (pp. 350–71). Washington, D.C.: NASW Press.

Sprang, G., Secret, M., and Bradford, J. (1999). Blending work and family: A case study. *Affilia* 14(1), 98–116.

Steele, K., and Berman, C. (2001). *The day the voices stopped: A memoir of madness and hope.* New York: Basic Books.

Stellman, J. M., and Daum, S. M. (1973). *Work is dangerous to your health.* New York: Vintage.

Stevenson, R. W. (2000). Roots of prosperity reach past Clinton-Gore years. *New York Times,* October 9, A14.

Stoesz, D. (1986). Corporate welfare: The third stage of welfare in the United States. *Social Work* 31, 245–50.

Straussner, S. L. A. (1988). Comparison of in-house and contracted-out EAPs. *Social Work* 33(1), 53–55.

——. (1989). Occupational social work today. *Employee Assistance Quarterly* 5(1), 1–17.

——. (Ed.). (1990). *Occupational social work today.* New York: Haworth Press.

Straussner, S. L. A., and Phillips, N. K. (1988). The relationship between social work and labor unions: A history of strife and cooperation. *Journal of Sociology and Social Welfare* 15(1), 105–18.

Strom-Gottfried, K. (1999). When colleague accuses colleague: Adjudicating personnel matters through the filing of ethics complaints. *Administration in Social Work* 23(2), 1–16.

Sum, A., et al. (2004). The unprecedented rising tide for corporate profits and the simultaneous ebbing of labor compensation: Gainers and losers from the National Economic Recovery Act in 2002 and 2003. Center for Labor Market Studies, Northeastern University, Boston, Mass. Available at http://www.nupr.neu.edu/4-04/corporate_profits.pdf.

Swenson, C. R. (1995). Clinical social work. In R. L. Edwards et al. (Eds.), *Encyclopedia of social work* (19th ed.) (1:502–13). Washington, D.C.: NASW Press.

Sze, W., and Ivker, B. (1986). Stress in social workers: The impact of setting and role. *Social Casework* 67 (March), 141–48.

Tambor, M. L. (1994). Containment, accommodation, and participative management in agency-union relations. *Journal of Progressive Human Services* 5(1), 45–62.

———. (1995). Unions. In R. L. Edwards et al. (Eds.), *Encyclopedia of social work* (19th ed.) (3: 2418–26). Washington, D.C.: NASW Press.

Tanner, R. (1991). Social work: The profession of choice for EAPs. *Employee Assistance Quarterly* 6(3), 71–84.

Terkel, S. (1972). *Working*. New York: Avon.

Thomas, K. (Ed.). (1999). *The Oxford book of work*. Oxford: Oxford University Press.

Thomlison, R. J. (Ed.). (1983). *Perspectives on industrial social work practice*. Ottawa: Family Service Canada.

Thurow, L. C. (1995). Companies merge; families break up. *New York Times*, September 3, sec. 4, p. 11.

———. (1999). *Building wealth: The new rules for individuals, companies, and nations in a knowledge-based economy*. New York: Harper Collins.

Thyer, B. A. (2002). Evidence-based practice and clinical social work. *Evidence-based mental health* 5, 6–7.

———. (2003). Empirically based interventions. In R. A. English (Ed.), *Encyclopedia of social work* (19th ed.) (2003 supplement, pp. 21–29). Washington, D.C.: NASW Press.

Titmuss, R. M. (1968). *Commitment to welfare*. New York: Pantheon.

Tobin, D. R. (1993). *Re-educating the corporation*. Essex Junction, Vt.: Oliver White.

Toossi, M. (2002). A century of change in the U.S. labor force. *Monthly Labor Review* 125(5), 15–28.

Tower, K. (1994). Consumer-centered social work practice: Restoring client self-determination. *Social Work* 39(2), 191–96.

Towle, C. (1987). *Common human needs* (rev. ed.). Silver Spring, Md.: NASW Press.

Tracy, M. B., and Ozawa, M. N. (1995). Social Security. In R. L. Edwards et al. (Eds.) *Encyclopedia of social work* (19th ed.) (3:2186–95). Washington, D.C.: NASW Press.

Tulgan, B. (2001). *Winning the talent wars*. New York: W. W. Norton.

UAW (United Automobile Workers). (1998a). *Washington Report* 38(15, August 14), 1–2.

———. (1998b). *Washington Report* 38(17, September 18), 4.

———. (1999). *Washington Report* 39(1, January 15), 2.

Uchitelle, L. (1996). More downsized workers are returning as rentals. *New York Times*, December 8, pp. 1, 34.

———. (1997). Strike points to inequality in 2-tier job market. *New York Times*, August 8, p. A22.

Ulrich, D. N., and Dunne, H. P. (1986). *To love and work: A systematic interlocking of family, workplace, and career.* New York: Brunner-Mazel.

Underground economy (1998). Editorial. *Nation*, January 19, pp. 3–5.

United Nations. Department of Economic and Social Affairs. (1971). *Industrial social welfare.* New York: Author.

Urban B., and Bennett, L. (1999). When the community punches a time clock: Evaluating a collaborative workplace domestic abuse prevention program. *Violence against Women* 5(10), 1178–93.

U.S. Department of Health and Human Services. (1992). *Aging America, 1991.* Washington, D.C.: Author.

U.S. Department of Labor.(1998). Bureau of Labor Statistics. *Number of jobs, labor market experience, and earnings growth: Results from a longitudinal survey.* Washington, D.C.: Author.

———. (2000). Employment and Training Administration. Apprenticeship E-tools, Registered apprenticeship brochures, Building a skilled workforce in the 21st century. Retrieved July 26, 2004, from http://www.doleta.gov/atels_bat/e-tools.cfm#brochures.

———. (2004). Bureau of Labor Statistics. Occupational outlook handbook, 2004–05 edition, social workers. Retrieved July 9, 2004, from http://stats.bls.gov/oco/ocos060.htm.

———. (2004). Bureau of Labor Statistics. Union members summary. Retrieved January 21, 2004, from http://www.bls.gov/news.release/union2.nr0.htm.

U.S. Equal Employment Opportunity Commission. (1999). Charge statistics FY 1992 through FY 1998. Retrieved February 2, 1999, from http://www.eeoc.gov/stats/charges.html.

U.S. General Accounting Office. (1998). *Welfare reform: States are restructuring programs to reduce welfare dependence* (GAO-HEHS-98–109). Washington, D.C.: Author.

Vigilante, F. W. (1982). Use of work in the assessment and intervention process. *Social Casework* 63, 296–300.

———. (1993). Use of work in the assessment and intervention process. In J. Rauch (Ed.), *Assessment: A sourcebook for social work practice* (pp. 105–11). Milwaukee, Wisc.: Families International.

Vigilante, F. W., and Mailick, M. D. (1988). Needs-resource evaluation in the assessment process. *Social Work* 30, 101–4.

von Bertalanffy, L. (1968). *General systems theory: Foundations, development, applications.* New York: Braziller.

Vosler, N. R. (1994). Displaced manufacturing workers and their families. *Families in Society* 75, 105–15.

Vourlekis, B., Edinburg, G., and Knee, R. (1998). The rise of social work in public mental health through aftercare of people with serious mental illness. *Social Work* 43(6), 567–75.

Wagner, A. G., Queen, S. A., and Harper, E. B. (1930). *American charities and social work* (4th ed.). New York: Thomas Y. Crowell.

Walden, T. (1978). Industrial social work: A conflict in definitions. *NASW News* 23(5), 3.

Wallen , J. (2002). *Balancing work and family: The role of the workplace.* Boston: Allyn and Bacon.

Warr, P., Jackson, P., and Banks, M. (1988). Unemployment and mental health: Some British studies. *Journal of Social Issues* 44, 47–68.

Warren, J., and Johnson, P. (1995). The impact of family support on work-family role strain. *Family Relations* 44(2), 163–77.

Weinbach, R. (1998). *The social worker as manager: A practical guide to success* (3rd ed.). Boston: Allyn and Bacon.

Weiner, H. J., Akabas, S. H., and Sommer, J. J. (1973). *Mental health care in the world of work.* New York: Association Press.

Weiner, H. J., Akabas, S. H., Sommer, J. J., and Kremen, E. (1971). *The world of work and social welfare policy.* New York: Columbia University School of Social Work, Industrial Social Welfare Center.

White, M. (2000). Think ability: Disabilities in the diversity agenda. *Diversity Factor* 8(2), 2–9.

Whyte, W. H. (1972). *The organization man.* New York: Simon and Schuster.

Wilensky, H. L., and Lebeaux, C. N. (1965). *Industrial society and social welfare.* New York: Free Press.

Williamson, S. H. (1992). U.S. and Canadian pensions before 1930: A historical perspective. In J. A. Turner and D. J. Beller (Eds.), *Trends in pensions* (pp. 35–57). Washington, D.C.: USGPO.

Wilson, W. J. (1987). *The truly disadvantaged.* Chicago: University of Chicago Press.

———. (1991). Studying inner-city social dislocations. *American Sociological Review* 56, 1–14.

———. (1996). *When work disappears: The world of the new urban poor.* New York: Alfred A. Knopf.

Winfield, L., and Spielman, S. (1995). *Straight talk about gays in the workplace.* New York: American Medical Association.

Winslow, W. W. (1966). Some economic estimates of job disruption. *Archives of Environmental Health* 13(2), 213–19.

Witkin, S. (1998). Editorial: Human rights and social work. *Social Work* 43(3), 197–201.

Witte, E. (1962). *Development of the Social Security Act.* Madison: University of Wisconsin Press.

Woititz, J. (1987). *Home away from home.* Pompano Beach, Fla.: Health Communications.

Wolf-Jones, L. R. (1995). Unemployment compensation and workers' compensation. In R. L. Edwards et al. (Eds.), *Encyclopedia of social work* (19th ed.) (3:2413–17). Washington, D.C.: NASW Press.

Women at work. (2003). *Monthly Labor Review* 126(10), 49.

Work in America. (1973). A report of a special task force to the U.S. Secretary of Health, Education, and Welfare. Cambridge, Mass.: MIT Press.

World Health Organization. (1976). Document A4/INFDOC/1. Geneva, Switz.: Author.

Wrong, D. H. (1971). The meaning of work in Western culture. *Humanitas* 7, 215–22.

Zanz, S. (1998). Resiliency and burnout: Protective factors for human service managers. *Administration in Social Work* 22(3), 39–54.

INDEX

Bloom, M., 11
Boeing, 74
Bok, Derek, 97
Bombyk, M., 123
Boston Globe, 197
Bourdieu, P., 41
Bradford, J., 152
Brager, G., 182
Brenner, M. Harvey, 24–25, 40, 108
Briar, K. H., 123
Burghardt, S., 60
burnout: definition of, 203, 230; elements
    leading to, 202–3; empowerment link
    to, 204; initiatives to reduce, 217–18;
    social worker, 202–4, 217–18, 230
Bush, George H. W., 110

capitalism: exploitation by, 57; success of,
    56–57; values of, 222
Carnoy, M., 129–30
carpal tunnel syndrome, 140
Carson, Rachel, 106
Carter, Betty, 24
Carter, Jimmy, 81
Castellino, D., 143
Caterpillar, 74
Center for Labor Market Studies, 51
CETA. *See* Comprehensive Employment
    and Training Act
Chamber of Commerce, 140
Charity Organization Societies, 8
Chase Manhattan Bank, 61. *See also* J. P.
    Morgan Chase Manhattan Bank
Chemical Bank, 61
Chestang, L. W., 27
child care, 22, 109–12, 168
Child Labor Act (1916), 77
chronic unemployment, 107. *See also*
    unemployment
CIO. *See* Congress of Industrial Organiza-
    tions
Civil Rights Act (1964), 38–39, 95, 146
Civil War, 77
Civil Works Administration (CWA), 78
Clinton, Bill, xix, 70; welfare support by,
    110, 112–13
Cloward, Richard, 137
coaching: executive, 223; life, 223–24;
    qualities needed for, 224
Code of Ethics (NASW), 118, 120, 197;
    diversity and, 206; unethical behavior
    and, 211; unionization and, 217, 227
Cohen, J. A., 198

Columbia University, 95, 171, 191
commitment and perspective concept:
    embeddedness notion and, 13; empow-
    erment and, 12; population at risk and,
    13
Common Human Needs (Towle), 70
Communication Workers of America
    (CWA), 197
community: disability social work and,
    184–92; labor's involvement with,
    234–35; organizational change impact
    on, 162–63; work-family integration
    with, xviii, 13–18, 106, 236; workplace
    socialization and, 111; work relation
    to, 13–18, 111, 167–68, 184–92
Comprehensive Employment and Training
    Act (CETA; 1973), 80
conceptual framework, OSW: commit-
    ment and perspective, 12–13; focus and
    orientation, 10–12; method and model,
    8–10. *See also specific concepts*
Congress of Industrial Organizations
    (CIO), 72, 96
contingent work: advantages of, 65, 67;
    disadvantages of, 63; job conversions
    to, 64; tier system and, 63
Cooke, P. W., 57, 81
Coolidge, Calvin, 109
core workforce, 62, 63
corporations: downsizing of, 59, 161–63;
    employee conversions by, 62–65;
    employee disposability in, 59–61; merg-
    ers and acquisitions of, 59; philan-
    thropic giving by, 234–35; profit
    growths of, 51; taxes paid by, 56, 82.
    See also organizations, work
Cotter, C., 213
Council on Accreditation for Children and
    Family Services, 154
Council on Social Work Education
    (CSWE), xvi, xxi; policy guidelines by,
    12; social work accreditation by, 196
CPS. *See* Current Population Survey
Crump, C., 158
CSWE. *See* Council on Social Work Edu-
    cation
Cunningham, G., 89
Current Population Survey (CPS), 230
CWA. *See* Civil Works Administration
cyclical unemployment, 107. *See also*
    unemployment

Davidson, J., 148

Deitch, C., 139
delivery systems, social work, 146–48;
assessment of, 171–72; EAPs as,
151–57; interrelation, worlds (of living)
and, 167–68; managed care, 164–67;
MAPs as, 151–57; occupational social
welfare, 148–51; organizational change
initiatives as, 161–63; specialized work
programs as, 157–61. *See also specific
systems*
Denisovich, Ivan, 22
Denning, P., 154
Depression. *See* Great Depression
Detroit Free Press, 74
*Diagnostic and Statistical Manual of Men-
tal Disorders*, 9, 60
dilemma(s), social work: confidentiality, 5;
occupational focus, 5; social worker's
role as, 6; work context issue, 29–33
disability(ies): case example of, 175–76;
compensation for, 43–44, 133–34; consensus points regarding, 187; contributions of workers with, 190; costs of,
175; definitions of, 173–74; emotional
responses to, 134; insurance for, 43–44,
134; legal mandates for, 175, 179–80;
policy threats regarding, 189; positive
aspects regarding, 176–77; resource
collaboration for, xviii; social construct
of, 178–79; work-created, 174–75;
worker ambiguity during, 181; workplace issues on, 133–35. *See also* mental health conditions; social work, disability; workers' compensation
disability policies, workplace: case finding
and, 183; case management services for,
183–84; guidelines for, 182; implementation of, 182–83; maintenance needs
for, 184; recording system for, 184;
team coordination for, 182
discrimination: gender, 35, 52, 142; mental health, xx; racial, 35–38, 142; sexual orientation, 38–39, 142; work value
and, 33; workplace, 35–39, 137–39,
141–43
diversity, workplace: American, 222; gender, 34–35; management of, 224; paraprofessional staffing for, 207–8; race,
35–38; sexual orientation, 38–39;
social agency, 206–8; stages of, 206–7;
structural changes for, 207
Donovan, R., 93, 102
downsizing, 233; community impact of,

162–63; job loss statistics on, 59; work-
ers released through, 161–62; workers
surviving, 162
Drucker, P., 205
Drug Free Workplace Act (1988), 131
Dunlap, L., 153
Dunlop, John, 97
Dunn, E. F., 13

EAPs. *See* employee assistance programs
Eastern Airlines, 74
ecomaps, 29
Economic Opportunity Act (1964), 79
Economic Policy Institute, 51, 108, 114
economy: children's roles in, 55; transition
of, 55–57; work's relation to, 39–41
Edinburg, G., 189
education, 22
Edwards, R. L., 57, 81
EEOC. *See* Equal Employment Opportunity Commission
effectiveness, social work: agency leadership for, 208–9; diversity achievement
for, 206–8, 217; human resources
process for, 205–6; supervisory support
for, 209–11; team building empowerment for, 211–17
Ehrenreich, B., 137
Electronic Data Systems, 113
1199: National Health and Human Services Employees Union/SEIU, 72,
101–2, 105, 123
Ellison, Ralph, 21
Employee Assistance Handbook, 153
employee assistance programs (EAPs), xiii;
availability of, 228; expansion of, 10,
154–55; incentives, labor union, for,
97–98, 101–3, 105; incentives, management, for, 93–96, 103–5, 151–52; internal v. external, 120–22; mental health
conditions and, 155–56; motivation
behind, 151–52; origins of, 151; services of, 152, 228–29; staffing for, 228;
substance abuse and, 151, 153–54. *See
also* labor union incentives, EAP; management incentives, EAP; specialized
work programs
Employee Retirement Income Security Act
(ERISA; 1974), 43, 91
Encyclopedia of Social Work, xvi
environment, social agencies, 195–96;
burnout in, 202–4, 217–18, 230; case
study on, 199–202; diversified, 206–8,

approach in, 8–9; PIE system approach in, 9; social system evolution and, 10; social work roots and, 8
Meyer, Carol H., 9, 28, 46, 114
Microsoft, 64, 116–17
Milford Conference, 6
Mills, C. Wright, 96, 226
Molloy, D. J., 76, 235
Mor Barak, M., 114
Motor Voter movement, 137
Mount Sinai Hospital, New York, 169, 213
Moynihan, Daniel Patrick, 80
Mutual of New York, 234

NASW. *See* National Association of Social Workers
National Alliance for the Mentally Ill, 233
National Association of Manufacturers, 140
National Association of Social Workers (NASW), 9, 28, 226; eligibility for, 196, 230; publications by, 118, 120; substance abuse and, 154
National Conference on Social Welfare, 120
National Directory of Corporate Giving, 234
National Health and Human Service Employees Union. *See* 1199 National Health and Human Service Employees Union/SEIU
National Institute of Mental Health (NIMH), 24
National Labor Relations Act (Wagner Act) (1935), 72
National Labor Relations Board (NLRB), 72
National Voter Registration Act (1993), 137
Neff, W. S., 30
Neighborhood Youth Corps, 79
New Deal, xvii, 222; work benefits through, 22, 42, 46
Newhill, C., 210
New York Labor Coalition for Home Care Workers, 102
New York State Vocational Educational Services for Individuals with Disabilities (VESID), 169
New York Times, 35, 113
Nickel and Dimed (Ehrenreich), 137
Nixon, Richard, 80, 109–10

NLRB. *See* National Labor Relations Board
nonstandard jobs: contingent work as, 63–65, 67; emergence of, 61; supplemental work as, 62–63; tiers of work and, 62, *63;* union coverage of, 61, 64
nonwork. *See* unemployment
Norfolk Family Service Agency, Virginia, 170
Norris-LaGuardia Act (1932), 72

OASI. *See* Old Age and Survivors Insurance
occupational issues, OSW: internal v. external EAPs as, 120–22; labor-management, 117–20; people v. profits as, 122–23; practice location v. mission as, 114–17; whistle-blowing, 118–19. *See also* presenting problems, OSW
Occupational Safety and Health Act (1970), 91
Occupational Safety and Health Administration. *See* OSHA
occupational social work (OSW): accommodation issues in, 46–47; benefit mentality in, 188; conceptual framework for, 8–13; definition of, 3–4, 88–89; disability roles of, 177–84; diversity response in, 34–39, 206–8, 224; issues and dilemmas in, 5–6, 29–33; labor setting use of, 101–3, 105; labor's incentive for, 96–100, 225–27; literature on, xv–xvi; management setting use of, 103–5; management's motivation for, 93–96; nonoccupational social work relation to, 5–6, 105–6, 167–71; practice influences and, 13–18; roles of, 189–90; skills required for, xx, 171–72; texts on, 4; transitions of, 90–93; work context issues for, 29–33; world (of living) integration and, 5–6, 13–18, 105–6, 167–71, 189–90. *See also* assessment, social work; conceptual framework, OSW; dilemma(s), social work; effectiveness, social work; future, social work; presenting problems, OSW; social work (non-occupational); social work, disability
occupational welfare system, 2; definitions of, 148–49; evolution of, 149–50; income redistribution impact and, 150–51